THE QUEENS AND ROYAL WOMEN OF SWEDEN, c. 970–1330

This is the first major piece of scholarship to provide an overview of the lives of Sweden's earliest documented queens, together with some of their most influential female relatives, who lived between 970 and 1330.

Spanning a period over 350 years, approximately 40 biographies are included from the semi-legendary Viking queen Sigrid Storråda to Duchess Ingeborg of Norway, the first female de jure and de facto ruler of Sweden. Rather than merely summarising previous research, this study offers new perspectives on the evolution of queenship in medieval Sweden. It tracks the different religious, political, and socio-economic trends which defined and shaped the office of queen and identifies three main phases of development which led to royal women's economic and political emancipation by the mid-fourteenth century. The study's main strength lies in its close reading and novel interpretation of the surviving primary sources, enabling readers to understand the importance of these women and wider themes such as state formation, Christianisation, and international politics.

The Queens and Royal Women of Sweden, c. 970–1330 is of interest to scholars of queenship and gender studies, medieval historians in general, those with an interest in ecclesiastical history, and anyone studying medieval Scandinavia.

Caroline Wilhelmsson is a historian of state formation, urban history, and military architecture. She teaches Viking history at the University of Aberdeen, UK, and is a postdoctoral researcher at University College Cork, Ireland, where she investigates walled towns. She previously held a Bernadotte Fellowship at Uppsala University, Sweden.

Lives of Royal Women

Series Editors:
Elena Woodacre, Ellie.Woodacre@winchester.ac.uk
Louise Wilkinson, LWilkinson@lincoln.ac.uk

This series features academic, yet accessible biographies of royal women - consorts, dowagers, royal mothers and female sovereigns - inclusive of all periods, cultures and geographic regions. These biographies include a deep engagement with the premise of queenship studies and the exercise of the queen's office (or equivalent), in addition to covering the lives of particular women. The series is divided into three sub-strands: Queens of England (blue), Queens and Empresses of Europe (purple), and Royal Women of the World (red).

Joan of Navarre
Infanta, Duchess, Queen, Witch?
Elena Woodacre

Early English Queens, 850–1000
Potestas Reginae
Matthew Firth

Berengaria of Navarre
Queen of England, Lord of Le Mans
Gabrielle Storey

The Queens and Royal Women of Sweden, c. 970–1330
Their Lives, Power, and Legacy
Caroline Wilhelmsson

THE QUEENS AND ROYAL WOMEN OF SWEDEN, c. 970–1330

Their Lives, Power, and Legacy

Caroline Wilhelmsson

Routledge
Taylor & Francis Group

LONDON AND NEW YORK

Designed cover image: 14th or 15th century painting of Saint
Ragnhild in Enånger Old Church © The Picture Art Collection /
Alamy Stock Photo

First published 2025
by Routledge
4 Park Square, Milton Park, Abingdon, Oxon OX14 4RN

and by Routledge
605 Third Avenue, New York, NY 10158

Routledge is an imprint of the Taylor & Francis Group, an informa business

© 2025 Caroline Wilhelmsson

British Library Cataloguing-in-Publication Data
A catalogue record for this book is available from the British Library

ISBN: 9781032491158 (hbk)
ISBN: 9781032491172 (pbk)
ISBN: 9781003392200 (ebk)

DOI: 10.4324/9781003392200

Typeset in Sabon
by codeMantra

To all the women, everywhere, that no one ever writes about.

CONTENTS

FIGURES

ACKNOWLEDGEMENTS

I would like to thank the *Kungliga Gustav Adolfs Akademien för Svensk Folkkultur* and the *Bernadotte Programme* for their generous financial and academic support throughout this project. It has been very inspiring to be part of the Academy's community for a year, and I will forever cherish this experience. Writing this book would have been much more difficult without the valuable help and encouragement of my four mentors: Louise Berglund, Stefan Brink, Thomas Lindkvist, and Christine Ekholst. Thank you for your guidance. I am also extremely grateful to *Uppsala University* and to everyone at the *Historiska Institutionen*, who hosted me for the duration of my Bernadotte Fellowship and welcomed me as part of their research community. Their encouragement and camaraderie provided me with the boost I needed whenever this project felt impossible. Many thanks to Annika Björklund as well for allowing me to use her maps. They look infinitely better than mine! Finally, my deepest gratitude to Elena Woodacre and Louise Wilkinson, the editors of this wonderful series, for trusting me all along.

NOTES

Names have been given in their modern Scandinavian form according to the kingdom from which a character originated or with which they are most associated ("Ingegerd Haralds*datter*" from Norway but "Ingegerd Sverkers*dotter*" from Sweden, "*Svend* Estridsen" but "Blót-*Sven*," "*Canute* the Great" but "*Knut* of Sweden"). In some cases, a queen's name is spelled in various ways throughout the sources. The most common rendering of the name was thus chosen to ensure consistency. In the rare instances where a person's native name is not known, the name under which they are most often identified in literature will be used. Similarly, place-names are given their modern spellings in the corresponding language. The names of modern-day countries are sometimes used for convenience ("Sweden," "Germany"), but it is obviously a simplification of the much more complex medieval situation, and specific details will be given where relevant.

1

INTRODUCTION

A children's tale cannot have a king without a queen, and a prince without a princess. From the glamorous young queen to the bitter queen mother, and from the shy princess to the adventurous one, royal women have been portrayed in different ways throughout the ages. These common tropes are often based on real historical customs. While the image of queenship has been distorted in popular culture to fit set narratives, their ubiquitous presence in literary works, art, and other media shows that queens are important characters in history, in fiction, and in the public psyche. Yet, they have typically remained secondary to their male counterparts and understudied, despite theirs being a distinct role with distinct expectations, and distinct responsibilities.

Fortunately, the number of studies about women, both present and historic, has exploded in recent years. Scholars and the public have realised the value in investigating the role that women, who have traditionally remained hidden in men's shadows, have played in all areas of society since times immemorial. The book series that this monograph is part of has chosen to focus on queens and royal women all over the world, throughout time. Some of these queens have certainly received more attention than others in scholarship so far. As will be shown in the literature review, in a European context, much has been written about French, English, and Spanish queens in particular. These are large, well-documented kingdoms which have been at the forefront of European politics for centuries. It is therefore perfectly understandable that more should be known about them than about

DOI: 10.4324/9781003392200-1

the women that I will be discussing in this book. Indeed, up to c. 850, the paucity of written sources means that the study of early medieval Sweden is mainly the realm of archaeology. It is only later, after c. 1000, that runestones, annals, ecclesiastical accounts, diplomas, and eventually sagas begin to exist in larger numbers. While written primary sources remain scarce and fragmentary, they do allow us to piece together a basic image of how the kingdom looked like, and how it developed. It is during these five centuries that the kingdom was Christianised, that its administration developed, that its borders consolidated, and that a sort of proto-nationalism emerged.[1]

No monograph, in either English or Swedish, has been written before about the Swedish queens of that period. While there have been studies concerning elite women in medieval Scandinavia, especially in the fourteenth and fifteenth centuries, very little has been written about royal women. This is partly the result of limited sources, but is also due to traditional and outdated discourses which ignored women's capabilities and framed them as secondary to their husbands, and powerless. Many undoubtedly were: medieval society was highly patriarchal, and most women never reached their full potential as the constraints of the world they lived in hampered their personal ambitions. However, to think that Swedish queens were powerless would be factually untrue, and it is time to revise the outdated view that powerful female leaders were rare and exceptional in the Middle Ages.[2] As will become clear in this book, many directly influenced Swedish politics, religion, and culture; and helped shape a monarchy which aimed to emulate European examples. This is the interesting fact about medieval Swedish queens (and, indeed, many others across Europe): most were not Swedish at all and instead brought with them their own customs, education, and prestige. This book, therefore, will be telling the stories of several generations of women without whom Sweden would not have become the powerful, sophisticated, and Europeanised kingdom that it had become by the end of the Middle Ages.

The introduction will firstly give an overview of what has been written about queens in medieval Europe, and which aspects of queenship have received most attention so far. The next step will be to briefly discuss the history of early medieval Sweden and define its characteristics. Indeed, it is impossible to understand queenship without first understanding kingship, and the notion of kingdom in a Swedish context. Because the period studied here was so tumultuous, precise definitions will be given for some of the recurring terms employed throughout this book, and significant trends such as the realm's Christianisation, state formation, and Europeanisation, will need to be contextualised. This section will ensure that the framework within which this monograph was written, and the circumstances within which these women lived are as clear as possible. It will also acknowledge the necessary limitations of the present study, chiefly the uncertainty which results from the nature of sources available for medieval Swedish history. The methodology employed and sources used in this study will be introduced at this stage.

Following this introduction, we will dive straight into the lives of some of Sweden's most illustrious royal women. The first core chapter will focus on the period between c. 970 and 1050 during which written sources about the kingdom are scarce and unreliable. The first historically attested queens of Sweden lived during that time. While little is known about them, they can nevertheless help us understand attitudes towards women and towards the nascent monarchy in what was still a very obscure and isolated period in Swedish history. The second core chapter will focus on the years during which monasticism grew at increasing speed throughout the kingdom, from about 1100 to 1210. Many women sponsored monastic institutions and these, in turn, were hugely influential in the consolidation of royal power during the twelfth and thirteenth centuries. While it is not possible to discuss all women connected to religious institutions, those that were so while also leveraging royal connections will be studied in the context of a fringe kingdom that was becoming increasingly connected to the rest of Europe and Christendom. The third core chapter, covering the years between 1210 and 1330, will investigate these women who had explicit political power, culminating in the accession of the first *de facto* female leader in Swedish history, Duchess Ingeborg of Norway. From the second half of the thirteenth century, it became increasingly common for some women to play an openly political role and shoulder public responsibilities. While these women remained marginal compared to their peers, they nevertheless paved the way for later generations of strong, internationally recognised female rulers in Scandinavia. The aim of these three chapters is to show the evolution of royal women's powers and roles over the course of these centuries, and to draw comparisons between attitudes prevalent in pre-Christian times, and women's status in a kingdom fully integrated into Latin Christendom. This monograph is not so much about showing progress or improvement in any way. Indeed, it will be shown that in some aspects of women's lives, earlier times may have been more "progressive" – in a modern sense – than later periods. It is therefore not the superfluous goal to come to any conclusion, but more simply to tell, in chronological and thematic order, the story of these women.

1.1   Literature Review

Before delving straight into the subject matter, it is necessary to survey the scholarship produced so far on medieval queens. While it can be perceived as a specialised area of study, it has grown in popularity in recent times, and excellent work has been carried out which must be introduced. Firstly, Elena Woodacre's *Queens and Queenship* (2021) provides an excellent, concise, and accessible introduction to queenship throughout the world.[3] This otherwise small book packs an impressive amount of information about what was expected of queens in various locales and various time periods. Queenship almost never simply meant being married to a king: queens were required to follow codes and rules, set examples for society, produce and educate heirs, serve as diplomatic tools, and sometimes also had a very important role in the management of the court. *Queens and Queenship* summarises all this to provide the foundation for more in-depth study of specific kingdoms.

Going back in time, the first major works focusing on royal women include Pauline Stafford's *Queens, Concubines and Dowagers: The King's Wife in the Early Middle Ages* (1983) which was particularly influential for the field.[4] Also noteworthy are

Anne Duggan's *Queenship in Medieval Europe* (1997), and John Carmi Parsons's *Medieval Queenship* (1990).[5] These two edited volumes compile a range of essays discussing various aspects of medieval queens. The breadth of topics studied in these two books reflects the sudden enthusiasm which ignited the field in the last quarter of the century. Duggan's book includes papers on Hungary, France, Britain, the Low Counties, Byzantium and the Latin East; and touches upon architecture, literature, ecclesiastical history, art history and others. Carmi Parsons's work is more focused on lineage, succession, and the legal aspect of queenship, and is very efficient at illustrating that nothing in the definition and conduct of queenship, was random. The essays presented in his book underlined the highly sophisticated and structured nature of queenship, which may have helped underscore the fact that queens could be as important and influential as some kings. Most interestingly, these two books brought together locales and subjects which had rarely been studied together before.

Indeed, it is more common for queenship studies to focus on certain individuals or periods – and it is what the present monograph does as well. It is of course convenient: scholars tend to be specialised, and readers are usually interested in specific areas. However, it also makes it easier to lose track of the bigger picture. Very few areas existed in a vacuum, and many of the questions discussed in this book in relation to Swedish queens also apply to other European women. There is thus no point for the present author in reviewing a catalogue of essays, articles and books which have been written throughout the decades about individual queens. Instead, it may be useful to look at what sort of questions research has tried to answer when it comes to medieval queenship. Theresa Earenfight has recently published an updated generalist monograph about queenship which is noteworthy for the depth of its analysis of the theoretical frameworks in which queenship studies have developed. Her 2017 book, titled *Queenship in Medieval Europe*, covers a wide geographical area, like the two previously mentioned, and is the first of a textbook series covering queenship and power.[6] She organises her work in thematic sections, and provides a brief overview of the early history of Scandinavia. By pulling examples from all over Europe, she tries to answer specific problems in the history of European monarchy, many of which apply to Sweden as well. Some of these questions are basic and yet so difficult to answer. Where did ideas and expectations of queenship come from? What role did royal women play in the family unit? How did one become queen in the first place?

A first obstacle to queenship which many women experienced in the early medieval period, when institutions were still changing and Christianity was still spreading, was the question of legitimacy. As will be shown in the first part of this study, in Scandinavia, where concubinage remained common until the late eleventh century, multiple women could claim similar privileges. It is only after monogamy became the norm that royal women gained a clearer path to power. The issue of queens' legitimacy and authority has been much explored notably in the context of French medieval laws, which were some of the most sophisticated in Europe, and influenced several other law codes.[7] In the heavily patriarchal societies of medieval Europe, it is fundamental to establish through which mechanisms a woman could become queen, and whether the title (when it was granted) came with any actual power at all. Significant works include Marion Facinger's pioneering article from 1968, "A Study of Medieval Queenship: Capetian France, 987–1237," while more recent research includes Kathleen Nolan's *Capetian Women* (2003) and Éliane Viennot's *La France, les femmes et le pouvoir: l'invention de la loi salique (V-XVI siècle)* (2006).[8]

Late medieval, and early modern English and Scottish queens too have been studied at length in the context of legitimacy and authority. Scholars such as Lois Huneycutt and John Carmi Parsons have written more articles about queenly power and attributes than can be mentioned here, but their influence will be felt throughout this study. The development of queenship in England is a particularly insightful subject because late Anglo-Saxon and early Norman England was one of medieval Europe's most sophisticated and well-organised kingdoms. Many studies have of course investigated the circumstances of Elizabeth I's reign, but also her lesser-known predecessors. Helen Castor's *She-Wolves: The Women who Ruled England before Elizabeth*

(2010) and Marjorie Chibnall's *The Empress Matilda: Queen Consort, Queen Mother and Lady of the English* (1991), which was the first study of all aspects of Matilda as a woman and not just as a political character, have helped shed light on how successive generations of high-status women, some of whom lesser-known, worked to improve their status in medieval times.[9] Louise Wilkinson's "Royal Daughters and Diplomacy at the Court of Edward I" (2020) shows how royal women other than queens could still play an important political role and were an integral part of the monarchy. The distinction between queens and royal women here is very important, notably because this book will also study women who were of royal pedigree but not necessarily queens. Charles Beem's *The Lioness Roared: The Problems of Female Rule in English History* (2008) is a convenient overview of the obstacles faced by English queens throughout the history of the kingdom, although the book also offers a specific analysis of medieval circumstances. Many of the problems that they encountered were the result of basic gender bias and patriarchal customs, and they can thus be transposed into almost any time period and any locale.[10]

There is, however, a significant gap in European queenship studies, as it is mostly the queens of well-documented kingdoms such as Spain, France, and England, who have been studied. Iberian royal women have been particularly intensely scrutinised, not least because of the vast number of surviving sources available, and because the region saw the rise of strong and influential public women such as Isabella of Castille in positions of power for significant periods of time. Few other European kingdoms can claim such a strong female figure during the medieval period. Scholarly works about the queens of Spain include Therese Martin's *Queen as King: Politics and Architectural Propaganda in Twelfth-Century Spain* (2006) and *Queenship and Political Power in Medieval and Early Modern Spain* edited by Theresa Earenfight (2005), as well as the recent works of Elena Woodacre.[11] Other southern monarchies on the edge of Europe, including the kingdoms of Jerusalem and Antioch, and Middle-Eastern polities (such as the Yemeni and Fatimid caliphates) have also received attention. These kingdoms have in common that they are extremely well documented and were at the heart of the seismic religious developments witnessed during the Middle Ages – not least the Crusades. Nevertheless, there is comparatively very little, if anything, about royal women in smaller, more isolated realms such as the Nordic countries, or eastern Europe.

In fact, studying queenship in eastern and central Europe is useful for understanding it in an east Scandinavian context, because many of the queens that will be discussed in this book had close ties to the Baltic kingdoms, and central Europe including Kyivan Rus. The author's grasp of literature concerning these areas is limited because of the language barrier, but some English-language works concerning royal studies in this this geographical sphere are nevertheless of particular interest. While Przemysław Wiszewski's *Domus Bolezlai: Values and Social Identity in Dynastic Traditions of Medieval Poland (c. 966–1138)*, published in 2010, is not directly related to Sweden, it nevertheless helps us understand the cultural background of some of Sweden's earliest queens at a time when the Scandinavian kingdom entertained many commercial, political and diplomatic links with this part of the Baltic region. Grzegorz Pac's 2022 English edition of his monograph about medieval Polish royal women, *Women in the Piast Dynasty: A Comparative Study of Piast Wives and Daughters (c. 965–c.1144)*, is a valuable addition to the corpus of scholarship about women of that period, and provides a foray into a little-known and yet extremely powerful early medieval dynasty.[12]

Relevant to Sweden's early queens are also attitudes towards queenship in Kyivan Rus, with which Scandinavia had strong commercial and ethnic ties. Slavic women generally had a lot less agency than Scandinavian – or indeed other European – women. While shedding light on female power is important, it is equally necessary to acknowledge the serious limitations that many faced, notably in Slavic areas. Talia Zajac's recent chapter, "The Social-Political Roles of the Princess in Kyivan Rus', ca. 945–1240" (2021), is a valuable piece of scholarship which carefully analyses the role and power (or lack thereof) that royal women had in this part of Europe. In this paper, Zajac investigates kingly attitudes towards their partners, and the dismissive and inherently imbalanced nature of their relationship. This provides an interesting contrast with the Swedish queens of this period, at least a couple of which hailed from Slavic areas, who had significantly more power. Zajac has also written in "Gloriosa Regina or 'Alien Queen?'" (2016) about the eleventh-century queen Anna Yaroslavna, who was the wife of the French king Henry I. She describes how Anna has been systematically underestimated and dismissed as an "alien queen" whose foreign origins limited her influence and importance within the French court and society in general. Zajac argues instead that the queen did exercise power notably by participating in civic life and sponsoring ecclesiastical institutions. Similar strategies were employed by the queens of Sweden during the same period, and studies about Anna are valuable to Scandinavian scholars in that her life is much better documented than any of the women who will be discussed in the present book. Literature about her, both contemporary and more recent, can thus help us get a clearer view of the situation in Sweden.[13]

In a strictly Scandinavian context, rather more has been written about Denmark's early queens than about those of Norway or Sweden. Inge Skovgaard-Petersen's "Queenship in Medieval Denmark" (1998) was an important starting point in establishing this new field of studies in relation to Scandinavia.[14] By today's standards, her article can seem merely introductory – which is great, as it shows how much scholarship has progressed. It was, at the time, one of the first serious studies of the subject which also accounted for structural sexism in both the medieval period itself but also, crucially, in historians' perception of medieval women. It is interesting to note that Skovgaard-Petersen was a historian of state formation, like many of the people writing about queenship. It is hardly surprising that it is the scholars specifically studying state institutions and identity formation which primarily write about royal women: it is indeed impossible to understand the birth of kingdoms without understanding their foundation, of which women were literally, biologically part.

Therefore, much of what has been written about Nordic queens can be found in studies of state formation. Peter Sawyer *När Sverige blev Sverige* (1991) was the first overview of state formation in medieval Sweden, and covers the development of offices such as kingship, jarlship, and to an extent queenship from the Viking Age to the thirteenth century. Sverre Bagge's book *From Gang Leader to the Lord's Anointed* (1996) provides insights into twelfth- and thirteenth-century Scandinavian political ideology. Philip Line's *Kingship and State Formation in Sweden: c. 1130–1290* (2007), which gives a detailed account of the kingdom's development between 1130 and 1290, is a precious mine of information about Swedish royal women.[15] His monograph mentions many of the women which will be covered here. However, as in almost all other secondary literature, they are only ever studied secondarily to their male partners, or family members. While Fredrik Charpentier Ljungvist's *Lagfäst kungamakt under högmedeltiden* (2016) is not directly concerned with women, by analysing in detail the power structures in place in Scandinavia during the early medieval period, the subject of kinship, social circles, and therefore the role of women, is discussed at length. It is very useful from a comparative perspective as his study makes clear that different attitudes were prevalent across Scandinavia not just towards female but male power as well.[16]

Lars Hermanson's body of work provides valuable insights into friendship, kinship, and other social networks in medieval Scandinavia. His doctoral thesis, *Släkt, vänner och makt: en studie av elitens politiska kultur i 1100-talets Danmark* (2000), is notably helpful in understanding women in medieval Sweden. While it focuses on Denmark, his study of social networks is highly relevant to Sweden which may have followed a similar system during the same period. Particularly significant is Hermanson's analysis of maternal lineage and its role in establishing kin groups.[17] He has also written about the relationship between lay and ecclesiastical elites, notably in respect of Vreta Abbey, which will be a recurrent subject of discussion in this study. In *Medeltidens genus: Kvinnors och mäns roller inom kultur, rätt och samhälle. Norden och Europa ca 300–1500* (2016), which Hermanson edited with Auður Magnúsdóttir, men's dependence on women is underlined. To be more precise, the book underlines the interdependence of both genders. It is well established that women and men had well-defined roles and were confined to their respective areas in society (mainly domestic life for women, everything else for men), but one aspect of this *status quo* which is often ignored is the simple fact that one could not exist without the other. It would be very easy for scholars of women's studies to exaggerate female impact to try and make up for centuries of neglect, but the present book's main goal, like Hermanson and Auður Magnúsdóttir's book, is to rectify this imbalance rather than create a new one.[18]

Auður Magnúsdóttir has written extensively on concubinage in medieval Iceland, which may inform our understanding of the practice elsewhere in Scandinavia. Her work includes "Frillor och fruar. Politik och samlevnad på Island 1120–1400" (2001) and "Friends, Foes, and Follower. Power, Networks, and Intimacy in Medieval Iceland" (2020).[19] Birgit Sawyer also wrote several studies about the mechanics of female influence in social circles, notably through maternal inheritance. In *Kvinnor och familj i det forn- och medeltida Skandinavien* (1992), she gives an overview of the development of women's roles across the Middle Ages, from the Viking Age until well into the period studied here. Of particular importance to her study is the influence of Christianity on the legal framework within which women lived, as well as the new roles and norms which were expected of them.[20] One of the strengths of her book is the comparative nature of it, as she discusses women from all three Scandinavian kingdoms, and also provides elements of comparison with the rest of Europe. While she does not focus on queens *per se*, much of what she writes would have applied to women of various social statuses. She also wrote more specifically about elite women's economic power in several unpublished essays. Notable papers include "Marriage, Inheritance and Property in Early Medieval Scandinavia" and "Viking-Age Rune-Stones in Scandinavia" (both 2001), in which she discusses runic evidence pointing to female inheritance. Sawyer's work has played an important role in shedding light not just on the theory of women's role in society but on the practical expression of it.

William Layher's *Queenship and Voice in Medieval Northern Europe* (2010) is one of the works on medieval Scandinavian queenship most closely related to the present monograph. It also provides multiple biographies of queens, and focuses on some of the strategies that they used to make themselves heard.[21]

He writes about the voice that medieval queens had in the public sphere and the authority that it afforded them, the physical performativity of queenship, and how patronage and the commission of art and literature allowed women to spread messages which they otherwise may not have been allowed to share out loud. Layher's work takes on a different approach by using surviving literary texts as the basis of his study, as concrete manifestations of queenship from which he builds his analysis. The main issue, however, is that despite Layher's originality in his handling of the source material, he does not write about Swedish queens and instead focuses on better-documented figures from Denmark and Norway.

Some generalist works dealing with the kingdom's earlier queens were published in the nineteenth and early twentieth centuries. While not scholarly in nature, these were symptomatic of the sudden revival that medieval and early modern history enjoyed. An early pioneering effort to focus on women is Wilhelm Malm's book from 1844, *Svenska drottningar: porträtter och biografier*, which gives the biographies of some of Sweden's queens chronologically. Unsurprisingly, however, Malm ignores medieval queens, and instead starts in the sixteenth century, during the time of the Vasa dynasty's ascent to power. While his study is superficial, it does give a sense of continuity which sheds light on the developments in women's condition which led to the arrival of Queen Christina. Nanna Lundh-Eriksson wrote a great deal about the queens from this period and her works, which include *Sveriges drottningar, 1531–1860* (1916) and *Den glömda drottningen: Karl XII:s syster Ulrika Eleonora* (1976), were very popular with non-academics. Lundh-Eriksson's works managed to capture the intrigue and sensationalism associated with such a glamorous time, but lack the depth required of academic publications. Wilhelmina Stålberg's and Per Gustaf Berg's *Anteckningar om svenska qvinnor* (1864) represents a more serious attempt at presenting some of the medieval women discussed in this monograph, although queens are not the main subject, and entries remain superficial and uncritical. There is thus a staggering lack of specialised scholarly literature about Sweden's medieval queens as individuals.

Of course, Christina is partly to blame. The iconic seventeenth-century monarch, who reigned over the kingdom and its dominions for over 50 years and broke the rigid gender norms of her time, has attracted an unquantifiable level of attention.[22] Very few queens ever became so famous anywhere in the world. She is on par with England's Victoria, its Elizabeths, and Catherine II of Russia. However, a consequence of her fame is that her predecessors have received much less accolade. Early modern women in general have been well covered in scholarship, not least because they are rather well documented in primary sources too. The Early Modern period in Europe was dominated by strongmen, such as Gustav I (Vasa) but also Henry VIII, Charles V, and Francis I, who all carefully crafted hyper-masculine public personas by which they are still defined today. In this particularly patriarchal context, therefore, female perspectives have always been attractive subjects for scholars, and the public as well. Modern scholars of early modern Swedish queens include Karin Tegenborg-Falkdalen, whose works include generalist titles such as *Sveriges Drottningar* about the queens from the Vasa dynasty until today, targeted studies such as *Vasadrottningen: En biografi över Katarina Stenbock 1535–1621*, and group biographies such as *Vasadöttrarna* (2010) which looks at Gustav Vasa's daughters, who have typically been overlooked in favour of their brothers, and father. An important part of the latter is the constant plotting and political ongoings within which these women had to survive. Women's influence in intellectual life and courtly culture in Sweden has also been studied in Kristoffer Nevile and Lisa Skogh's edited volume *Queen Hedwig Eleonora and the Arts Court Culture in Seventeenth-Century Northern Europe* (2017), in which female patronage takes centre stage.

The late Middle Ages, in between the arrival of the Vasa dynasty and the period studied here, have received increased scholarly attention in recent times as well. Louise Berglund has written extensively about the queens and elite women from this period. She has notably worked on female influence in a religious context, and has carried out extensive investigations of how women could hold and sway power in monastic institutions. Some of her notable articles about the topic include "Medeltidens diskreta makthavare: om abbedissan Ragnhild och andra kvinnor i Riseberga kloster" (2008) and "Queen Philippa and Vadstena Abbey: Royal Communication on a Medieval Media Platform" (2009).[23] Berglund has demonstrated how monastic institutions provided women with a public platform which they could use to take part in politics. Choosing a cloistered life was also one of the only ways a woman could remain unmarried and therefore free of the influence of a husband, while retaining status in society as well as a certain level of autonomy. While Berglund's work focuses on a later period than that studied here, it is nevertheless extremely useful in helping us understand how monastic institutions could directly impact on the kingdom's politics. They played a similar role in previous centuries as well, although they are of course less well-documented. The question of royal women's religious influence will be at the heart of the second chapter, which will focus on the eleventh and twelfth centuries, when nunneries, abbeys, and monasteries first developed in Sweden.

As mentioned previously, the nineteenth century saw an important uptick in the study of Sweden's earlier medieval period, from the Viking Age to the fourteenth century. Bror Emil Hildebrand and his son Hans Hildebrand were two of the first important medieval historians and archaeologists of Sweden, whose many works and pioneering archaeological methods greatly impacted on various academic disciplines. They notably wrote about women. Hans Hildebrand, specifically, wrote an influential series in two volumes titled *Sveriges Medeltid* (1879) in which he discussed women's condition without the misogyny or flippant attitude which was otherwise prevalent in his nineteenth-century milieu.[24] Hans Hildebrand, it should be noted, was the first president of the Fredrika Bremer Association, founded in 1884, which is the oldest women's rights association in Sweden. In *Sveriges Medeltid*, while Hildebrand acknowledges the social constraints experienced by women notably following Christianisation, he points out the relative prestige that they enjoyed in pagan times, when women were considered to be closer to nature and more in touch with the gods.[25] He does not, however, discuss queens in detail. The only exception is Margaret, who formed the Kalmar Union in the fourteenth century. Hildebrand mentions her but insists on the exceptional nature of her reign.[26] This seems a rather diminutive view with modern scholars such as Steinar Imsen instead insisting on the impressive power that the so-called "union-queens" yielded in the fourteenth and fifteenth centuries.[27] Much in the same vein, part of this book's aim is to show that Margaret's coming to power should not have been that surprising or unexpected considering the development of queenship in preceding years. The most thorough scholarly writings about Sweden's earliest known queens can be found in encyclopaedias such as *Svenskt Biografiskt Lexicon* and *Svenskt Kvinnorbiografiskt Lexicon*. The main problem with these entries is of course their brevity, but they manage to condense an enormous amount of information into just a few lines. They are especially precious for their listing of the various primary sources most relevant to a given woman, and in several cases they served as the starting point for the extended biographies presented here.

It should be clear by now that there is little written about Swedish queens between 970 and 1330. One exception is Sigrid Storråda, the first historically attested queen of Sweden, about whom a decent amount of work has been done. She is one of the best-documented women in this monograph, but she is also the one whose historicity is the most debated. This will be discussed in the next chapter. Apart from her, women are rarely afforded more than a footnote or a comment. The methodology employed here is therefore rather simple. Each biography gathers as much superfluous reliable information as possible about all queens who lived between the tenth and fourteenth centuries. In some particularly badly documented cases, sections will consist of little more than fact-gathering, but these women's lives will be contextualised as far as feasible and discussed in relation to wider events, trends, and societal factors which may have affected the biography's subject. Because the aim of this monograph is to provide reliable information, legendary and mythical facts will only be given if they are relevant. Unlike most of the works discussed so far, women with royal connections who otherwise were not queens will also be studied. This is partly because, as will be detailed shortly, the characteristics and attributes of kingship in medieval Sweden are quite difficult to define, especially during the

Viking Age, when this monograph begins. Concubinage was commonplace, and the social and marital structure associated with medieval European monarchies and courts took much longer to develop in Sweden than elsewhere in Scandinavia. In addition, the period studied saw state formation, and the spread of ecclesiastical institutions, towards which different types of elite women contributed. A coherent and comprehensive picture of this formative period in Sweden's history requires a study of all relevant actors, and not only those who were given an elusive title (in several cases not even confirmed on paper). The constant expansion and transformation of Sweden's institutions led to several different types of women exercising power in the public sphere, and these will therefore be discussed too. Their selection was as objective as possible, but some, whose identities or biographical details cannot be confirmed, have been excluded to keep the book straightforward and digestible.

1.2 Historical Context: Kingship, Kinship, and State Formation

Understanding basic facts about medieval Sweden is our first step. Until the thirteenth century, kingship was not a stable concept in Sweden. As there was no centralised administration until then, multiple kings could vie for power and claim different territories at the same time. This was certainly the norm during the Viking Age, not just in Sweden but elsewhere in Scandinavia as well, where local magnates and overlords created a web of elite networks reigning over many different petty kingdoms and small polities. Well into the Christian era, as Swedish kingship was slow to consolidate, instances of multiple kings reigning at the same time are recorded. A letter from Pope Gregorius VII, writing in 1080, for instance, is addressed to *Visigothorum regibus*, Inge and Halstan, who reigned concurrently in Västergötland.[28] It suggests that even within one province, different factions could have different political preferences, or that kings could collaborate. Many other examples will be shown throughout this monograph. In the absence of consolidated borders and centralised administration, nothing stopped clans or groups of villages from electing their own king. Another example of how this worked can be seen in the election and subsequent murder of Ragnvald Knaphövde. Elected by the people of Uppland in the 1120s, Ragnvald embarked on a tour of the various provinces that tradition dictated needed to approve his appointment. However, Ragnvald's flouting of the rules by not taking hostages in Västergötland offended the population, which led to his murder. *Västgötalagen* tells us this was because he broke with tradition.[29] Yet, Saxo Grammaticus implies that this had been a political manoeuvre all along, as the people of Västergötland wanted to elect Magnus Nielsen, a Danish nobleman of Swedish ancestry, as king instead.[30] This likely had to do with Magnus' being the grandson of a Swedish king, as well as the strong economic links which the province had with its southern neighbours.

While extreme, Ragnvald's fate was not surprising, because power in medieval Sweden was negotiated. Provincial assemblies held much power and sway in political decisions. Consisting of free landowners and spearheaded by a lawspeaker, these assemblies (called *thing*) discussed local affairs, settled disputes, and served as intermediary between the population and overlords. Newly elected kings needed all provincial assemblies to approve their election and even after that, had to work in cooperation with them. Assemblies had a significant amount of power until the early thirteenth century, after which their judicial powers were progressively replaced by ecclesiastical courts.[31] It remains unclear to what extent early medieval kings in Sweden exerted power, and what specific role they played. Recent scholarship suggests that they essentially worked as mediators between the provinces, and as a sort of spokesperson for the entire realm. They certainly seem to have played an important role when larger exterior threats required the mustering of a fleet or army, in which case the king became a military leader.[32] "Kings" in the long Viking Age should therefore be seen as overlords: particularly powerful noblemen who achieved a certain level of recognition, even if only locally.

A magnate's claim to kingship relied on his social networks – especially at a time when hereditary monarchy was not the norm and other factors influenced someone's popularity. Before Christianity became firmly established in the second half of the twelfth century, people could derive their social status from both parents, which is of course relevant to the study of queenship. As Christian customs took hold, maternal lineage declined in importance for questions of inheritance, but until the late twelfth century, one's kin on the maternal line could be as influential as those on one's paternal line.[33] This impacted greatly on early Swedish kings' choices in partners, as will be shown throughout this book. It also means that one's allegiance could get complicated. Kin groups, in medieval Scandinavia, did not revolve solely around blood family. Friends were very important too, although in a medieval context, they could quickly turn into enemies, because they were not necessarily people that you got on with at a personal level. They were people who might have done you a favour, thus tying you into bounds of loyalty which contemporary codes of honour expected you to respect. Or they were perhaps former business associates of your late great-uncle, and thus you were expected to maintain the relationship. Betraying friends or otherwise failing to honour friendships could lead to the (literal) burning of bridges. The sagas are littered with stories of bloody battles sparked by such feuds. Generally, the friends of your friends were also your friends, and you were automatically enrolled into your parents' social circles. Interestingly, marriage between clans or kingdoms, perhaps as a peace exercise, meant that some people could end up belonging to rival social circles, and yet were bound by the same ties of loyalty to both sides. It could be that one sometimes had to choose friends over family, depending on the strategic or economic importance of the relationship itself, rather than one's personal connection with the other party. Much has been written about this subject and I defer to Hermanson's work, for instance, and the more recent series *Nordic Elites in Transformation c. 1050–1250* (2019–2022).[34] As mentioned, Christian customs, which emphasised blood family and the sanctity of marriage, helped streamline social networks in medieval Sweden. They restricted women's rights, and cemented their rigid role within the family unit.[35] For our purposes, however, this is convenient, as it means that the relationship between king and queen (or mistress) becomes much clearer and better documented from the late twelfth century onwards.

Kingship, the monarchy, and therefore the state developed together. As a result, some of the terminology usually associated with state formation, and which will be employed throughout this monograph, should be explained. "Sweden" itself needs to be contextualised. While its borders to the east and west were roughly settled by the end of the eleventh century, the provinces to the south which constituted Skåneland (modern-day Skåne and Blekinge) belonged to Denmark until the seventeenth century. The borders to the north were unclear even at the time, as thick forests virtually cut off entire self-governing regions such as Jämtland, which was also disputed with Norway. The island of Gotland functioned on the periphery, and it remains debated how integrated it was with the rest of the kingdom.[36] Finland, which was conquered during the first Baltic Crusades which took place in the early twelfth century, was also a fully recognised province until Sweden lost it to Russia in the nineteenth century.[37] The realm's borders and the main towns within it were therefore quite similar in the high Middle Ages to what they are today. Yet the power afforded to the local assemblies, and the influence exerted by local magnates, kept it from gelling. Sweden, in sum, did not function as one cohesive unit until the late twelfth century, when it started being treated as such, chiefly by the Papacy. This subject requires its own book, but in summary, the advent of the Crusades and the growing threat of Orthodox Christianity may have led the Church to double down on its efforts to fully integrate Sweden within Christendom. It was certainly a convenient ally to have, with Finland and Gotland now serving as buffer zones between Russia and the rest of northern Europe.[38] The fragmentary nature of Sweden, in addition, also made ecclesiastical hegemony all the more attractive, as it faced virtually no competition from any other centralised authority. In supporting the Church, local magnates saw an opportunity to increase their own power and legitimacy in the public eye – something which will be discussed in the second chapter of this monograph. The process of state formation in Sweden was therefore intrinsically linked to the development of the Church in that region.

There has been, however, considerable debate about whether the term "state" should apply to a medieval kingdom. One of the main problems with the word is the connotations that come with it. In modern parlance, states are highly organised and centralised entities, with a full legal and financial infrastructure in place, and with a state army.[39] Very few places in medieval Europe had all these characteristics before the early modern period, and it is indeed from the sixteenth century onwards that most European kingdoms started calling themselves "states." However, it took hundreds of years for these early modern states to develop their attributes, and the expression "state formation" has been rightfully applied to the medieval period. In fact, Rees Davies pointed out that the kingdoms and polities of the Middle Ages could be as sophisticated as later states.[40] Yet, he also remarked that by using the same word to describe medieval and early modern polities, historians may apply the same criteria to both periods, which might lead to a simplification of the various layers of power which existed throughout medieval Europe. Admittedly, using the word "state" to discuss medieval kingdoms – an increasingly common practice from the nineteenth century onwards – may have helped rehabilitate these very polities, which had long been seen as primitive.[41]

Unsurprisingly, different definitions of statehood emerged according to individual historians' interpretation. Pre-Conquest England, for example, has been characterised as an "elaborately organised state" by James Campbell due to the rulers' advanced control of coinage, tax assessment and collection, and extensive royal legislation. None of these are true of Sweden before the end of the thirteenth century. Susan Reynolds instead proposed the following definition: "an organisation of human society within a more or less fixed area in which the ruler or governing body more or less successfully controls the legitimate use of physical force."[42] As will be shown in the second and third chapters, this definition can apply to Sweden from the thirteenth century onwards, when the Crown went increasingly unopposed. Thomas Bisson, in order to avoid anachronistic connotations, preferred the use of more general terms such as "lordship" and "power" rather than "administration" and "government."[43] He argues that "lordship," for instance, can be used to discuss all relations of subordination, whether between a king and his subjects, or landed people and their tenants. Following Bisson's example, this book will prefer general terms such as "central power," "the Crown," and "centralised administration" when discussing medieval Swedish politics. This will also help avoid unnecessary anachronisms when discussing these emerging institutions, while still efficiently conveying their nature and basic functions.

Considering how little is understood of early kings' actual influence, authority, and role in early medieval Sweden, it is to be expected that even less is known about their wives and partners. As mentioned, men could have multiple partners who, in pagan times, all held near equal status. The situation was somewhat simplified after Christianity, but the lack of sources about some of the women studied makes it difficult to establish what their position was, whether they were officially married to the king, and other such important information. In any case, queens have been defined in various ways. In medieval Scandinavia, the term referred to a woman lawfully married to a king. Imsen points out that the use of the word *drottning* is derived from the Old Norse *drótt*, which refers to a lord or prince, and should therefore be translated as "lady" or "princess."[44] *Drottning* was reserved for the lawful wife of a king from the Viking Age onwards. From that perspective, in fact, some female monarchs should not be called queens at all in modern parlance, as some were not married to a king. Margaret I, for instance, was never married to a "union-king" but rather created the union and reigned over it herself.[45] "Female monarch" is more appropriate in a Scandinavian context, although in line with contemporary usage, the term "regnant queen" will be used as well. However, it is interesting to note that historical usage may have been less restrictive than it is now. This is certainly a result of the stringent social roles imposed by Christian monarchical customs which have moulded an image of queenship which is much more simplistic than the Viking Age reality. The monograph will therefore also include women who seem to have been the main partner of a given king, although they may not have been formally afforded the title in writing and might not have been religiously married. In cases where the connection with a king is present but less formal, or not as close – an influential sister or mother, or a concubine – "royal woman" will be used instead.

As mentioned previously, medieval Sweden is notoriously difficult to study because of the scarcity of sources available. This is true of many regions in the Middle Ages, but the situation was made significantly worse by the destruction of Tre Kronor, the royal castle in Stockholm which held all royal archives and burned down in 1697. Copies were kept in Åbo, the capital city of Finland until 1827, when a fire also reduced the city to ashes (and its set of archives with it). What historians of medieval Sweden rely on, therefore, consists of a very limited number of charters, private correspondence, and other documents which had been kept outside of these two repositories. This includes private documents kept within families, copies of Swedish charters made abroad – many of our sources are preserved in Germany, for instance – and ecclesiastical records, which were typically kept in churches and monasteries. The latter are rather scarce too, however, as the Reformation led to the destruction of many monasteries and their libraries with them. We do have, nevertheless, a significant number of legal texts and political documents such as treaties – which were nearly always copied, with the different parties involved all receiving a duplicate. While physical editions of these sources exist, they can also be searched online as they have been digitised by Riksarkivet.[46] Wills and charters documenting land transactions, while they may seem boring, are usually useful in revealing the power dynamics at play within society, as well as the different ways in which women were involved in the economy. Unsurprisingly, however, some of our most important sources for medieval Sweden are its laws. Several provincial laws have survived. All were written down in the thirteenth and fourteenth centuries, although they may reflect older practices as well as many show clear signs of being based on older, sometimes oral tradition.[47] This makes them useful as sources for the Viking Age, and to an extent for pre-Christian customs as well, despite their being written well into the Christian era.

The oldest surviving example is *Västgötalagen*, which exists in two versions, one being slightly older than the other. They were written down in the 1220s and 1280s, respectively. It was the law of Västergötland, the western side of Götaland, where Gothenburg is located. *Västgötalagen* is fascinating because of its breadth, but also because of the various amendments and extras which were added to it in its later version. These include a list of all law-speakers of the region, but also a list of kings, and other precious information about the region's elite families. These appendices were added in by a priest, about whom little is known, but who may have been a cleric at the diocese of Skara involved in the updating of the law. He no doubt had access to sources which are now lost.[48] Another law text surviving from the first half of the thirteenth century is *Gutalagen*, the law of the island of Gotland. From the late thirteenth and early fourteenth centuries, we have *Upplandslagen*, the law of Uppland which is often considered Sweden's traditional historic core; *Östgötalagen*, from the eastern part of Götaland; *Hälsingelagen*, the law of Helsingland, a region which functioned autonomously longer than the rest of the king-dom; *Södermannalagen* which covered the region south-west of Uppland; and *Tiohäradslagen* in what is now Småland. An addi-tional legal code has survived which did not apply to provinces but merchant cities. This is called the *Bjärköarätt* but will not be particularly useful for the purpose of our study.[49] The provincial laws were all edited in the nineteenth century and first half of the twentieth century, and translations in modern Swedish are available as well. Recently, Thomas Lindkvist also published an English translation of *Västgötalagen*.[50]

Despite the survival of several laws and many charters, much of what we know about early medieval Scandinavia comes from later sources, and as a result of the lack of contemporary sources highlighted above, it is impossible not to use later literature. The Icelandic sagas, which were written down roughly from the thirteenth century onwards, provide us with some insight into Viking Age and twelfth-century Scandinavia. They are by no means always factual, however, and scholars have long recog-nised that the historicity of the events and characters they depict must always be questioned. The sagas mostly deal with Viking Age, pre-Christian stories, and they are therefore most relevant to Sweden's earliest queens, although they can be useful too in iden-tifying basic genealogical information about later queens. Most details about the life of Sweden's first historical queen, Sigrid, are found in the early thirteenth-century compilation *Heimskringla*, for instance – more on this below. For later royal women, other sources can be more enlightening, including both domestic and foreign annals and chronicles, as well as poetic writings such "Erikskrönikan," which is Sweden's oldest surviving chronicle, having been written during the first half of the fourteenth century. It deals with the history of Erik, Duke of Södermanland, who was a son of Magnus Ladulås. This chronicle will be useful in understanding the political role that women played in the thirteenth century, notably in terms of forging alliances through marriage. It is not to be confused with "Erikslegenden," composed in the late thirteenth century in support of the canonisation of the twelfth-century crusader king Erik Jedvardsson (Saint Erik).

As mentioned previously, ecclesiastical records are important, and some of our most precious sources regarding medieval Sweden and its royal dynasties were written by foreign ecclesiastics. Two sources will be used extensively in the first part of this book: Adam of Bremen's *Gesta Hammaburgensis Ecclesiae Pontificum* (*The History of the Archbishops of Hamburg-Bremen*), composed between 1073 and 1076, and Saxo Grammaticus' *Gesta Danorum* written in the second half of the twelfth century.[51] Both works extensively discuss Scandinavia's prehistory. Adam's treatise is a thorough description of the lands belonging to the archdiocese of Hamburg-Bremen in the eleventh century, which included the whole of Scandinavia until the diocese of Lund was elevated to the status of archdiocese in 1104. It was entirely written outside of Scandinavia and there is no evidence that Adam ever visited the regions that he wrote about. As such, some of his accounts are nearly fictional, or at least vastly exaggerated. In spite of this, others are still routinely used as primary sources, such as his description of pre-Christian Norse beliefs and traditions, as well as his discussion of some diplomatic events and geographical regions such as the Oder estuary.[52] While his focus was on discrediting pre-Christian customs and its actors, his work will nevertheless be very useful when dealing with the earliest queens of Sweden, some of whom he directly wrote about. Saxo's *Gesta*, which unlike Adam's was written from within Scandinavia by a Scandinavian man, presents the history of Denmark. It is a nationalistic history and as such is a work of propaganda. It is nevertheless useful in that it gives us information about events, battles, dynastic struggles, and the general political landscape of early medieval Scandinavia. While Saxo's word should not always be trusted, it allows us to cross-reference with other sources. Saxo is also good for comparing different receptions of the same events, and it will therefore be used throughout this monograph.

Another early surviving source for Scandinavian history is *Chronicon Thietmari* compiled between 1013 and 1018 by the bishop Thietmar of Merseburg.[53] Thietmar's work is more concerned with political happenings during the reigns of German emperors Henry I, all three Ottos, and Henry II. This is relevant to us because that leads him to discussing matters of inheritance and fighting over Slavic lands, from whom several Swedish queens hailed during this period. His work therefore provides the background information required to contextualise some of the dynastic marriages that took place during the tenth and eleventh centuries. Other ecclesiastical writings of a less narrative nature have also been produced which can help with early Swedish history. Censuses, for instance, which gather financial information, sometimes reveal nuggets of information which give us clues as to the economic relations between families, dynasties and so on. For instance, Danish King Valdemar II's *jordebog*, discussed shortly, is a crucial source in the study of Sigrid, the first attested queen of Sweden. Chronicles and annals centred on specific nunneries or dioceses also give biographical information about royal women who may have chosen a religious existence – a fascinating aspect of women's lives which will be investigated in the second chapter. Martyrologies, necrologies, and other lists of names and events will also be used throughout the monograph.

To a lesser extent, archaeological sources can help us understand women's lives, especially for those least documented periods of the Viking Age. Runic inscriptions, in particular, can help reconstruct the economic landscape of a given area, and shed light on the roles played by women within it. This is admittedly a very limited application of archaeology, but it is nevertheless an important tool which comes in handy where nothing else remains. Archaeological investigations can also sometimes help confirm or refute information given in written sources. As we shall see in the next chapter of this monograph, much has been written about some semi-historical queens about whom little is really known. Archaeology can at least help confirm the likelihood of their owning particular estates or having lived in certain areas as per the sagas and other written sources.

1.3 Mythical and Ancient Royal Dynasties

The biographies covered in this book start in the mid-tenth century because there is virtually nothing written down about Swedish royal women from earlier than this period. It is not to say that the first queen studied here – Sigrid Storråda – was the first ever; she is merely the first properly documented. Ancient historians and geographers had some knowledge of Scandinavia and wrote extensively about its populations. In the first century AD, Tacitus wrote the earliest surviving mention of the native tribes dwelling in modern-day Sweden in his work *Germania*. Tacitus' account is in fact very interesting for the purposes of the present study. In his description of what roughly corresponds to Sweden and part of Finland, he mentions the Sitones, a tribe that he considers similar to the Suiones, and both are now usually considered to be likely ancestors of the Swedes. About the Sitones, he writes that they were ruled by women, an unsurprisingly uncommon phenomenon which he thought worth a mention.[54]

This particular line has attracted considerable attention and scholars usually belong to one of two sides. There are those who have adopted the view that it is highly unlikely that such a situation could have taken place so early in history. Kemp Malone, for instance, interpreted this passage of Tacitus' work as a metaphor for the downfall of the Sitones, whom Tacitus was unfavourably comparing to other Germanic tribes.[55] More recently, Axel Kristinsson described the statement as "rather fanciful" and even doubted the existence of the Sitones.[56] Writing 1100 years after Tacitus, Saxo Grammaticus also took the Danes' temporary submission to a queen as evidence of the downfall of the kingdom.[57] There might therefore be a literary motif here whose historicity is questionable. Yet, others have taken the statement at face value and drawn a linguistic correspondence between the Sitones and

Situne, the Latin spelling for the early medieval capital city of Sigtuna.[58] The merits of this theory as well as the reconstructions of the various ethnonyms applied to this region have been studied elsewhere, but there is little doubt that there must have been some sort of continuity – even if indirect – between the Suiones and the Sitones, and the medieval Swedes.[59] The relative power that medieval Swedish women had compared to their peers elsewhere in Europe in the later medieval period also seems to sustain the theory that Tacitus' statement was at least partly accurate. The truth might lie in the middle: Tacitus may well have overstated the political importance of women in an attempt to discredit the Sitones, but it is nevertheless possible that women were already held in higher regard than in other tribes.

Unfortunately, Tacitus is the only source in which this informa-tion about women's ruling power is given and therefore our inter-pretation remains speculative. In Ptolemy's *Geography*, written around 150 AD, the various groups which lived in Scandinavia are described again with no significant departure from Tacitus' own observations, although nothing is said about ruling women.[60] Much later on, in the sixth century, we know that Roman politi-cian Cassiodorious wrote a history of the Gothic people, who are thought by the majority of the scholarly community to have emi-grated from Sweden around the time when the Western Roman Empire fell. This work is now lost.[61] However, it was used by the Romano-Gothic writer Jordanes as basis for his own history of the Goths, *De origine actibusque Getarum* which provides the most detailed account of Sweden ever written before Adam of Bremen, although he does not mention Sweden's women.[62]

While these accounts were written several centuries before the first queen studied here was born, their description of Sweden and Tacitus' observation of women is a good reference to keep in mind, as neither Scandinavia nor the Slavic and Baltic popu-lations were Christianised for another 300 years after Jordanes, and therefore it is plausible that little changed in the way of cus-toms, gender expectations, and behaviours. These descriptions also informed and influenced later ecclesiastical writings such as Adam of Bremen's eleventh-century account, and it is thus impor-tant to know the origins and sources for some of the stereotypes about Scandinavian women which were widespread in the later medieval period.

Legendary dynastic lines going back to the third century AD have been reconstructed thanks to sources such as "Ynglingasaga" among others.[63] However, the earliest king of Sweden whose name is known and considered reliable is Björn, who was said in the ninth-century *Vita Anskarii* written by Rimbert to have ruled over Birka.[64] Birka is known to have been an extremely important Viking Age settlement and port before declining in the second half of the tenth century when the nearby town of Sigtuna took off instead.[65] We do not know whether Björn was recognised as overlord by the wider population dwelling in modern-day Sweden, or whether he was just one of many petty kings ruling over small territories. Considering the frailty of the concept of "Sweden" before the twelfth century, it is more likely to be the second option. Nonetheless, the fact that his reign is documented shows that his status was established enough and recognisable enough for an external observer to count him as a legitimate ruler among the many other monarchs and emperors discussed in the *Vita Anskarii*.

Several legendary kings are known before Björn and Erik Segersäll (Sweden's first official king), although the veracity of their life stories as told by Adam of Bremen, Saxo, the Icelandic sagas and later medieval authors cannot be proven beyond doubt due to the severe paucity of contemporary sources. "Lilla Rimkrönikan," composed in the fourteenth century, gives a list of legendary kings which is so obviously far-fetched that it can only be fictional.[66] Consequently, almost nothing is known about their alleged partners and daughters. Several legendary Swedish royal women are mentioned by Saxo. One is Sigrith, who according to him was the daughter of King Yngve of Götaland.[67] We are told how Yngve's son Alf married a princess named Alfhild, herself the daughter of another king, also in Götaland. Alf and Alfhild supposedly had a daughter named Gurid, whose son Harald became king of Denmark.[68] This is all reportedly taking place sometime in the fifth or sixth century, and proponents of the idea that this is historically accurate have noted that these events may directly precede those mentioned in the Anglo-Saxon epic *Beowulf*.

It should be remembered that neither *Beowulf* nor Saxo's *Gesta Danorum* are considered completely accurate and while there is some overlap in the events depicted, *Beowulf* was mainly written for entertainment, while Saxo's work is highly politically charged and biased.[69]

Elsewhere, prior to Erik Segersäll, Adam of Bremen mentions three kings: Ring, and his sons Emund and Erik. All three are said to have ruled at the same time, and they were supposedly succeeded by Erik Segersäll.[70] The Icelandic sagas give us yet more names: the thirteenth-century "Hervarar saga ok Heiðreks" provides Erik's family tree several generations back, none of whom can be reliably confirmed.[71] Several sagas relate the existence of one Olof Björnsson, a brother and alleged co-ruler of Erik Segersäll. According to Saxo, Olof's daughter is said to have been named Gyra, and to have married King Harald of Denmark mentioned above, who reigned in the second half of the tenth century, thereby becoming Queen of Denmark.[72] Yet, despite the fact that co-kings were common in early medieval Scandinavia, this Olof Björnsson only appears in this saga as well as in some of those compiled in *Heimskringla* and a short story named "Styrbjarnar þáttr Svíakappa," all of which were written several centuries later, and the rest of his lineage can therefore not be proven beyond doubt in spite of its plausibility. This is a recurring problem in the study of Sweden's early queens.

As nothing else is known about any of the aforementioned women's lives, it is impossible to confirm or disprove any of the little information we have. They might not have existed at all, as no surviving contemporary source mentions them. Despite this, they tell us a few things, regardless of their historicity. Firstly, these stories are evidence that multiple kings could reign in the same region at once, which means that there were necessarily multiple royal lines in existence at any given time. Considering that literary records did not appear before the twelfth century in Sweden, this also means that it is impossible to trace all the royal women who lived prior to that period. Secondly, women could play (or be portrayed as playing) an important diplomatic role across their kingdom's boundaries, and this will be a recurrent theme throughout this study. Finally, the fact that some women are mentioned by name in medieval works about Scandinavia, even if they are fictional, shows that they were not systematically ignored. This may seem like a self-evident, even superfluous observation, but the main reason why most historical women throughout the world have been so little studied is because they have routinely been erased from history – thus giving the impression of a world nearly exclusively populated by men. Writing about women therefore reflects the recognition by some medieval authors of Scandinavian history that female characters could be important and worth naming. Some of the likely reasons for this will be explored throughout the book.

In conclusion, research into the queens of early and high medieval Sweden needs an update from a strictly historical perspective – as opposed to a literary or mythological approach. This study is divided into three chapters: Viking Age women, who are all problematic in that little is known about them; queens of the twelfth and early thirteenth centuries, whose reigns were characterised by a close relationship with the Church; and the women who lived in the thirteenth and early fourteenth centuries, many of whom enjoyed significant political and economic agency. The main objective of these biographies is to identify these women, provide accurate information about them as far as feasible, and contextualise them within Europe. Several recurring patterns will emerge, not least queens' continued role as intercessors. It will become clear that although Sweden was slow in developing royal institutions, administration, and an ecclesiastical framework, its queens were very much integrated within Europe's cultural fabric.

Notes

1 As it did elsewhere in Europe during that time. See the contributions to Simon Forde, Lesley Johnson, and Alan V. Murray, eds., *Concepts of National Identity in the Middle Ages* (Leeds: University of Leeds, 1995).
2 Heather J. Tanner, Laura L. Gathagan, and Lois Huynecutt, "Introduction," in *Medieval Elite Women and the Exercise of Power, 1100–1400: Moving beyond the Exceptionalist Debate*, ed. Heather J. Tanner (Cham: Springer, 2019), 1–6.

3 Elena Woodacre, *Queens and Queenship* (Leeds: ARC Humanities Press, 2021).

4 Pauline Stafford, *Queens, Concubines and Dowagers: The King's Wife in the Early Middle Ages* (Athens: University of Georgia Press, 1983). A discussion of the importance of this monograph has been provided by a group of scholars consisting of Valerie L. Garver, Penelope Nash, Elena Woodacre, Janet L. Nelson, Charlotte Cartwright, Theresa Earenfight, Phyllis Jestice, Simon MacLean, Lucy K. Pick, Dana Polanichka, Katherine Weikert, and Megan Welton, "Forum: Pauline Stafford's Queens, Concubines, and Dowagers Thirty-Five Years On," *Medieval People* 35, no. 1 (2020), article 3. Available at: https://scholarworks.wmich.edu/medpros/vol35/iss1/3, accessed 23 April 2024.

5 Anne Duggan, ed., *Queenship in Medieval Europe: Proceedings of a Conference Held at King's College London April 1995* (Woodbrige: The Boydell Press, 1997). John Carmi Parsons, ed., *Medieval Queenship* (New York: Palgrave-Macmillan, 1990).

6 Theresa Earenfight, *Queenship in Medieval Europe* (New York: Palgrave-Macmillan, 2017).

7 Katherine Fischer Drew, *The Law of the Franks* (Philadelphia: University of Pennsylvania Press, 1991).

8 Kathleen Nolan, *Capetian Women* (New York: Palgrave Macmillan, 2003). Éliane Viennot, *La France, les femmes et le pouvoir: l'invention de la loi salique (V-XVI siècle)* (Paris: Perrin, 2006). Marion Facinger, "A Study of Medieval Queenship: Capetian France, 987–1237," *Studies in Medieval and Renaissance History* 5 (1968), 3–48.

9 Marjorie Chibnall, *The Empress Matilda: Queen Consort, Queen Mother and Lady of the English* (Oxford: Blackwell, 1993). Helen Castor, *She-Wolves: The Women Who Ruled England before Elizabeth* (London: Faber and Faber, 2010).

10 Louise Wilkinson, "Royal Daughters and Diplomacy at the Court of Edward I," in *Edward I. New Interpretations*, ed. Andy King and Andrew Spencer (York: York Medieval Press, 2020), 84–103. Charles Beem, *The Lioness Roared: The Problems of Female Rule in English History* (New York: Palgrave Macmillan, 2008).

11 Therese Martin, *Queen as King: Politics and Architectural Propaganda in Twelfth-Century Spain* (Leiden: Brill, 2006). Theresa Earenfight, ed., *Queenship and Political Power in Medieval and Early Modern Spain* (Abingdon: Routledge, 2005).

12 Przemyslaw Wiszewski, *Domus Bolezlai: Values and Social Identity in Dynastic Traditions of Medieval Poland (c.966–1138)* (Leiden: Brill, 2010). Grzegorz Pac, *Women in the Piast Dynasty: A Comparative Study of Piast Wives and Daughters (c. 965–c.1144)*, trans. Anna Kijak (Leiden: Brill, 2022).

13 Talia Zajac, "The Social-Political Roles of the Princess in Kyivan Rus," in *A Companion to Global Queenship*, ed. Elena Woodacre (Amsterdam: Amsterdam University Press, 2018), 125–146. By the same author, see "Gloriosa Regina or 'Alien Queen'? Some

Reconsiderations on Anna Yaroslavna's Queenship (r. 1050–1075),"
Royal Studies Journal 3, no. 1 (2016), 28–70.

14 Inge Skovgaard-Petersen, "Queenship in Medieval Denmark," in
Medieval Queenship, ed. John Carmi Parsons (New York: Palgrave-
Macmillan, 1990), 25–42.

15 Peter Sawyer, *När Sverige blev Sverige* (Alingsås: Viktoria Bokförlag,
1991). Sverre Bagge, *From Gang Leader to the Lord's Anointed:
Kingship in* "Sverris saga" *and* "Hákonar saga Hákonarsonar"
(Odense: Odense University Press, 1996). Philip Line, *Kingship and
State Formation in Sweden: c. 1130–1290* (Leiden: Brill, 2007).

16 Fredrik Charpentier Ljungvist, *Lagfäst kungamakt under högmedeltiden: en komparativ internordisk studie* (Stockholm: Institutet för
Rättshistorisk Forskning, 2016).

17 Lars Hermanson, "Släkt, vänner och makt: en studie av elitens
politiska kultur i 1100-talets Danmark" (PhD Diss., Gothenburg University, 2000).

18 Lars Hermanson and Auður Magnúsdóttir, eds., *Medeltidens genus:
Kvinnors och mäns roller inom kultur, rätt och samhälle. Norden och
Europa ca 300–1500* (Gothenburg: Acta Universitatis Gothoburgen-
sis, 2016).

19 Auður Magnúsdóttir, "Frillor och fruar: politik och samlevnad på
Island 1120–1400" (PhD Diss., Gothenburg University, 2001),
and "Friends, Foes, and Follower. Power, Networks, and Intimacy
in Medieval Iceland," in *Nordic Elites in Transformation, c. 1050–
1250, Volume II: Social Networks*, ed. Kim Esmark, Lars Hermanson, and Hans-Jacob Orning (Abingdon: Routledge, 2020), 215–236.

20 *Kvinnor och familj i det forn- och medeltida Skandinavien* was first
published in Skara by Viktoria bokförlag in 1992 but was subsequently
reworked by the author in 2015. A new version is available online
at: https://www.academia.edu/15124871/Kvinnor_och_familj_i_det_
forn-_och_medeltida_Skandinavien, accessed 23 April 2024. It is this
new version which will be used in the present monograph.

21 William Layher, *Queenship and Voice in Medieval Northern Europe*
(New York: Palgrave Macmillan, 2010).

22 For an introduction to the larger-than-life character that Queen
Christina was, see Veronica Buckley, *Christina, Queen of Sweden:
The Restless Life of a European Eccentric* (New York: HarperCollins,
2004).

23 Louise Berglund, "Medeltidens diskreta makthavare: om abbedissan Ragnhild och andra kvinnor i Riseberga kloster," in *Patroner,
gästgivare och andra kvinnor*, ed. Gunnela Björk, Håkan Henriksson,
and Sture Isaksson (Örebro: Lokalhistoriska sällskapet i Örebro län,
2008), 7–20. By the same author, "Queen Philippa and Vadstena
Abbey: Royal Communication on a Medieval Media Platform," in
Media and Monarchy in Sweden, ed. Mats Jönsson and Patrik Lundell
(Göteborg: Nordicom, 2009), 21–32.

24 Hans Hildebrand, *Sveriges medeltid: kulturihistorisk skildring* (in
2 vols) (Stockholm: P. A. Norstedt & Söner, 1879).

25 Hildebrand, *Sveriges medeltid vol. 1*, 90–92.
26 Hildebrand, *Sveriges medeltid vol. 1*, 88–89.
27 Steinar Imsen, "Late Medieval Scandinavian Queenship," in *Queens and Queenship in Medieval Europe*, ed. Anne Duggan (Woodbridge: Boydell Press, 1997), 53–74.
28 Svenskt Diplomatariums huvudkartotek (SDHK) nr 169, https://sok. riksarkivet.se/SDHK, accessed 23 April 2024.
29 Thomas Lindkvist, ed. and trans., *The Västgöta Laws* (Abingdon: Routledge, 2021), 197.
30 Karsten Friis-Jensen, ed., and Peter Fisher, trans., *Saxo Grammaticus. Gesta Danorum: The History of the Danes, Volume I* (Oxford: Clarendon Press, 2015), 919.
31 Caroline Wilhelmsson, "The Concept of Swedish Identity, 800–1288" (PhD diss., University of Aberdeen, 2022), 239–241.
32 Wilhelmsson, "The Concept of Swedish Identity, 800–1288," 44–50.
33 Jón Viðar Sigurðsson, "The Viking Age and the Scandinavian Peace," in *Viking Encounters: Proceedings of the Eighteenth Viking Congress*, ed. Anne Pedersen and Søren Sindbæk (Aarhus: Aarhus University Press, 2020), 24–25.
34 Bjørn Poulsen, Helle Vogt, end Jón Viðar Sigurðsson, eds., *Nordic Elites in Transformation, c. 1050–1250, Volume I: Material Resources* (Abingdon: Routledge, 2019). Kim Esmark, Lars Hermanson, and Hans Jacob Orning, eds., *Nordic Elites in Transformation, c. 1050–1250, Volume II: Social Networks* (Abingdon: Routledge, 2020). Wojtek Jezierski, Kim Esmark, Hans Jacob Orning, and Jón Viðar Sigurðsson, eds, *Nordic Elites in Transformation, c. 1050–1250, Volume III: Legitimacy and Glory* (Abingdon: Routledge, 2022).
35 This will be detailed later in this book. Also, see Birgit Sawyer's numerous works about the subject.
36 Wilhelmsson, "Swedish Identity," 109–152.
37 Line, *Kingship and State Formation*, 433–467.
38 Wilhelmsson, "Swedish Identity," 232–236.
39 Rees Davies, "The Medieval State: The Tyranny of a Concept?" *Journal of Historical Sociology* 16, no. 4 (2003), 284.
40 Davies, "The Medieval State," 284–286; 287–293.
41 Davies, "The Medieval State," 280–281.
42 Susan Reynolds, "The Historiography of the Medieval State," in *Companion to Historiography*, ed. Michael Bentley (London: Routledge, 1997), 118.
43 Thomas Bisson, "Medieval Lordship," *Speculum* 70, no. 4 (1995), 743–759.
44 Imsen, "Late Medieval Scandinavian Queenship," 53.
45 Imsen, "Late Medieval Scandinavian Queenship," 53.
46 Svenskt Diplomatariums huvudkartotek (SDHK), https://sok.riksarkivet. se/SDHK, accessed 23 April 2024. Physical editions have also been published in the series *Diplomatarium Suecanum*.

47 Stefan Brink, "The Creation of a Scandinavian Provincial Law: How Was It Done?," *Historical Research* 86 (2013), 5–11.

48 Lindkvist, *The Västgöta Laws*, 11–12.

49 Fredrik Charpentier Ljungqvist, *Quantitative Approaches to Medieval Swedish Law* (Newcastle: Cambridge Scholars Publishing, 2022), 27–38.

50 Lindkvist, *The Västgöta Laws*.

51 Georg Waitz, ed., *Adami Gesta Hammaburgensis ecclesiae pontificum ex recensione Lappenbergii* (Hannover: Impensis Bibliopolii Hahniani, 1876). The standard English translation is Francis Tschan, trans., *The History of the Archbishops of Hamburg-Bremen* (New York: Columbia University, 1959).

52 See contributions to Grzegorz Bartusik, Radosław Biskup and Jakub Morawiec, eds., *Adam of Bremen's* Gesta Hammaburgensis Ecclesiae Pontificum: *Origins, Reception and Significance* (Abingdon: Routledge, 2022).

53 For Thietmar's chronicle in Latin, see Robert Holtzmann, ed., *Die Chronik des Bischofs Thietmar von Merseburg und ihre Korveier Überarbeitung* (Berlin: Weidmann, 1935). In English: David Warner, trans., *Ottonian Germany. The Chronicon of Thietmar of Merseburg* (Manchester: Manchester University Press, 2001).

54 The standard translation, originally published in 1948, is James Rives, ed., and Harold Mattingly, trans., *Tacitus. The Agricola and the Germania* (London: Penguin Classics, 2010). For the description of Scandinavia, see chapters 44 and 45. For a Latin edition with commentaries, see J. G. C. Anderson, ed., *Tacitus. Germania* (Bristol: Bristol Classical Press, 1998).

55 Kemp Malone, "The Suiones of Tacitus," *The American Journal of Philology* 46, no. 2 (1925), 173–174.

56 Axel Kristinsson, *Expansions: Competition and Conquest in Europe since the Bronze Age* (Reykjavik: Reykjavíkur Akademían, 2010), 177.

57 Friis-Jensen and Fisher, *Gesta Danorum I*, 551–553.

58 "Sitones," in *Real-Encyclopädie der classischen Altertumswissenschaft in alphabetischer Ordnung, vol. 6. Pra-Stoai*, ed. August Pauly, Christian Walz and W. S. Teuffel (Stuttgart: Metzler, 1852), 1226.

59 Ludwig Rübekeil, "Scandinavia in the Light of Ancient Tradition," in *The Nordic Languages: An International Handbook of the History of the North Germanic Languages vol. I*, ed. Oskar Bandle (Berlin: De Gruyter, 2002), 602.

60 Multiple versions of Ptolemy's *Geography* survive in Greek and Latin, having been copied and reproduced multiple times throughout the centuries. There is, however, no scholarly English translation of the entire work in print, except for a flawed attempt by Edward Luther Stevenson from 1932. An excellent online and user-friendly edition of the maps and their descriptions produced by Bill Thayer can be found on the University of Chicago's server: https://penelope.uchicago.edu/Thayer/E/Gazetteer/Periods/Roman/_Texts/Ptolemy/home.html#Text, accessed 23 April 2024.

61 S. J. B. Barnish, "The Genesis and Completion of Cassiodorus' 'Gothic History'," *Latomus* 43 (1984), 336–361.

62 Peter Van Nuffelen and Lieve Van Hoof, trans., *Jordanes. Romana and Getica* (Liverpool: Liverpool University Press, 2020). For a Latin edition, see Theodor Mommsen, ed., *Iordanis. Romana et Getica* (Berlin: Weidmann, 1882).

63 Åke Ohlmarks, *Våra Kungar från äldsta till våra dagar* (Stockholm: Sturefölaget, 1972), 31–78.

64 Charles H. Robinson, trans., *Anskar, the Apostle of the North, 801–865* (Toronto: Toronto University Press, 1921), 13.

65 Charlotte Hedenstierna-Jonson, "Spaces and Places of the Urban Settlement of Birka," 23–31; Sten Tesch, "Sigtuna: Royal Site and Christian Town and the Regional Perspective, c. 980–1100," 115–132, both in *New Aspects on Viking Age Urbanism c. AD 750–1100: Proceedings of the International Symposium at the Swedish History Museum, April 17th–20th 2013*, ed. Lena Holmquist, Sven Kalmring, and Charlotte Hedenstierna-Jonson (Stockholm: Stockholm University Press, 2016).

66 Gustaf Edvard Klemming, ed., *Svenska Medeltidens Rimkrönikor* (Stockholm: Norstedt & Söner, 1865), 215–231.

67 Friis-Jensen and Fisher, *Gesta Danorum I*, 687.

68 Friis-Jensen and Fisher, *Gesta Danorum I*, 471–477.

69 Emily Lyle, "The Scylding Dynasty in Saxo and Beowulf as Disguised Theogony," in *Myth and History in Celtic and Scandinavian Traditions*, ed. Emily Lyle (Amsterdam: Amsterdam University Press, 2021), 235–246.

70 Tschan, *History of the Archbishops of Hamburg-Bremen*, 52.

71 Christopher Tolkien, ed. and trans., *Saga of King Heidrik* (London: Thomas Nelson & Sons, 1960), 60–61.

72 Friis-Jensen and Fisher, *Gesta Danorum I*, 464–471.

2

SEMI-HISTORICAL WOMEN

970–1090

This chapter introduces Sweden's earliest known historical royal women. These are Sigrid Storråda, the first known Swedish queen; Estrid and Edla, King Olof Skötkonung's wife and concubine; Gunnhild, wife of King Anund Jacob; Estrid Njalsdatter, wife of King Emund; and "Ingamoder," the nameless wife of King Stenkil and matriarch of his dynasty. As expected, these women are some of the most mysterious figures studied in this book. Concubinage was still common in the late Viking Age, and it is possible that other women, who are not mentioned in this work, were equally active in royal circles of this period. However, the lack of sources drastically restricts the number of individuals which can be reliably identified and meaningfully studied here. During the tenth and eleventh centuries, Sweden was undergoing a slow process of Christianisation, and the realm was fractured into traditional provinces which functioned independently. This resulted in an unstable political situation in which royal structures were ill-defined and sometimes non-existent, which significantly complicates our understanding of the period.

An additional hurdle to the study of these early women is their treatment in medieval sources. As will be shown in this chapter, one woman could be known under different names, and basic facts about her life could differ from one source to another. These discrepancies may have resulted from the author's genuine confusion – most sources regarding Viking Age Sweden were written much later, or abroad – but are also the product of medieval history-writing. Indeed, medieval attitudes towards the study

DOI: 10.4324/9781003392200-2

of history radically differ from ours. Accuracy was considered less important than the overall message conveyed, meaning names and facts could be changed according to the author's chosen narrative. As a result, the following biographies are confusing: they cannot be otherwise, as our understanding of linearity and factuality is at odds with the way medieval authors thought about and represented their subjects. Much can nevertheless be learned from these women especially in terms of gender roles and expectations.

2.1 Sigrid Storråda

While it is obvious that there were queens before her, the first queen of Sweden for which there is both sufficient and consistent historical evidence is Sigrid Storråda who, according to the sources discussed below, was first Queen of Sweden as the wife of Erik Segersäll and then Queen of Denmark as the wife of Svend II Tveskæg. While Sigrid primarily appears in Icelandic sagas as a literary character, she is also mentioned in non-fictional historical documents – which will be analysed below – which suggests that she might have existed. There has nevertheless been considerable debate about whether she should be studied as a historical character or remain confined to the realm of fiction, and arguments from both sides of the question will be discussed here. While we have to start with Sigrid as per the chronological nature of this monograph, she is by far the most complex woman discussed in this monograph – not least because she might, in fact, be no fewer than three different women mashed together.

The primary sources available give conflicting information about her family history and background. "Óláfs saga Tryggvasonar" tells us that she was the daughter of a Swedish magnate named Skoglar Toste (ON Skǫglar-Tósti). "Haralds saga Gráfeldar" and "Óláfs saga Helga" both confirm that ancestry, too.[1] *Heimskringla*, in which these three sagas appear, is however the only source to give us that information, and Skoglar Toste himself is a legendary character whose historicity has not been confirmed. His case illustrates the problem of the sagas' value as historical sources. Indeed, many saga characters are based on real people, and many of the events depicted may hold some historical truth.

Nevertheless, we also know that saga writers aimed to entertain their audiences and frequently mixed stories and amalgamated characters to create a more compelling narrative.[2] There is no evidence that a magnate called Skoglar Toste had a daughter who became Queen of Sweden, but there is also little to prove otherwise. There is one runestone in Uppland mentioning a successful Viking called Tosti, and some scholars have equated both men.[3] This, however, is a sort of self-fulfilling prophecy: both sources are used to justify the other. Icelandic writers (and indeed all medieval writers) relied heavily on local knowledge and oral tradition, and this saga's author might have known about the runestone and spun a story around it. Nonetheless, the chronology does not make sense. On the runestone, Toste is said to have been contemporary with King Canute the Great. This is unlikely because Toste, if he had been the father of Sigrid, who herself was old enough to be Canute's mother (and reputed to be so, as discussed further shortly), would have been a very old man at the point of his expedition. It should also be noted that Toste was a rather common name, which underlines the fragility of the link between runestone and saga. It is therefore likely, considering the lack of corroboration of the Toste ancestry from independent sources, that this relationship is fictional.

Instead, other historical documents can help shed light on Sigrid's ancestry. This is where, however, the investigation gets slightly more complex, as many of the sources which are about to be discussed do not use her name, but rather describe her according to her social relationships. Writing in the tenth century, Thietmar of Merseburg (who was contemporary with Sigrid), tells us that Svend Tveskæg's wife was the daughter of Mieszko I of Poland, and sister of Boleslaw the Great – who was a known ally of Erik Segersäll.[4] Writing a century later, Adam of Bremen writes that King Erik of Sweden was married to a Polish princess – "[Boleslaw's] daughter or sister," and that it is this princess who gave birth to Olof.[5] Neither author gives a name for the princess, but considering that Sigrid is said in the sagas to have first married Erik, given birth to Olof, and then married Svend, it is probable that these accounts all refer to the same person. However, as with any early medieval source written by an outsider who never actually met the people that he wrote about, it is possible that Thietmar misunderstood the exact nature of her relationship with Mieszko. It is likely, nevertheless, that he was mostly right when identifying her with a member of his close entourage.

There are several reasons why her identification with a Slavic princess is more trustworthy than the claim that she was the daughter of Skoglar Toste. Firstly, we discussed the fact that there is no evidence that the latter was her father, whereas her alleged links to specific, well-known Polish leaders are at least plausible. This is partly because it was extremely common, in the Viking Age, for Scandinavian magnates to marry Slavic women. There were numerous cultural and economic links between Sweden and the Baltic and Slavic regions during this period. Expeditions and raids towards the areas which now form the Baltic republics, as well as excursions towards eastern and central Europe via the Volga, Vistula, and Dniper Rivers, had led to Scandinavian settlements emerging in these areas as early as the eighth century, and perhaps earlier.[6] In this context, it is also impossible not to mention the Rus, a people of Swedish origin established in what is now roughly modern-day Ukraine and Belarus. Ethnically mixed by the ninth century, the Rus were the direct descendants of east Scandinavian travellers some of whom were engaged in trade, while others were on their way to Byzantium to serve in the Varangian Guard.[7] People of Scandinavian descent quickly formed a cultural and political elite centred around a chief named Rurik. While Rurik himself is a partly legendary figure, Slavic sources such as the *Novgorod First Chronicle* and the *Russian Primary Chronicles* do suggest that the earliest rulers of the dynasty were of Scandinavian origin.[8] Unsurprisingly then, over the next few hundred years, numerous alliances took place between eastern Scandinavians, the Rus, and their Baltic neighbours.

Secondly, recent research notably undertaken by archaeologists and mythologists has suggested that there was more than foreign politics at play when choosing foreign wives and partners in the Viking Age. It has been shown that elsewhere in Europe, kings sometimes chose low-born or alien women precisely to avoid creating dependency relations with other grandees.

This gave the king and his descendants some exclusivity regarding inheritance and avoided the type of feuds which became common in the Christian period. This strategy was notably adopted by Merovingian kings.[9] By taking Slavic wives, thus, early Swedish kings could avoid conflict with other local powerful families. This is completely incompatible with the hypothesis that Sigrid was the daughter of Toste. In addition, these women's foreign character itself may have been attractive. Indeed, many of the literary motifs found in Norse mythological texts include the idea that something foreign is powerful, mystical, to be respected. Foreigners are portrayed as a link between far-away worlds, sometimes supernatural. In more down-to-earth terms, being foreign or maintaining close relationships with foreigners showed a king's connection to societies far beyond what the regular Scandinavian farmer could possibly imagine.[10] It also gave them an excuse for disrespecting local power dynamics that they found inconvenient, allowed them to keep a distance from their subjects and, as mentioned previously, avoid conflict with local dynasties.[11] It would have therefore been much more advantageous for Erik to marry a foreign woman.

Thirdly, and on a more pragmatic level, neither Adam nor Thietmar wrote for entertainment. Or rather, it may not have been their primary focus. All writers aim to engage with an audience, and Adam for instance is known for his exaggerated descriptions of events, people, and beasts, which are sometimes more metaphorical than literal in nature.[12] Notwithstanding, they were both first and foremost ecclesiastical writers and would have gained little by purposefully misrepresenting Sigrid's ancestry who, because of her gender, remained a secondary character in the wider political landscape of the time. Saga writers, however, might have preferred to portray her as the wild daughter of a fierce and successful seafaring Viking, rather than as the court-educated daughter of a foreign prince with whom thirteenth-century Icelandic readers would not have identified. Indeed, as will be discussed shortly, the Sigrid from the sagas is systematically described as fierce, determined, and strong-willed, to the point of impertinence. From a narrative perspective, her character is flamboyant and engaging, but this may overstate her actual historical importance and certainly bend the truth. It is important to remember that saga writers composed their works long after Thietmar and Adam wrote theirs.

In most of the sagas in which she appears, her name is given in Old Norse as Sigríðr *ina stórráða* (or a close variant). It is transcribed in modern Swedish as Sigrid Storråda, and she is also known in English as "the Haughty." In "Yngvars saga víðförla," which was written in the twelfth century, it is said that she was the lawful wife (and apparently the first as well), of King Erik Segersäll (ON *inn sigrsæli*, "the Victorious").[13] This fact also appears in "Hervarar saga," in which she is briefly mentioned as the king's wife.[14] Similar information is given in "Óláfs saga Helga," "Haralds saga Gráfeldar," and "Óláfs saga Tryggvasonar," all of which are part of *Heimskringla*, compiled in the 1230s. Writing at the end of the twelfth century, Saxo Grammaticus calls her *Syritha*, the Latin form for Sigrid, and also names her as Erik's wife.[15] While Erik also appears in several fictional sources whose historicity cannot always be confirmed, Adam of Bremen, writing in the eleventh century, does tell us about him. His account, which he claims is supported by an interview with King Svend Estridsen of Denmark, places Erik's death between 992 (his ally's Boleslaw the Great of Poland's accession to the throne) and 995, when the first coins in Sweden were minted in Sigtuna by his son, Olof.[16] This makes Sigrid a late Viking Age queen at a time when Swedish elites were still mostly pagan but gradually shifting towards Christianity and Europeanised modes of governance. Erik's own conversion to Christianity, however, was most probably only political and evidently short-lived.[17]

Through her marriage to Erik, Sigrid is repeatedly presented as the mother of Olof Skötkonung, who became the first Christian king of Sweden at the very end of the tenth century. He is the only historical figure whose mother is systematically given as Sigrid. She might have had other children, including a daughter called Holmfrid with Erik, but as will be shown shortly, it is difficult to trace her kin because she has been associated with other women whose identities might have been mixed up over the centuries. The sagas further tell us that following Erik's death and Olof's accession to the throne of Sweden around 995, Sigrid married

the king of Denmark, Svend Tveskæg ("Forkbeard"), which formalised an alliance between the two kingdoms.[18] With Svend, she
may have had more children including Estrid Svendsdatter and
Canute the Great, although this is also disputed, as will be shown
below.

It must be said that the question of Sigrid's religion is an intriguing one. While all sources portray her as a staunch defender of
pre-Christian beliefs, if she truly was a daughter of Mieszko, one
may expect her to have been Christian.[19] Indeed, Mieszko I was
the first Christian ruler of Poland and, while he had been raised
as a pagan, he worked hard to spread the new faith in his realm.
In this context, it is difficult to see how it would have been acceptable for Sigrid to carry on with pre-Christian traditions and, as a
daughter of Mieszko, she would have probably not been exposed
to them in the first place.[20] Both of Mieszko's wives were openly
Christian as well, although there is no evidence that they gave
birth to Sigrid. As the exact identity of her mother is unknown,
it is equally possible that she might have been a pagan herself.
However, this discrepancy puts in doubt the theory that she was
Mieszko's daughter. It is unlikely that the daughter of a Christian
public figure would openly admit to being a pagan. It might be,
therefore, that she was not his daughter but perhaps another close
relative. A more radical explanation is that Sigrid might not have
been pagan at all, but saga authors might have written her as a
pagan character to embody pre-Christian beliefs – this will be
discussed again shortly. This would also explain why she is presented as a Swedish Viking's daughter, as it would be impossible,
for the reasons just mentioned, to introduce a Polish pagan princess in the story.

Viking Age women could play an important ritualistic role
in pre-Christian customs. While queenship during this period is
extremely difficult to define, an important aspect of it seems to
have been the queen's role as a drink-bearer during feasts. Feasts
were not solely a social occasion. It was during these lavish parties that business was conducted, that alliances were struck, and
that economic affairs were concluded. The hall was the most
important domestic building and had religious connections. The
central role that the hall plays in the concept of Valhall in Norse

mythology reflects its significance in real life.[21] The custom of feasting in a hall was not confined to Scandinavia, and similar practices can be found in Anglo-Saxon England too, for instance. In this context, the image of Viking Age queens and noblewomen projected in the sagas is that of intercessors between chieftains and their allies (and enemies), whose main role during feasts was that of a hostess who poured the men's drinks.[22] Far from being a reductive domestic role, this should be seen as a diplomatic function, which hints at the intercessory nature of a queen's position – which will be a recurring pattern in this study. Lavishly serving drinks to guests reflected well on a hostess whose own status benefitted from this expansive show of wealth. A hostess's status may have also reflected that of her guest with queens serving high dignitaries, and lower-class women serving correspondingly lower-class guests.[23] Our understanding of this aspect of women's role in the Viking Age remains patchy but this role may mark the beginning of the institutionalisation of queenship in the early medieval period.

We should note, however, that this role took place in the domestic sphere (if we consider the hall as a part of the home environment devoted to politics), and only took on its full symbolism when performed in relation to male guests and a male chieftain. It therefore should not be taken as evidence of female agency. In addition, whether this hosting function was unique to the lawful wife of a chieftain or could also be performed by other women is unclear, but as suggested above, less prestigious guests would have probably been served by women of a similar status. This further muddles the distinction between queen and mere noblewoman, and points to the drink-serving role as a womanly role in general, and not a specific characteristic of queenship. However, the sagas and later legal texts show that the lawful wife of a landowner could, in some circumstances, act as head of the household. This was particularly true when the king was away or when he died, and some women may have earned significant power through this avenue.[24] It is this rather than the drink-bearing itself which might point to a true characteristic of Viking Age queenship: that of holding authority over the running of the king's estate and its users during his absence. Nonetheless, we must also remember that these texts were written down much later, at a time when the wife as mistress of the house was indeed the common perception. It is therefore unclear whether these episodes accurately reflect Viking Age mores, and this question may be best answered by archaeologists.

In any case, there are various sources in which an unknown, historically attested noblewoman appears who fits many of Sigrid's characteristics. There is, firstly, the tenurial survey commissioned by Danish king Valdemar II, known as the *jordebog* (or *Liber Census Daniæ*). Valdemar's *jordebog* was compiled in the first half of the thirteenth century (he reigned between 1202 and 1241). It is an official record of the Crown's income and properties in Denmark as well as in other neighbouring areas, and how they came to its ownership. It is similar to the type of tenurial surveys commissioned by the kings of England and other powerful landowners precisely during the same period.[25] Of lands located in the southern region of Blekinge (then part of Denmark but now belonging to Sweden), *jordebog* says that some belonged to "Sigrydhlef," or the inheritance of Sigrid.[26] This is not only plausible but logical as well. "Óláfs saga Tryggvasonar" tells us that she owned land in her own name.[27] A later fourteenth-century list of kings claims that the "Sigrydhlef" is specifically named after the mother of Olof Skötkonung.[28] If Sigrid did marry Svend, as the sagas say and as Adam and Thietmar suggest, then it is to be expected that some of her possessions should have fallen into the hands of the Danish Crown.

Indeed, maternal inheritance was a regular occurrence in medieval Sweden, and women could not only own property independently of a man but also pass it on. This is related in later medieval laws but in a Viking Age context, most of the direct evidence for maternal inheritance relies on runic inscriptions. A significant portion of Swedish runestones indicate that women had the power and authority to raise memorials and own land. They could inherit either directly from their father, when there were no surviving sons (a common scenario in raiding dynasties), or indirectly from more distant family members such as an uncle. In turn, women could pass property onto their children, including daughters.[29] It should be noted, however, that historians such as Christian Lovén have cast doubt on the identity of the Sigrid whose name was given to the "Sigrydhlef." Indeed, there is another historically attested Sigrid who, in the mid-twelfth century, owned the land on which Varnhem Abbey was built. She was apparently a close kinswoman of Queen Kristina, the wife of Saint Erik. Her exact identity remains unknown, but the dating and written evidence of her links to royalty have led to the theory that it might be her who lent her name to the Sygridhlef. This remains inconclusive.

As has become obvious by now, much of Sigrid's biography requires to be reconstructed from different – and sometimes contradictory – sources. Unsurprisingly, therefore, there remains much confusion about Sigrid's exact identity, and she has been equated with several other women. It has been hypothesised that she may be the same person as Gunhild of the Wends. "Óláfs saga Tryggvasonar" tells us that Svend Tveskæg was forced to marry the daughter of Burislav, King of the Wends, as part of peace negotiations. That daughter is named as Gunhild and is said to have been the mother of Canute the Great.[30] This description (bar the specific mention of a link between the princess and Canute), also fits that given in the works of Adam and Thietmar. However, Saxo writes that it is Sigrid, as Svend's wife, who gave birth to Canute.[31] As a result, some have concluded that Gunhild was real and Sigrid fictional, some have come to the opposite conclusion, and others think that both women were mixed up, which seems likely.

Concerning the mysterious woman's link to Canute, scholars of medieval Poland have further posited that she might have been called Świętosława, a supposed daughter of Mieszko I of Poland whom we have shown has already been proposed as Sigrid's father. The theory assumes that Canute's sister may have been named Świętosława after her own mother. Evidence for the name of Canute's sister is found in the *New Minster Liber Vitae*, which records visitors to the New Minster in Winchester. A list of guests reads: "Santslaue, soror, Cnut regis nostris."[32] There are examples across northern Europe of royal daughters named after their living mothers, and the idea is that her name might shed light on her mother's identity. Most historians of Sweden remain sceptical about this assumption, as are other modern Polish scholars such as Rafał Prinke, but it is correct that Canute's mother was a Slavic princess.[33] This is evidenced in *Gesta Cnutonis Regis* which tells about Canute and his brother's trip to "the land of the Slavs" to bring back their mother.[34] It is nevertheless unclear in what context this expedition would have taken place. Thietmar, nonetheless, did write that Svend had eventually banished his Polish wife, who had perhaps gone back home.[35] However, Canute's mother could also have been any one of Svend's concubines. In any case, Canute's Polish ancestry also explains the presence of Polish troops in England during his reign.[36]

In conclusion, it is very likely that some facts about Sigrid's biography were misrepresented in medieval literature, either willingly for narrative effect or because of Svend's complicated family history. It was common for Scandinavian men to marry Slavic women of high rank during the Viking Age, due to the many cultural and economic exchanges that took place between the Slavic and Baltic territories, and Scandinavia from the eighth century through to the eleventh.[37] It is therefore entirely possible, and in fact likely, that Svend may have married several distinct Slavic princesses. To make matters worse, the norm in medieval literature was to ignore women's names. Few women are ever named, simply because they were not considered important enough to be remembered. This is of course hugely problematic when dealing with genealogy, not just for modern scholars but for later medieval writers as well, such as the author of *Heimskringla*, who were left to piece together the family trees of people long gone. Nevertheless, the mention of a woman called Sigrid in a legal text such as the *jordebog* as well as the fact that most sources agree that she did marry Erik and then Svend, give us enough reasons to treat her as at least partially historical.

One of the main reasons why many scholars still consider her wholly fictional is, of course, the fact that some important aspects of her life remain unclear, and that primary sources relay such contradictory information about her. Her image as a combative and volatile character has also contributed to her dismissal as fictional. Scholars of previous generations were particularly scathing in their assessment of her historicity. In 1911, Lauritz Weibull completely dismissed her as the product of late medieval authors' imagination.[38] In his *History of the Vikings*, originally published in 1968, Gwyn Jones makes a point of twice labelling her "the non-existent Sigrid the Haughty" and "the non-existent lady" within the same page.[39] Jones does not provide any explanation for his dismissal.[40] Doubting Sigrid's life is of course rational, and even the most optimistic of scholars will be fully aware that some episodes of her biography may be entirely fabricated. However, this is true of a great many medieval characters especially considering that the medieval concept of history-writing was significantly different from ours. Facts and chronological accuracy mattered less, and they were readily manipulated to achieve a particular effect on the audience, much akin to propaganda. Yet, comparatively few figures from Norse literature have been as systematically dismissed as Sigrid has. For example, while there is no doubt that Sigrid's first husband Erik existed, many aspects of the main events of his reign remain heavily debated, and the circumstances of his birth remain virtually unknown. Yet he is always taken more seriously as a historical figure than Sigrid. There is certainly a double standard when assessing the veracity of historical figures' lives, and Sigrid's treatment in scholarship is evidence of this.

Regardless of the exact details of Sigrid's life, or indeed whether she existed or not, there is immense scholarly value in studying what her literary treatment tells us about what was expected of royal women in Viking Age Sweden – and how these were perceived by both scholars and the public. In *Heimskringla*, Sigrid is a pagan, free-spirited and independent woman who quite literally does whatever she wants, whenever she wants. After the death of Erik, we are told that she was courted by several high-profile men, as she remained a high-quality widow of strategic value – being the mother of a king and owning plenty of land. The story goes that she was particularly ruthless with the poor suitors who dared ask for her hand. "Óláfs saga Tryggvasonar" in *Heimskringla* tells us that when King Vissavaldr came with his retinue from Garðaríki (eastern Europe) to ask her for marriage, "Queen Sigríðr had an attack made on them during the night with both fire and weapons," and that she said "that thus would she make petty kings stop going from other countries to ask to marry her."[41] It is frankly unlikely that this could have happened. Murdering kings would have had serious political implications, and yet *Heimskringla* does not mention any consequences for Sigrid's actions. This is more likely to be for narrative effect and to underline her independence.

However, *Heimskringla* (and Adam of Bremen) also tell us that she eventually agreed to marry Olaf Tryggvason, King of Norway, but that they fell out when she refused to convert to Christianity. After he called her a "heathen bitch" and threw his glove into her face, she allegedly threatened him: "that could well cost you your life."[42] Saxo's version of events is even more dramatic. He writes that Olaf, who had initially wanted to marry Sigrid to form an alliance with Sweden against King Svend of Denmark, purposefully humiliated Sigrid in public by having his men throw her into the sea. According to Saxo, the Danes had treacherously convinced Olaf that he could marry Thyra, Svend's young daughter (other sources have her as his sister). Olaf had preferred the prospect of marrying "an unspoilt virgin" rather than a "a woman in matron's garb." Capitalising on Sigrid's understandable anger, Svend then married her, refused Thyra's hand to Olaf, and entered into a conflict with him.[43] Some of the details of this story differ from one source to another. "Oláfs saga Tryggvasonar" in *Heimskringla* claims that Thyra did eventually marry Olaf, although against Svend's wishes.[44] In any case, all sources which mention this event agree that Sigrid exacted revenge on Olaf.

Indeed, it is said that Sigrid subsequently urged her son Olof and her new husband Svend to go to war against Olaf at the Battle of Svolder (presumably fought around the year 1000) during which Olaf lost his life.[45] The result seems to have been that Sigrid held sway over two kings at once. She is thought to have directly influenced Svend's politics, while Saxo himself admits that her son King Olof of Sweden "controlled the kingdom, albeit under her ascendancy."[46] Whether any of this is historically accurate is difficult to ascertain. In any case, this is particularly cunning behaviour by any standard, and certainly coming from a woman. This might be fictional, obviously, but still shows a willingness to portray her as a strong female character who held political

FIGURE 2.1 Illustration of Sigrid Storråda and Olaf Tryggvason. Drawing by Erik Werenskiold, 1899.

sway over powerful men – a rather rare phenomenon in medieval literature (Figure 2.1).

The language used to describe Sigrid's personality reveals a lot about differing attitudes towards women. *Heimskringla*, although written by a Christian author, aimed to partly capture the attitudes of a bygone era. At the beginning of her royal career, she is described in translation as "young and fair," and "very haughty."[47] This is a mixed description which is not entirely positive, but which also explains how she carved a legacy for herself independently of her husbands and suitors – more on this shortly. After Erik's death, she is said to be the "wisest of women and prophetic about many things."[48] This observation is in line with the idea notably supported by Hans Hildebrand that pagan women were seen as closer to nature and wiser than men.[49] It also tells us that Sigrid was someone worth listening to, and although temperamental, she is not represented as capricious. She is shown as being thoughtful, calculating, but also deeply aware of her responsibilities as a royal widow and landowner. Talking with her foster brother King Harald Grenski of Vestfold (in Norway), she is said to have emphasised that she valued her possessions within Sweden as much as his possessions in Norway, which underlines the fact that she considered herself a stateswoman of equal status to a man.[50] Her confidence might have arisen from her alleged background. If she was indeed a close relative of Mieszko I, then she certainly was well above Harald Grenski in social status, despite her gender. Indeed, Mieszko was the first attested ruler of Poland, which at that time was known as a duchy. In the 960s, it was rapidly expanding and consolidating as a state, and Mieszko can be credited with making Poland a serious political player in eastern Europe.[51] His possessions certainly dwarfed those of Harald Grenski who was no more than a petty king.

We do not know where Sigrid lived with Erik – and neither do we have that information for any of the women studied here prior to the twelfth century. The primary sources which discuss Erik associate him with Uppland, and during the tenth century, we know that Birka and Old Uppsala were two important central places. Remains of what may have been a large and luxurious residential complex have been found in Old Uppsala, although its precise function and years of use remain debated.[52] This nevertheless points to the general area where Erik may have dwelt, and he is said to have died in Uppsala.[53] It is difficult to talk about a "royal court" during the time of Erik and Sigrid. There is no evidence that such a concept existed, and indeed it is not before the twelfth century and the reign of Sverker the Elder that evidence starts to emerge of a group of courtiers living together with the king and his family (this is discussed in the next chapters).

Let us now return to the question of religious expectations at the time of Sigrid Storråda. To get an idea of what a good Christian woman was expected to be in the tenth century, we may want to compare Sigrid with the English royal Saint Edith of Wilton who was born around 961 and died at the age of 23, making her precisely contemporary with the Swedish queen. She was a daughter of King Edgar of England who had been dedicated to a religious life and was widely portrayed as the ideal nun.[54] Yet, she also played an important public role as a high-profile member of the royal family. She was considered a good and humble Christian woman while also being known as a glamorous and extremely wealthy figure who was always magnificently dressed due to her royal status. Edith is a great illustration of what was considered an ideal Christian royal woman in the tenth century. Contemporary commentators wrote that she was skilled at embroidery, reading, calligraphy, painting and composing music. She is also shown as being helpful, assisting the masons working in the abbey by carrying stones for them. She is also known to have designed and manufactured furniture for herself, as well as made some of her own vestments. Her piety is shown through her copying of prayer books – a task usually considered a chore and undertaken partly as penance by monks. However, for all her humility, she was also a great ambassador for the Crown, and spent a considerable amount of time at the court of her father, notably to advance the interests of her abbey. When offered the throne of England, she refused, choosing instead to devote herself to her holy mission. Whether this is a true representation is unknown, although monk Goscelin's account, from which much of Edith's life story is known, is considered serious and believable by many scholars.[55]

None of this is said about Sigrid Storråda. She is presented as precisely the opposite of Edith, with her alleged selfishness and pretentiousness being obvious from her nickname ("the haughty"). Even considering her pagan beliefs, no mention is made of her piety or devotion to her religion. There is also no mention of any domestic skills, and her positive personal characteristics are limited, which puts her at odds with a figure like Edith, whose moral attributes elevate her among her peers. Edith's royal heritage is also evident in her behaviour, although she never seems to overstep her station. Instead, Sigrid is exclusively represented through her combativity and stubbornness. Nevertheless, while she is presented as an extreme example of pre-Christian female behaviour, she was not unique in being a non-conforming queen by Christian standards. Only about 20 years or so before Sigrid's accession to queenship, Queen Thyra of Denmark also went against the gender norms expected of a Christian-era queen – and it is worth pointing out that she may have been English like Saint Edith, although her ancestry is uncertain.[56] She reigned in the mid-tenth century and may have died around the time when Sigrid was born. Like her, Thyra was probably not a Christian, as it is her son – Harald Bluetooth, whom she had with King Gorm the Old, who is credited with Christianising Denmark. She was also an admired military figure. Saxo describes her prowess as a fighter and praises her as bearing "a man's heart beneath a feminine exterior."[57] She is said to have built the Daneverk, a network of fortifications in northern Germany (in reality, it already existed, but she most probably extended it).[58] She is also said to have led an army in battle – whether she was on the battlefield herself is not clear, but she is presented as the army's leader nonetheless. This is certainly not the behaviour expected of a Christian woman, but instead Thyra's fierceness is reminiscent of Sigrid's. The Danish queen was renowned for it as well, as evidenced by a tenth-century runestone raised by King Gorm in her memory whereby she is described as "Denmark's flower." The Old Norse term, *bod*, could also mean "repair," and it is possible that exaggerations were made about Thyra's connection to the Danevark to explain the nickname.[59] In any case, while the extent of her deeds is unclear, Thyra's popularity is known to be historically accurate, which suggests that Sigrid's behaviour might not have been totally out of place either.

Even though Sigrid was probably just a regular Scandinavian woman of her time, there is no doubt that her character later served as exemplar for what women should *not* be in Christian times. Christian women, in the later Middle Ages, were expected to be obedient, chaste, and humble. Whether they were all these things in private is not always clear, of course, but this was the image that they were expected to project – and the behaviour which became the norm for Swedish queens in the following centuries, as we shall see throughout this book. Sigrid was the exact opposite of this: she was stubborn, made decisions for herself which often went against the interests of her male counterparts, and certainly knew herself powerful, and did much to maintain her status and that of her family. While Jones' dismissal of her existence is too harsh, he is certainly right when remarking that the author of *Heimskringla* made a point of underlining Sigrid's incompatibility with the Christian morals prevalent at the time of writing in the thirteenth century.[60] As noted previously, the writing is ambiguous enough so that some of Sigrid's personality traits are presented in a relatively positive, or at least neutral manner. However, a contemporary reader, familiar with the moral code of the High Middle Ages, would have certainly understood *Heimskringla*'s version of Sigrid as an anti-Christian character. Her refusal to convert to Christianity, while completely unproven historically, would have underlined this idea.

Saxo, despite his Christian background, is surprisingly generous in his description of her in the face of Olaf's humiliation. He opposes Olaf's image of Sigrid, which he expresses in sexist and ageist terms to reflect Olaf's mindset, with his own positive perception of the queen.[61] One might have expected the author, writing long after the Christianisation of Denmark was complete, to side with Olaf who, despite his abusive behaviour, nevertheless represents Christianity. Yet, what this passage shows is that beyond religious affiliation, there was also a specific code of conduct to respect, notably between genders, but also towards people of high-status in general. Widows were respected in Norse society, and there are examples of former queens in Norway and Denmark remaining active within political circles even after theoretically losing their royal status.[62] This is also true of Sigrid whose own son was now king. She was thus not only a royal widow but also a queen-mother. She thus enjoyed the prestige of being directly related to two illustrious kings.

It is also possible that Saxo implicitly drew a comparison between Sigrid and the Virgin Mary, in that both were mothers.[63] Olaf's hostility towards Sigrid supposedly because she was a "matron," at a time when both motherhood and widowhood were highly respected, may therefore have been a step too far.[64] Olaf's behaviour is clearly depicted as dishonourable and improper for a king. Sigrid's response, on the contrary, is considered natural and acceptable; and her revenge, enacted lawfully through her marriage to Svend, is shown as a proportionate reaction to the shame to which she was subjected. It is not to say that the Danish author was good to women in his writings, however, and *Gesta Danorum* is known for its harsh treatment of female characters. Instead, Saxo clearly uses the event and his praise for Sigrid to underline what he considers good royal behaviour and give a moral lesson to his reader.[65]

Heimskringla, instead, uses the event to set up the scene for an explosive narrative which involves Sigrid enacting violent revenge through blood and fire – a dimension that is absent from Saxo's work. Icelandic author Oddr Snorrason, writing in the twelfth century from an overtly Christian stance – he was a Benedictine monk – is less amiable than *Heimskringla* and certainly a lot less gentle than *Gesta Danorum*. He writes that she was a quarrelsome and difficult woman, whom Erik had sought to divorce.[66] There is no evidence that this was the case, and other sources such as *Heimskringla* instead claim that she was widowed as Erik died of sickness.[67] Oddr Snorrason's description of Sigrid projects the typical image of a "bad woman" by Christian standards: disobedient, aggressive, and the mention that she received Götaland, presumably as divorce gift, implicitly accuses her of being greedy and demanding.[68]

The dichotomy in the literary (and subsequently scholarly) treatment of Sigrid's character is best illustrated by the two nicknames by which she is remembered. In modern Swedish, she is known as Sigrid Storråda, which is based on the Old Norse *Sigríðr innar stórráðu* ("the Ambitious"), a rather neutral nickname that she is given following the tale of her assassinating suitors in *Heimskringla*, as well as in "Hervarar saga ok Heiðreks."[69] In English, she is instead known as "the Haughty," which is self-explanatory and clearly more critical. Unlike *innar stórráðu*, which is how she is formally introduced in parts of *Heimskringla*, the origin of the use of "Sigrid the Haughty" in English is less clear. She is never named as such in any primary source which mentions her. Most English translations of *Heimskringla* do describe her as "haughty," but the original Old Norse term is in fact *svarkr mikill* which would be most correctly translated as "[who] talks back a lot," or "much defiant."[70] It is not quite the same, and while combativity is inherent in both translations, the use of "haughty" is an editorial choice which inadvertently reinforces a sexist, but common, misconception that a woman who stands her ground is necessarily pretentious.

It is not only Sigrid who suffers from this image. This expression is used in other Old Norse sources to describe other strong-willed women.[71] In England just a century later, Empress Matilda is another example of a strong female leader whose behaviour has been routinely described both in contemporary sources (such as the *Gesta Stephani*) and in later English-written scholarship as "haughty" and "intolerably proud." Matilda's main fault was to have tried to rule in her own right following the death of her father King Henry I (as per his wishes), rather than quickly pass the throne to her son Henry II.[72] In both Sigrid's and Matilda's cases, there is no evidence that they behaved worse than any other royal figure of their period. In fact, concerning Sigrid, Saxo's description of the events surrounding her meeting with Olaf Tryggvason depicts her as a victim and not as a bully.

Even more interesting is the fact that other characters in the sagas compiled in *Heimskringla* are routinely called "haughty" in English as well. Olof Skötkonung himself is called "haughty" in the same English translation of the saga when he is criticised for not being diplomatic enough. His wife, Queen Estrid, is also termed "haughty" when she is herself criticised for mistreating her stepchildren, which is quite a serious fault as a maternal figure. Yet, the Old Norse term used in both cases is different from that used to describe Sigrid. Estrid is *ríklundað* and Olof is *ríklundaðr*.[73] This has been translated as "high-spirited," "proud-minded," "imperious" or "severe," most of which are at least as negative as *svarkr mikill*.[74] It is thus worth noting that other characters directly related to Sigrid exhibited much worse behaviour than her, not least Olaf Tryggvason; and many others throughout Old Norse literature have been described as *svarkr mikill* (or variants), or otherwise stubborn and severe, and yet only Sigrid inherited this characteristic as a permanent nickname. This must have therefore been coined by later, English-speaking writers who wanted to portray the queen in a more negative light than historical evidence suggests. Again, a comparison with Matilda sheds light on what may be a widespread phenomenon. It has been pointed out notably by Helen Castor that the men around

Matilda all engaged in similar behaviour and in many cases were much more violent, and yet none is remembered as insufferable. It is one of these great historical injustices which are difficult to untangle. It remains unclear when the nickname first appeared, but Sigrid was already known as "haughty" in 1863, when the American poet Henry Wadsworth Longfellow mentioned her in his work and popularised the nickname.[75] It is during the same period that some of the most vitriolic criticism aimed at Matilda was published too, which suggests that in both hers and Sigrid's case, this treatment might reflect Victorian gender ideals.[76]

Ever since she first entered the record, Sigrid Storråda, as a character, has served as the ideal of a pagan queen, as well as the antithesis of Christian femininity. Her story has endured in popular culture, and a revival of pre-Christian Norse culture first witnessed in the nineteenth century also brought about a range of fictional works in which she plays an important role. Poets and novelists incorporated her into their works. Longfellow made her the central character of one of his famed Norse ballads, "Queen Sigrid the Haughty."[77] She appears in Swedish novels as a character.[78] She even makes an appearance in Karen Blixen's short story "The Deluge at Norderney," which relates the legend according to which she murdered her suitors. In Poland, too, her life has fascinated readers, with no less than three novels based on her life.[79] While they all distort her biography to fit their narratives, it is clear that the mythology surrounding this mysterious queen still resonates with modern people. In sum, Sweden's first attested queen might not have existed in the way she is described, and some will argue that she did not exist at all, but it is nevertheless necessary to know about her if only because of the influence that she has had on the perception of women and queenship. Furthermore, as shall be discussed in the rest of this chapter, her probable Slavic connections may have also impacted the development of Sweden's monarchy.

Sigrid had several children, not least Olof Skötkonung whose partners are studied in the next section. She may also have had at least one daughter with Erik, who is known as Holmfrid. However, very little is known about her, except for her alleged marriage to a son of a Norwegian jarl. This is related in both "Ólafs saga Helga" and "Óláfs saga Tryggvasonar," but she is hardly mentioned in any other literature.[80] It is therefore unlikely that she ever led a royal life, as one would have expected her to be named in other sources if this had been the case, and thus she will not be studied here. With Svend, if we consider that Gunnhild and Sigrid were the same person, she might have been the mother of Estrid Svendsdatter, about whom considerably more is known. Estrid had an illustrious career as a noblewoman and lent her name to the "Estridsen" royal dynasty in Denmark. There is no evidence that she had any dealings in Sweden, however, and she is best studied in a Danish context.

2.2 Estrid and Edla

Sigrid's son, Olof (known as Skötkonung), who became King of Sweden upon the death of his father Erik in the last few years of the tenth century, had two partners which are well documented. These are Estrid of the Obotrites, his lawful wife, and Edla, one of his concubines. These two women are interesting for they help illustrate the different roles and expectations of both roles in an early medieval context. Both were Slavic and are widely accepted as having existed, although their native names have not survived. Before lawfully marrying Estrid, Olof is known from "Óláfs saga Helga" to have had a concubine known as Edla with whom he is said to have fathered Emund and Jacob, who later became kings, and daughters Holmfrid and Estrid, who will be briefly discussed shortly. We are told that Edla was the daughter of a Slavic jarl who was captured and taken to Sweden, where she became Olof's mistress.[81] This must have happened after he became king but before he married Estrid, which gives us a date range of 995–1000.

Estrid of the Obotrites's family background is unclear as well, although Adam of Bremen tells us that she came from the land of the Obotrites.[82] The Obotrites were a confederation of Slavic tribes dwelling mostly in the coastal areas of modern-day Germany.[83] "Óláfs saga Helga" also claims that she was kidnapped and brought back to Sweden where she married Olof.[84] As mentioned, this may have happened around the year 1000, shortly after Edla's own arrival in the kingdom. As with Sigrid, the question of what constituted such an early "marriage" is problematic. It is not known whether this was a lawful marriage contracted according to the Church's criteria, or another type of arrangement more akin to pre-Christian unions which were much less codified. In Anglo-Saxon England, for instance, leading men also routinely had concubines, sometimes alongside a wife. Margaret Clunies Ross remarks that "there were several ways of entering into a recognized sexual connection with a woman," and that such unions were not "not legally ratified but acknowledged by custom."[85] Concerning the taking of official wives, Ross identifies several traditional methods used by Anglo-Saxon leaders, some of which are completely incompatible with Christian ideals. These include the purchase of a woman, and abduction as might be the case here with Estrid.[86] It is possible that Olof's relationship with Estrid was interpreted by Christian writers as a form of marriage because it closely resembled it, and because she was considered the most senior of his partners. Nevertheless, contemporary examples provided by the Anglo-Saxons show that there existed other types of recognised unions outside the ecclesiastical framework, and it is likely to have been similar in Sweden. With Estrid, his alleged wife (or senior partner in any case), Olof is said to have fathered Ingegerd (who later became Saint Anna in Kievan Rus), and Anund, who like his illegitimate brothers, also became king.

Because Estrid was married to Olof, she is referred to as *dróttnigin* ("the queen") whereas Edla is only known as *ambótt*.[87] The term *ambótt* can be translated in several ways, some of which are significantly less respectful than "concubine." Indeed, it can also be taken to mean "slave woman," "serving woman," "handmaid," and in a Christian context, "nun."[88] *Heimskringla* leaves therefore no ambiguity as to the hierarchy among Olof's partners. Interestingly, however, *Heimskringla* gives Edla's name but only refers to Estrid as "the queen" whereas Adam only names Estrid and makes no mention of a concubine until much later in his work, when he briefly mentions that King [Anund] Jacob was "born of a concubine by Olaf."[89] Each author's respective omission is certainly not a coincidence. Adam is clearly being careful in his description of Olof and wants to present him as a good Christian king. When introducing his family, it is likely that he purposefully ignored Edla because concubinage went against the Church's teachings. Mentioning a concubine in this passage would have revealed a less polished side to Olof which would have damaged his reputation as a Christian. Adam is not in total denial either, and he readily admits that Swedish kings happily practised concubinage, and sometimes had many concubines.[90] This last comment is perhaps exaggerated to underline Adam's disapproval, but it is also possibly accurate. Interestingly, however, when Adam does mention Edla, much later in the text in connection with King Emund, he is critical of the new king, who he writes "took little heed of our religion."[91] Whether this is true is unknown, but it could be suggested that Adam's disapproval of the king's birth mother was partly motivated the cleric's criticism, which then serves to underline the incompatibility of concubinage with the exercise of royal power. As *Heimskringla* is less concerned with advancing Christian ethos than Adam's *Gesta*, Snorri may not have had any qualms about discussing the kings' concubines. On the contrary, it is possible that he made a point of giving as much literary value to mistresses as to lawful wives, because concubinage was such an important part of Viking Age warrior society, which Snorri is less shy to depict.

Indeed, concubines are an important concept in early medieval genealogical history, especially that concerning elite families, and taking female prisoners to marry them or take them as mistresses was common practice in the early medieval period, especially in pre-Christian times.[92] Kidnapping women was an important aspect of raiding culture which is notably associated with Viking leaders. It is perhaps surprising that a proudly Christian king should indulge in such a seemingly barbaric exercise, but this only serves as a reminder of Olof's position at the crossroads of cultures. Adam glosses over the fact that his relationship with Edla was the result of a kidnapping, and instead only focuses on his alleged piety, remarking that Olof had both his children, as well as his wife and (presumably) the rest of his entourage baptised.[93] While Edla is not mentioned, it is likely that she was baptised too, even if only nominally. It is also worth noting that both Edla and Estrid were noblewomen and not simple villagers. From this perspective, Olof's actions were closest to hostage-taking, common across northern Europe, whereby individuals of high political worth were given to a victor by the losing party as a token of peace.[94]

Concubinage in medieval Scandinavia is defined as "a semi-formal relationship in which men and women engage in sexual activity and sometimes cohabit without marrying."[95] Most human societies have at some point engaged in concubinage and it was far from being an exceptional practice in Viking Age Sweden. Vast amounts of literary sources, both contemporary and later, domestic and foreign, lay and ecclesiastical, point to concubinage being common in pre-Christian Sweden as well as in the early days of its Christianisation.[96] The details of how it functioned in practice, however, are more complicated to discern, and much remains unknown about how such relationships were viewed, lived, and what legal consequences they had, if any. It is also clear that concubinage meant different things in different societies and time periods, with concubines from a Roman law perspective providing a much more stable type of monogamous relationship than the concubines of Germanic tribes which were much closer to sex slavery.[97] Indeed, the Swedish medieval law codes mentioned previously suggest that concubines had the same status as slaves. As we mentioned previously, Edla is referred to in *Heimskringla* as *ambótt*, which may be translated as "slave girl." However, the thirteenth-century law codes may not accurately reflect Viking Age mentalities, and it has been pointed out previously that taking concubines could be a political act rather than a purely hedonistic one, and that such relationships could play a significant role in diplomacy and politics. As such, concubines themselves could be hugely important women.[98] It is perhaps from this perspective that Olof's relationship with Edla should be understood.

Several Slavic tribes were particularly powerful in the early medieval period, and regularly found themselves at war with the Scandinavians notably for dominance of the Baltic Sea, its resources, and its trade routes. These tribes are often indiscriminately referred to in Norse and Germanic literature as the "Wends." The history of the term "Wends" is complex and is best left for experts to discuss, but medieval Germanic writers mainly used it as a synonym for Slavic people living south of the Baltic coast, in modern-day northern Germany and further inland into central Europe.[99] The Wends are not the same as the Rus mentioned previously, or the Baltic peoples along the eastern coastline of the Baltic Sea, although they were also of Slavic origin. Proximity and similar strategic interests led to many instances of intermarriage between the Scandinavian and Wendish elites between the ninth and eleventh centuries, after which the influence of Wendish tribes declined, especially following the Baltic Crusades – which will be mentioned again in the next chapter. These marriages had long-term consequences not only in terms of the mix of cultures that they necessarily initiated but also because they created long-lasting diplomatic relationships, allegiances, and subordination. Like the later queens of Norwegian and Germanic origin who will be studied in the next chapters, the Slavic women who were introduced into Swedish royalty – either as official wives, concubines, or slaves – all inherently played a role as cultural mediators and diplomats within their social circles.[100] It should be noted, however, that it is unlikely that Viking Age queens played much of a direct role in politics. While comparatively freer than their continental counterparts, women were still very limited in what they could achieve in society, and the keeping of multiple partners evidences the primary use of women as objects of prestige and sexual commodities.[101]

What is interesting with Estrid and Edla is the relationship that they each had with Olof, and the way their respective children were raised. Namely, there was no evidence of a tangible difference between the king's treatment of the two and their offspring. Adam writes that Swedish kings treated their concubines as if they were lawful wives, and that the children born from these unions were legitimate.[102] This comment sheds some light on concubines' status in Viking Age Sweden. Olof's reasons for marrying Estrid and not Edla are unknown, although it might have had to do with the women's family backgrounds and their fathers' status within Slavic nobility. The distinction may have become more obvious when outside interests got involved. When discussing diplomatic relations, it was noted that Norway's King

Olaf II Haraldsson was inferior to the King of Sweden because of his marriage to Estrid, the illegitimate daughter of Olof.[103] In addition, the lawful queen, Estrid, is said to have mistreated her stepchildren, to the point that they had to be educated away from the court. Emund was sent to Vendland (a region in present-day northern Germany where Slavic peoples lived) to be raised by his mother's family, and Estrid was fostered in Västergötland by a powerful man known only as Egill.[104] However, Queen Estrid's mistreatment of the children might have reflected her jealousy and bitterness towards her rival, rather than being a faithful depiction of her attitude towards concubinage. One must also remember that this information is given to us in *Heimskringla* which could have exaggerated the animosity that Estrid felt towards Edla and her children. This passage suggests, nevertheless, that Edla must have died rather early as she did not raise her children and does not appear in the historical record again after this episode.

While this is not the place for an in-depth discussion of concubinage across the world's civilisations, it is worth noting that in many civilisations outside of Europe, concubines had a well-defined role with duties and rights enshrined in law or in some other sort of code of conduct. For example, in several Arabic societies, concubines formed part of a sultan's harem which followed a strict hierarchy. Accordingly, concubines' children also derived their status from their mother's place in this hierarchy.[105] In China, concubines were expected to follow a strict protocol. Far from being considered second-class women, they needed to be well educated and literate. A ruler's mother, who was commonly an ex-concubine or even a slave, could hold significant power within the court and effectively run it.[106] However, it is unclear whether concubinage was as strictly regulated in medieval Sweden. There is no surviving written evidence to help us elucidate the question, bar some accounts regarding the Rus. Indeed, several Arabic authors wrote about Rus customs. The most detailed account is that of tenth-century Muslim traveller Ahmad ibn Fadlan, thanks to whom we know that Rus leaders could have numerous wives and concubines, most of whom were young slave girls. The accounts' description of masters' relationships with their female slaves makes for horrific reading by modern standards. It tells us that young girls were routinely abused, raped, and burnt alive for ritual purposes all for the benefit (in this life, and the next) of their masters.[107]

Numerous graves have been found in eastern Europe, notably modern-day Ukraine, where grown men were buried with much smaller females who have been interpreted as being teenaged girls – possibly slaves. Whether these girls counted as concubines and formed "loving" relationships with their masters is unclear.[108] As per the Arabic accounts, they may have been sacrificed to accompany their lord in the afterlife. As archaeological interpretation of these sites remains speculative, one should also point out that in some instances, where the bodies' position does not suggest otherwise, the people buried together may be related in some other way through kinship, rather than being sexual partners. Some graves have also been shown to contain one man with multiple females which archaeologists suggest may be evidence of polygamous unions, or concubinage. However, no such grave has been found in medieval Sweden and runestones, which preserve much genealogical information, do not generally suggest that concubinage was widespread – or at least it is not recorded.[109] Overall, there is no evidence that Swedish society was as extremely patriarchal and violent towards women as that of the Rus. Indeed, it is important to remember that Rus society was itself the result of a mix of cultures, and Slavic customs were still prevalent among the elites despite its members' links to Scandinavia.[110] The result might have been something unique, and what was witnessed in Rus might therefore not reflect the situation in Sweden and in other eastern regions during the same period.

Nevertheless, official concubinage was certainly recorded in other Scandinavia royal families roughly contemporary with Olof. In Denmark, King Svend Estridsen is known to have had numerous partners. Adam of Bremen writes that following the dissolution of his marriage to a blood relative, he "took to himself other wives and concubines, and still others,"[111] and we know that he had dozens of children out of wedlock. This is clearly an extreme example and the number given by the sagas might need to be taken with a pinch of salt, although it remains conceivable that such a high-status figure could afford a virtually unlimited number of women. This particular issue – that of a few men "hoarding" all available women as trophies – may have been one of the driving factors behind the Church's outlawing of polygamy and concubinage. Indeed, an obvious consequence of the practice is the lack of women available to marry men of lower social status.[112] This led to tensions in society, of course, but also increased the risk of incest, as the pool of potential mates kept shrinking. It also contributed heavily to the concentration of wealth within the hands of a tiny elite,[113] although in Viking Age Sweden, this last point was partly addressed by women's inheritance rights, which were much more extant than elsewhere in Europe.

As mentioned previously, concubines were not always equal, and even within a monarch's group of mistresses, there may have been a hierarchy. We do not know whether such a system existed in medieval Scandinavia, but we do know that not all concubines were named in sources. None of Svend Estridsen's mistresses are known, for instance, despite his life being well documented, which suggests that they were not considered worth mentioning by contemporary commentators. However, King Harald Hardrada of Norway, who reigned between 1046 and 1066, is said to have married concubine Thora while still married to his wife Elisiv. There is no evidence of the Church's interference with the process, which would have been illegal in theory, and it is therefore unknown whether this was a formal marriage, or another type of union.[114] Thora is well known in literature and scholarship and is considered politically significant, which shows her high status. However, only Elisiv ever held the title of "Queen" in medieval sources.

In Edla and Estrid's case, the relatively equal status that both women enjoyed (at least in the private sphere), and the fact that their children were given similar dynastic rights is certainly a relic of pre-Christian practices. This is similar to medieval Wales where native law, in complete contradiction with Canon Law, allowed both legitimate and illegitimate sons to enjoy the same succession rights, in turn leading to dynastic conflicts.[115] In theory, Christianisation entailed stricter definitions of what constituted a legitimate family, and the sanctity and legal importance of marriage would have made it inconceivable that the children of an unmarried partner – bastards – could be treated as lawful heirs. This conundrum was already widely acknowledged and debated within medieval Wales. In Sweden, there is no evidence that this practice caused much unrest. This underlines Olof's position at the crossroads of religious beliefs and legal systems. During his reign, pre-Christian practices were still widespread and having multiple partners was a sign of power. However, Christian norms slowly being adopted also meant that the extreme accumulation of females by prominent individuals was increasingly falling out of fashion. There is certainly a major contrast between Olof's relationship with his mistresses and Svend Estridsen's. The women in Svend's life are completely unknown, and might have essentially only served as sexual objects, and incubators – many of Svend's children are known, with only one born to a lawful wife.[116] There is no suggestion that any of these women played a political role and Svend is portrayed by Adam of Bremen as a rather irrational and combative leader. Adam's description might be biased and the result of his antipathy for the Dane, who had openly defied ecclesiastical authority in relation to his doomed marriage,[117] but there is no doubt that Olof's limited number of concubines may have projected a more stable image of the family unit, at least in the eyes of their Swedish subjects.

We do not know what made a queen a good queen, and a concubine a good concubine in the late Viking Age. There is no mirror or code of conduct from that period to spell it out for us. What we know is what was considered ideal in Christianised European kingdoms (and indeed elsewhere): chastity, humility, charity, and physical beauty, all of which made a queen suitable as a ruler, a wife, and a leading example for the realm.[118] However, as has become clear by now, Sweden in the late Viking Age was at a cultural crossroad and it is unlikely that such idealised behaviours had been completely adopted yet. One may nevertheless suppose that the ability to bear children was a primordial criterion, as was a certain willingness to submit to one's husband. Nevertheless, as has been analysed elsewhere, expectations in terms of queenly behaviour were as much a reflection of personal values as they were a public display, and Christian queens were expected to serve as role models for women and girls across the realm.[119] This specific point cannot have applied in tenth and eleventh-century Sweden. The kingdom was barely formed, certainly not formalised or recognised legally in any way, and communication networks were so basic that the queen's image cannot possibly have mattered as much as it later would in subsequent centuries, as most of the population probably never even saw a pictorial representation of her. It is more probable that women adapted their natal customs to local traditions, which may have informed contemporary expectations regarding their behaviour.

As should be expected, there is also very little information about how exactly Estrid and Edla's children were raised. We know of course that Edla's son and daughter were sent away to be raised by other relatives and foster parents. However, their Slavic background must have had an impact on their education, ideas, and customs. Emund is even said to have failed to hold onto the Christian faith while living in Vendland, which is evidence that the new religion still competed with pre-Christian beliefs.[120] His mother and wives being Slavic must have intensely influenced King Olof's family and environment. The question of how to define "Swedishness" in this context is complex and better suited for a separate study, but it is worth noting that there is nothing to suggest that at such an early stage of Swedish monarchy, royal women were expected to foster specific cultural values. While later royal women were expected to fit in a cultural mould and assimilate within their new culture, Swedish identity was ill-defined in the late Viking Age, and it is possible that Edla and Estrid, and perhaps Sigrid before them too, passed their Slavic values and customs onto their children. Further research into Slavic influence in late Viking Age Swedish culture, which cannot be conducted within the scope of the present study, would be able to shed more light on this aspect of royal life in Sweden.

Of Olof's daughters, Ingegerd, now known as Saint Anna of Kiev, had the most exceptional life. Initially betrothed to King Olaf of Norway, she eventually married Yaroslav the Wise, Grand Prince of Kievan Rus. It is in Rus that she flourished and spent the most significant portion of her life, and she is therefore not a subject in this book. It is nevertheless worth mentioning that through her sponsoring of ecclesiastical institutions, and her impeccable conduct, she was canonised and is still today an important religious figure in Ukraine.[121] She is, in fact, one of Sweden's most famous royal women. Estrid did marry the king of Norway, now remembered as Olaf the Saint, in 1019 after his previous betrothal (to her sister Ingegerd) fell through. Like Ingegerd, most of her adult life was spent outside of Sweden and she is therefore not studied here.

2.3   Gunnhild of Sweden, Gunnhild of Denmark, and Gyda

As mentioned previously, both of Olof's sons became kings, despite having different mothers. The first to inherit the throne was King Anund Jacob, whom he fathered with his lawful queen, Estrid. Anund Jacob reigned for nearly 30 years (c. 1020–1050), which is testament to the stability of his kingship. As we just saw, his brothers-in-law were Yaroslav I of Kiev, and Saint Olaf of Norway, both of whom were strong Christian rulers. Anund Jacob's reign was important in helping cement Christianity in Sweden, and it is worth noting that he is the first Swedish king with a Christian name. He is also the first to be represented (on his coins) with a crown on his head.

He had one known wife, and while this is no guarantee that he did not have mistresses, none appears in surviving sources about his reign. According to different Icelandic sagas, her name was Gunnhild and she was the daughter of a Norwegian jarl named Sveinn Håkonsson.[122] Thus far, it is conceivable, and interestingly deviates from the norm in that she was not Slavic – a first sign that Swedish kings' political partners were changing. However, the rest of Gunnhild's biography as given by Icelandic authors is more problematic. Indeed, the sagas tell us that she was the daughter of Holmfrid, Olof Skotkonung's daughter mentioned above. This would make Gunnhild a very close relative of Anund Jacob, whose father was Olof. It seems extremely unlikely that this union could have been approved by the Church, whose definition of incest was wide-ranging (up to the seventh degree, including in-laws, step-parents and step-siblings).[123] Both Olof and Anund Jacob were deeply committed Christian kings who worked to establish good relations with the Church, and it is therefore hard to believe that Anund Jacob would be allowed to marry his own father's granddaughter. In addition to this dubious union, Gunnhild is said to have married King Svend Estridsen after the death of Anund Jacob, with Svend supposedly the grandson of Sigrid Storråda.[124] This made Gunnhild again a close relative of her new husband, being herself a great-granddaughter of Sigrid through Olof, and therefore a cousin of Svend. Adam of Bremen, who was contemporary, writes that the marriage had to be annulled as it was formally rejected by the Church. However, the degree of consanguinity (and therefore Gunnhild's true identity) is not detailed.[125] Considering the uproar that her union with Svend caused, it is difficult to explain why her first alleged marriage to Anund Jacob, to whom she was even more closely related, left so few traces in the historical record. This suggests that her genealogy, as established by Icelandic authors, might be incorrect. Another possibility is that the Gunnhild who married Anund Jacob was not actually the same Gunnhild who married Svend. Focusing on Adam of Bremen's account, which is likely to be more accurate than the sagas, may somewhat clarify the situation.

Indeed, a scholion in Adam's *Gesta* suggests the existence of three different women. There is first Gunnhild, Queen of Sweden: Anund Jacob's widow about whom little is said. Another Gunnhild is Svend's divorcee who came from Sweden and to whom he was related. The last is Gyda, Svend's eventual lawful wife who was murdered by a concubine.[126] Saxo Grammaticus tells us that Gyda was Anund Jacob's daughter, an information which is repeated in Icelandic annals too.[127] It is thus clear that this new wife cannot have been the widow of Anund Jacob. There are at least two different women here: Gyda and her mother (or stepmother if Gyda was born of a concubine).[128] This is also alleged in a fifteenth-century chronicle which claims that Svend's divorcee was his mother-in-law. While this chronicle's accuracy is difficult to determine, it may be based on now-disappeared sources.[129]

In addition, there is no indication in Adam's account that Svend's divorcee had anything to do with either Anund Jacob's widow, or his daughter. Adam writes that upon being separated from Svend, his divorcee Gunnhild retreated to her estates "across from Denmark." He refers to her as the "most saintly queen" (*sanctissima*) and highlights her pious deeds.[130] Expanding on this, Catholic bishop Johannes Magnus' sixteenth-century chronicle *Gothorum Sveonumque historia* claims that she lived in Västergötland where she supposedly finished her life, and founded the abbey at Gudhem.[131] This is known to be false, however, and there is no evidence that the abbey was founded before the mid-twelfth century, as will be seen in the next chapter. This is the result of Johannes Magnus' embellishment of Sweden's Catholic history in light of the Reformation. Intriguingly, Adam states that Stenkil, who was not king yet at that time, escorted episcopal legates "over the Swedish mountains" to Gunnhild after they were rejected by the Swedes.[132] This is odd considering that there are no mountains in the southern half of Sweden, and certainly not across from Denmark. This might thus refer to Norway or could simply result from Adam's lack of first-hand knowledge of Sweden's geography. It thus remains difficult to identify the region in which she retired.

As there is so little information about Anund Jacob's wife Gunnhild, who is the only one of these three women to be relevant to this study, it is impossible to determine whether she had any political influence over her husband(s). Perhaps the most interesting aspect of her contested biography is the fact that it illustrates the strategic importance of dynastic marriages in early medieval Sweden, and highlights the powerful duo that she formed with her daughter Gyda, as both may have been queens at roughly the same time.

2.4 Estrid Njalsdatter

Anund Jacob's half-brother, King Emund, inherited the throne around 1050 as it seems that Anund Jacob did not have any sons. Emund was the son of Olof Skötkonung's concubine Edla. Emund's reign was very short, however, and it is unclear whether he ever got lawfully married. The Norwegian noblewoman Estrid Njalsdatter has been touted as his queen by some scholars because

"Hervarar saga" claims that she gave birth to Stenkil, discussed below, who served as jarl and later king.[133] Adam of Bremen is not clear about Stenkil's family background, although he writes that he may have been a stepson of Emund.[134] Because he does not name Emund's wife, it has been speculated that she may have been Estrid. This is purely guesswork, however, and is not clearly enunciated anywhere. In fact, "Hervarar saga" claims that Stenkil inherited the throne thanks to his own wife's lineage, which goes against the hypothesis that his own mother was queen.[135]

A Norwegian ancestry would nevertheless be interesting, as her predecessor and sister-in-law Gunnhild was supposedly Norwegian too, as opposed to Slavic. This indicates a shift in Sweden's diplomatic relations with its neighbours, and presages the next chapter of this book, in which most queens were of Scandinavian origin. In any case, nothing else is known about the life of Emund's wife. Emund was not a popular king according to various sources, and this might be one of the reasons why so little is known about the royal couple.[136] He certainly fathered children, however, and two are known to historians: a son who died early and an unnamed daughter, known as "Ingamoder," who went on to contribute to the founding of the House of Stenkil.

2.5 Ingamoder

The daughter of King Emund, she is the mysterious figure known only as Ingamoder. "Ingamoder" is in fact not a name, but a modern nickname meaning "Mother of Inge," because except for the fact that she was a daughter of Emund, married to King Stenkil, and subsequently the mother of King Inge the Elder (who reigned between c. 1078 and 1112), nothing is known of her, not even her name. This makes a scholarly and accurate biography impossible to write. However, she remains an important woman to study not only because she was the mother of a king but also because despite the uncertainties surrounding her story, hers is the first clear example of a Swedish queen whose authority and fame were intrinsically linked to Christianity.

Indeed, like Sigrid Storråda, she has become a mythical character; but, where Sigrid is the stereotype of the strong, pagan Viking

Effigies veniti Iouis dicti Yngemokialla ad quem olim gentilismi et Papismi temporibus frequentes fiebant munusculorum oblationes Diis et Sanctis.

FIGURE 2.2   View of Ingemo's spring. Engraving by Erik Dahlberg and Jan van den Aveele, 1705.

woman, Ingamoder's figure is a deeply Christian one. She is specifically associated with a local saint from Västergötland named Saint Ingemo. The only trace of a cult of Ingemo is a sacred well, located in a rural area between Skövde and modern-day Tidaholm in Västergötland, named after her. Two early modern illustrations of the spring exist. The oldest is an engraving from Erik Dahlberg's mid-seventeenth century collection *Suecia Antiqua et Hodierna*. Johan Peringskiöld also drew the site a few decades later in *Monumenta Sveo-Gothicum*. It is described in literature of the same period including private correspondence,[137] and the saint's story was still known in the nineteenth century, at which point the spring's water was said to have long been thought to cure diseases.[138] The spring is still known today as "Ingemo källa," but nothing else is known of Ingemo, including when she lived, what she did to deserve sainthood, and when she was first venerated (Figure 2.2).

In truth, there is no definite evidence that Ingamoder was Ingemo, nor is there any surviving sources to explain when the theory originated. It is therefore prudent to take it with a degree of caution, although the present author finds the association extremely plausible. Ingemo is not a real name, and it does seem to be a nickname meaning "the mother of Inga or Inge" – Swedish *moder*, "mother," is often affectionately shortened to *mor* or *mo* even today. Though it could have been any other Inga or Inge, it is unlikely that just anyone could have become a saint. As will be shown shortly, early Christian royal or noble figures were readily canonised or venerated in some way. This was notably an attempt to create a natural link between God and the monarchy whose authority was then unquestionable. As will be discussed in depth in the next chapter, we also know that it was normal for local Christian magnates to sponsor ecclesiastical institutions and conduct themselves piously, including by being charitable towards their local population. Such people had to be widely popular, and there are several examples of laypeople becoming local saints as recognition of their efforts to support the Church, and/or their impeccable conduct.[139]

In addition to the fact that Ingamoder fits the probable profile of a local saint, Ingamoder's association with Västergötland is not only plausible but also very likely. Firstly, it is possible that Ingamoder came from Västergötland as following the Christianisation of Sweden, several leading families – usually influential landowners – grew in the region. Her grandfather was Olof Skötkonung, who was mainly based in Västergötland – where he was baptised – following the Svear's rejection of his authority on religious grounds.[140] It is unclear where her father Emund was based for the duration of his short reign, but by all logic he should have inherited land in the region by virtue of his father's establishment there. Furthermore, Ingamoder was married to King Stenkil, a wealthy man whose family history is unclear, but who may have used his wife's royal pedigree to shore up his legitimacy. Stenkil was strongly connected to Västergötland too. It is not known whether he was born there, but the list of kings attached to *Västgötalagen* indicates that he spent most of his time there and was very popular.[141] It is therefore perfectly understandable that the memory of Ingamoder would have somehow survived in Västergötland through the Ingemo character. Ingamoder/Ingemo must have been a convenient figure for the local population to hold onto as she was real enough for stories about her to be credible, but unknown enough that those stories could not be verified. This is much the same as Sigrid and as later women such as Ragnhild of Tälje and Ingrid Ylva, whose lives will be studied in the next two chapters.

As mentioned, Ingamoder/Ingemo may have been a local saint, which in fact means that she was not an official saint in that she was never recognised or canonised by the Church. However, the path to sainthood only became strictly regulated in the thirteenth century. Therefore, prior to this, local saints could be as important and as legitimate as saints recognised by the Church.[142] Local saints were made by the community for the community. Christianisation was still weak in eleventh-century Sweden, and it was common for respected members of the community to be recognised as "saints," in what should perhaps be seen as an updated, Christian version of the pagan veneration of ancestors. Local saints often filled a gap where the cult of regular, canonised saints did not serve the population's spiritual needs. And of course, it allowed them to keep aspects of their pagan customs alive, while conforming to new Christian practices. The veneration of local saints in Sweden was therefore more common in areas that were new to Christianity or where the Church was less present, because of lack of access, for instance.[143] Sweden was quite different from Norway and Denmark as female saints were more readily accepted. Sara Ellis Nilsson has posited that this may have been due to the Virgin Mary's significant popularity in early medieval Sweden, as evidenced by runic inscriptions.[144] Others have written better about sainthood and gender, and this is not the place to discuss this. However, there might be a link between the veneration of female saints in early medieval Sweden and the pre-Christian beliefs that women were more connected to nature as well as the realm of the supernatural than men. It may thus be suggested that female sainthood in Sweden should be seen as a Christian expression of a similar pagan attitude towards women.

Sweden only has two saints whose cult are documented as part of the official liturgy prior to 1300: Elin of Skövde (d. 1164), a noblewoman responsible for the building of the church in Skövde, and Ragnhild of Tälje (d. 1117), who was possibly a Swedish princess and later queen, who will be discussed in the next chapter in relation to her alleged husband King Inge the Younger.[145] This does not tell us that Ingemo was not venerated, however, simply that there is no evidence of it. There may have been many other local saints whose cult was so limited in time and geographically that they have left no trace behind them. It is noteworthy that Ingemo's spring is located reasonably close to Skövde, where Saint Elin was certainly venerated a century later. The region's population may therefore have been particularly open to the cult of female saints.

If one looks at female saints in the rest of Scandinavia before 1300, some similarities have been noted. Most of them were lay women of non-royal origins, they had all been married or widowed by the time they achieved sainthood, and none of them had had a formal relationship with a monastic institution. The first criterion may not apply to all female Swedish saints before 1300. Ellis Nilsson argues that the nobility of female saints was later exaggerated to underline their holiness, but in the case of Ingamoder/Ingemo, she most probably was a noblewoman already prior to her royal marriage. Similarly, Ragnhild of Tälje, discussed in the next chapter, was possibly a member of the illustrious Bjälbo dynasty, which owned large estates in Östergötland, prior to her marriage to King Inge the Younger. It has been theorised that early female saints had usually died as a result of domestic abuse or family feuds, and this seems particularly true of saints venerated in the dioceses of Lund and Uppsala (prior to Uppsala being elevated to archdiocese in 1164).[146] Ingemo was based in Västergötland and it is likely that the liturgy, and associated practices, was different there. As there is so little information available about Ingemo, nothing is known about the circumstances of her death. She was, however, queen during a turbulent time when the Swedish Crown was still a fragile institution.

Her husband Stenkil's succession was a complicated one. Adam of Bremen writes that it involved two men (both called Erik) and their followers fighting for the throne, with their struggle culminating in the violent deaths of both pretenders as well as large numbers of nobles.[147] Adam does not give any more precisions about the event and no other surviving source discusses it. It is notably unknown whether noblewomen were targeted too, to what extent the civilian population was concerned, and whether Ingamoder, as Stenkil's widow, played a role in the conflict. Thus, while there is no suggestion at this stage that Ingemo died due to familial tensions, it is worth noting that she did live in an unstable environment and that she may have been at the centre of what might be characterised as a civil war, albeit a short-lived one.

It is also possible to study local saints without going too deep into theological reasonings. Indeed, local saints could also be created for purely political purposes.[148] As the Church worked to advance its authority, creating saints and manipulating their story could serve as propaganda among a population that was still largely illiterate. As different towns fought to become the seat of new dioceses, monasteries, and other such new ecclesiastical institutions, new saints were produced to sway public opinion. Local saint's *vitae* ("lives" or hagiographical biographies) were written down to cement an area's role in the history of Sweden's Christianisation. The number of people declared martyrs grew dramatically throughout the eleventh and twelfth centuries as ecclesiastical and political authorities sought to highlight the struggle between the old and new faiths.[149] Different types of saints emerged, unofficially ranked in order of importance (and thus, influence). There were lay saints, who were regular people, often (but not always) lower class, who were recognised for their virtue. Even though the Church might have considered such saints secondary, they were probably the most important for the population as they were able to identify with these holy, common people. As Sweden was still undergoing Christianisation, it also produced missionary saints, who dedicated their lives to spreading the new religion. Consequently, there were also martyr saints, who had died as a direct result of persecution for their faith. There were royal saints, whose sainthood was usually political – see below – and sometimes completely manufactured as part of a family's propaganda. To these basic categories, one can add illustrious bishops, priests, and monks whose religious and/or political influence and diligence were recognised through sainthood.[150] It is unclear whether all medieval saints were considered saints by their contemporaries or whether a cult developed at a later stage.

It became increasingly important for elite families to boast at least one holy ancestor, and it is particularly true of these families which harboured royal ambitions. The canonisation of royal figures as a political act has been studied extensively, notably in connection with more developed kingdoms such as France and England but also Denmark where this phenomenon was much more common than in Sweden.[151] There will also be several examples of royal saints from Sweden mentioned in the present monograph, not least that of Saint Erik, whose wife Kristina will be studied in the next chapter. The Swedish Crown could be acquired in various ways which did not always entail hereditary succession. Medieval Sweden was an elective monarchy – although in effect only a handful of leading families were influential enough to vie for power. Competition was fierce, reputation was everything, and having a saint in one's family tree could help tremendously cement a family's position at the forefront of politics. It showed, first of all, that this was a good and respectable family by Christian standards. This is not dissimilar to pre-Christian times whereby elite families emphasised – and in some cases invented – their alleged blood link to ancient heroes, gods, and famous ancestors.[152] Secondly, medieval theology believed in the flow of grace, the idea being that a saint had been chosen by God to express His grace through them, and it was thought that this could be hereditary. This is why most kings were known as *rex gratia dei* or similar.[153]

Did Ingamoder/Ingemo become a martyr following the civil war that ensued her husband's succession? Or was she a royal saint whose cult aimed to promote her dynasty? Did she finish her life in a monastic institution and earned her sainthood this way? None of these answers can be given decisively, but her character seems to inscribe itself in a pattern alongside other local saints of medieval Sweden. It is entirely possible that her image played a political role long after her death, and she is the first queen of Sweden to be intrinsically linked to her Christian faith.

2.6   Concluding Remarks

As these first few biographies have shown, the Viking Age is a difficult period to study. The nature of the sources available to us – incomplete, contradictory, and often written much later – is a major obstacle to establishing even basic facts about the queens of this period. In addition, the social context itself was complicated: kingship was not yet a clearly defined concept. Instead, society was divided into factions headed by overlords who often had several partners: usually one lawful wife, and concubines. While having several women at his disposal allowed a man to show off his power and wealth, it also allowed him to maintain numerous social networks, which was an important aspect of medieval society, especially when lands, money, and authority were at stake. It is therefore impossible, considering the scarcity of sources, to track all royal women of this period. It is also very difficult to establish what their role entailed, although diplomatic skills seem to have been crucial for exercising power.

It is also clear that Sweden's earliest queens were of Slavic origin, which reflects the political situation of the time. There had long been contacts between modern-day Sweden, eastern Europe, and the Baltic region; and Viking Age Swedish consorts illustrate the diplomatic arrangements and political alliances in place in the tenth and early eleventh centuries. A shift is noticeable in the middle of the eleventh century, from which point Swedish consorts are chosen from within Scandinavia – a trend which carried on throughout the twelfth century, as will be shown shortly.

The late Viking Age was also a period of deep societal and cultural change. The transition from paganism to Christianity was a slow process which did not finish before the late twelfth century. Yet, a persistent Christian influence can nevertheless be seen already during the reign of Sigrid Storråda. One's religious background became an increasingly important consideration when choosing partners. It is during this period that tales of conversion among leaders become commonplace, and that the link between authority and piety becomes more obvious. Sigrid Storråda's refusal to convert is noted in many sources, for instance, while the ambiguity between pagan and Christian customs persisted for many decades after her, notably leading to mixed families in which the new faith progressively replaced the old. In the end of the chapter, this change culminates with the advent of King Stenkil's dynasty whose matriarch, the enigmatic Ingamoder, later became a strong Christian figure. While very little is known about her, she illustrates the completed transition from pre-Christian to Christian queenship, which the next chapter discusses.

Notes

1 Alison Finlay and Anthony Faulkes, trans, "Óláfs saga Tryggvasonar," in *Snorri Sturluson. Heimskringla Volume III. Magnús Óláfsson to Magnús Erlingsson* (London: Viking Society for Northern Research, 2015), 178. Alison Finlay and Anthony Faulkes, trans, "Óláfs saga Helga," in *Snorri Sturluson. Heimskringla Volume II. Óláfr Haraldsson (The Saint)* (London: Viking Society for Northern Research, 2014), 290. Alison Finlay and Anthony Faulkes, trans, "Haralds saga Gráfeldar," in *Snorri Sturluson. Heimskringla Volume I. The Beginnings to Óláfr Tryggvason* (London: Viking Society for Northern Research, 2011), 131.

2 Margaret Clunies Ross, "Realism and the Fantastic in the Old Icelandic Sagas," *Scandinavian Studies* 74, no. 4 (2002), 443–447.

3 Runestone U 344, located in Orkesta (Swede), reads *in ulfr hafiʀ o| |onklati ' þru kialt| |takat þit uas fursta þis tusti ka-t ' þ(a) ---- (þ) urktil ' þa kalt knutr* which is commonly translated as 'And Ulfr has taken three payments in England. That was the first that Tosti paid. Then Þorketill paid. Then Knútr paid'. More about this inscription is available through the Scandinavian Runic-text Data Base (https://rundata.info/, accessed 23 April 2024).

4 David Warner, trans., *Ottonian Germany. The Chronicon of Thietmar of Merseburg* (Manchester: Manchester University Press, 2001), 334–335.

5 Tschan, trans., *The History of the Archbishops of Hamburg-Bremen*, 78.

6 For an overview of the evidence for Scandinavian incursions in Baltic and central Europe, see Marika Mägi, *In Austrvegr: The Role of the Eastern Baltic in Viking Age Communication across the Baltic Sea* (Leiden: Brill, 2018).

7 Sverrir Jakobsson, *The Varangians: In God's Holy Fire* (New York: Springer International, 2020).

8 Samuel Hazzard Cross and Olgerg Sherbowitz-Wetzor, eds. and trans, *The Russian Primary Chronicle: Laurentian Text* (Cambridge, MA: The Medieval Academy of America, 1953), 59–62.

9 Stefan Brink, *Thraldom: A History of Slavery in the Viking Age* (Oxford: Oxford University Press, 2021), 171–172.

10 Andres Siegfried Dobat, "Viking Stranger-Kings: The Foreign as a Source of Power in Viking Age Scandinavia, or, Why There Was a Peacock in the Gokstad Ship Burial?," *Early Medieval Europe* 23, no. 2 (2015), 164–165.

11 Dobat, "Viking Stranger-Kings," 164–165.

12 An example is his treatment of the "Amazons" in northern Scandinavia. See Annett Krakow, "On the Influence of Adam's *Gesta* on Yngvars saga víðförla," in *Adam of Bremen's* Gesta Hammaburgensis Ecclesiae Pontificum: *Origins, Reception and Significance*, ed. Grzegorz Bartusik, Radosław Biskup, and Jakub Morawiec (Abingdon: Routledge, 2022), 147–149.

13 Oddr Snorasson, "Yngvar's saga," in *Vikings in Russia: Yngvar's Saga and Eymund's Saga*, Hermann Pálsson and Paul Edwards, eds. and trans., (Edinburgh: Edinburgh University Press, 1989), 44.

14 Christopher Tolkien, ed. and trans., *Saga of King Heidrik* (London: Thomas Nelson & Sons, 1960), 61.

15 Karsten Friis-Jensen, ed., and Peter Fisher, trans., *Saxo Grammaticus. Gesta Danorum: The History of the Danes, Volume I* (Oxford: Oxford University Press, 2015), 715–725.

16 Tschan, *The History of the Archbishops of Hamburg-Bremen*, 80–81. Brita Malmer, *Den svenska mynthistorien Vikingatiden ca 995–1030* (Stockholm: Kungliga Myntkabinettet, 2010).

17 Tschan, *The History of the Archbishops of Hamburg-Bremen*, 80–81.

18 Tschan, *The History of the Archbishops of Hamburg-Bremen*, 80–81. Finlay and Faulkes, "Óláfs saga Tryggvasonar," 213.

19 Philip Line, *Kingship and State Formation in Sweden: c. 1130–1290* (Leiden: Brill, 2007), 66–67.

20 Jerzy Kloczowski, *A History of Polish Christianity* (Cambridge: Cambridge University Press, 2000), 10–23.

21 Davide Zori, *Age of Wolf and Wind: Voyages through the Viking World* (Oxford: Oxford University Press, 2024), 114–135.

22 Zori, *Age of Wolf and Wind*, 121.

23 Zori, *Age of Wolf and Wind*, 121.

24 Ben Raffield, Neil Price, and Mark Collard, "Polygyny, Concubinage, and the Social Lives of Women in the Viking Age," *Viking and Medieval Scandinavia* 13 (2017), 189–193.

25 Mark Bailey, *The English Manor C.1200–c.1500* (Manchester: Manchester University Press, 2002), 23–24.

26 Oluf Nielsen, ed. and trans., *Liber census Daniæ, Kong Valdemar den andens jordebog* (Copenhagen: G. E. C. Forlag, 1873), 121.

27 Finlay and Faulkes, "Óláfs saga Tryggvasonar," 178.

28 Gustaf Edvard Klemming, "Catalogus Regum Sueciæ ad Annum Christi 1333," in *Småstycken på Forn Svenska* (Stockholm: Kungl. Boktryckeriet, 1881), 272.

29 Birgit Sawyer, "Late Viking-Age Rune-Stones in Scandinavia" (unpublished paper, 2001), 3–6.

30 Finlay and Faulkes, "Óláfs saga Tryggvasonar," 169.

31 Friis-Jensen and Fisher, *Gesta Danorum I*, 725.

32 Walter de Gray Birch, ed., *Liber Vitae: Register and Martyrology of New Minster and Hyde Abbey, Winchester* (London: Simkin & Co. 1892), 58.

33 Rafał Prinke, "Świętosława, Sygryda, Gunhilda. Tożsamość córki Mieszka I jej skandynawskie związki," *Roczniki Historyczne* 70 (2004), 83–85.

34 Alistair Campbell, ed. and trans., *Encomium Emmae Reginae* (London: Royal Historical Society, 1949), 18.

35 Warner, *Chronicon of Thietmar*, 334–335.

36 Michael Kenneth Lawson, *Cnut: England's Viking King* (Cheltenham: Tempus, 2004), 49.

37 This subject has attracted considerable attention in recent years. See, for instance, Marika Mägi, *In* Austrvegr, and Mats Roslund, *Guests in the House: Cultural Transmission between Slavs and Scandinavians 900 to 1300 AD* (Leiden: Brill, 2007).

38 Lauritz Weibull, *Kritiska undersökningar i Nordens historia omkring år 1000* (Lund: Lybecker, 1911), 108–120.

39 Gwyn Jones, *A History of the Vikings*, 2nd edn (Oxford: Oxford University Press, 2001), 136.

40 Jones, *Vikings*, 136.

41 Finlay and Faulkes, "Óláfs saga Tryggvasonar," 179.

42 Finlay and Faulkes, "Óláfs saga Tryggvasonar," 193.

43 Friis-Jansen and Fischer, *Gesta Danorum I*, 721–723.

44 Finlay and Faulkes, "Óláfs saga Tryggvasonar," 214.

45 Finlay and Faulkes, "Óláfs saga Tryggvasonar," 217–231.

46 Friis-Jansen and Fischer, *Gesta Danorum I*, 715.

47 Finlay and Faulkes, "Haralds saga Gráfeldar," 131. This translation is discussed a few paragraphs below, but regardless of the translation used, the original Old Norse remains quite negative.

48 Finlay and Faulkes, "Haralds saga Gráfeldar," 178.

49 Hans Hildebrand, *Sveriges medeltid: kulturihistorisk skildring (första delen)* (Stockholm: P. A. Norstedt & Söner, 1879), 90–92.

50 Finlay and Faulkes, "Haralds saga Gráfeldar," 178.

51 Patrice M. Dabrowski, *Poland: The First Thousand Years* (Ithaca: Cornell University Press, 2014), 12–19.

52 John Ljungkvist and Per Frölund, "Gamla Uppsala – The Emergence of a Centre and a Magnate Complex," *Journal of Archaeology and Ancient History* 16 (2015), 14–21.

53 Finlay and Faulkes, "Haralds saga Gráfeldar," 132.

54 Cynthia Turner Camp, *Anglo-Saxon Saints Lives as History Writing in Late Medieval England* (Cambridge: D.S. Brewer, 2015), 25–35.

55 Stephanie Hollis, ed., *Writing the Wilton Women: Goscelin's Legend of Edith and Liber Confortatorius* (Turnhout: Brepols, 2004).

56 For a biography of Thyra, see Leif Ingvorsen, *Mythen om Dronning Thyra* (Copenhagen: Wormanium, 1988).

57 Friis-Jensen and Fisher, *Gesta Danorum I*, 689.

58 Friis-Jensen and Fisher, *Gesta Danorum I*, 689. See also Inge Skovgaard-Petersen, "Queenship in Medieval Denmark," in *Medieval Queenship*, 2nd edn, ed. John Carmi Parsons (New York: St Martin's Press, 1998), 30–31.

59 Skovgaard-Petersen, "Queenship in Medieval Denmark," 31.

60 Jones, *A History of the Vikings*, 136.

61 Saxo writes that at the prospect of marrying the virgin daughter of King Sven Forkbeard of Denmark, "the Norwegian king was transported to the seventh heaven, reckoning it more desirable to wed an unspoilt virgin than a woman in matron's garb; he hankered after her chaste embraces because he could not bear to mar his early manhood in the bosom of a widow." In contrast, Saxo describes her as "a most noble female" and "a sovereign of unimpeachable distinction" (Friis-Jensen and Fisher, *Gesta Danorum I*, 723).

62 Stefan Olsson, *The Hostages of the Northmen: From the Viking Age to the Middle Ages* (Stockholm: Stockholm University Press, 2019), 160.

63 This possible reference to the Virgin Mary is not unique and is more readily identifiable in the twelfth and thirteenth centuries, as will be shown in the next chapters.

64 Judith Jesch, *Women in the Viking Age* (Woodbridge: The Boydell Press, 1991), 52.

65 Birgit Sawyer, "Valdemar, Absalon and Saxo: Historiography and Politics in Medieval Denmark," *Revue belge de Philologie et d'Histoire* 63, no. 4 (1985), 690.

66 Hermann Pálsson and Edwards, *Vikings in Russia*, 44.

67 Finlay and Faulkes, "Ynglinga saga," in *Heimskringla I*, 27.

68 Hermann Pálsson and Edwards, *Vikings in Russia*, 44.

69 Finlay and Faulkes, "Óláfs saga Helga," 438. Tolkien, *Saga of Heidrik*, 61.

70 Bjarni Aðalbjarnarson, ed., "Óláfs saga Helga," in *Snorri Sturluson. Heimskringla vol. 2* (Reykjavik: Hið Íslenzk Fornritafélag, 1945), 433.

71 For a range of translations and their literary and editorial contexts, see "svarkr" in the Dictionary of Old Norse Prose, https://onp.ku.dk/onp/onp.php?o77324#, accessed 23 April 2024.

72 Helen Castor, *She-Wolves: The Women who Ruled England before Elizabeth* (London: Faber and Faber, 2010), 125; 64–96; 100–103.

73 Bjarni Aðalbjarnarson, "Óláfs saga Helga," 130.

74 For a range of translations and their literary and editorial contexts, see 'rík·lundaðr' in the *Dictionary of Old Norse Prose*, https://onp.ku.dk/onp/onp.php?o65042, accessed 23 April 2024.

75 The poem can be found in the poetic compilation *Tales of a Wayside Inn* (Boston, MA: Ticknor and Fields, 1864), 83–88.

76 In *Lives of the Queens of England vol. 1* (1841), Agnes Strickland fails to find any redeeming quality in Matilda whom she constantly compares unfavourably with her contemporaries. In *The History and Antiquities of the County Palatine of Durham* (1857), William

Fordyce calls Matilda "a weak and haughty, but violent and rapacious woman."

77 Henry Wadsworth Longfellow, *Tales of a Wayside Inn* (Boston: Ticknor and Fields, 1864), 83–88.

78 See for instance Swedish journalist Johanne Hildebrandt's works, *Sigrid* (Stockholm: Forum, 2014), and *Estrid* (Stockholm: Forum, 2016).

79 For example, *Świętosława: Córka Mieszka I, żona, matka skandynawskich Konungów* by Maria Rawska-Mrożkiewicz (London: Oficyna Poetów i Malarzy, 1987), and more recently Elżbieta Cherezińska's *Harda* (Poznan: Zysk i S-ka, 2016).

80 Finlay and Faulkes, "Óláfs saga Tryggvasonar," 232; "Óláfs saga Helga," 295.

81 Finlay and Faulkes, "Óláfs saga Helga," 84.

82 Tschan, *History of the Archbishops of Hamburg-Bremen*, 81.

83 Michael North, *The Baltic: A History* (Cambridge, MA: Harvard University Press, 2015), 14–15.

84 Finlay and Faulkes, "Óláfs saga Helga," 84.

85 Margaret Clunies Ross, "Concubinage in Anglo-Saxon England," *Past and Present* 108 (1985), 11–13.

86 Clunies Ross, "Concubinage in Anglo-Saxon England," 11–13.

87 Bjarni Aðalbjarnarson, "Óláfs saga Helga," 130.

88 "Ambótt," in the *Dictionary of Old Norse Prose*, https://onp.ku.dk/onp/onp.php?q, accessed 23 April 2024.

89 Tschan, *History of the Archbishops of Hamburg-Bremen*, 125.

90 Tschan, *History of the Archbishops of Hamburg-Bremen*, 203.

91 Tschan, *History of the Archbishops of Hamburg-Bremen*, 125.

92 Olfsson, *The Hostages of the Northmen*, 208.

93 Tschan, *History of the Archbishops of Hamburg-Bremen*, 95.

94 Olfsson, *The Hostages of the Northmen*, 81–124.

95 Raffield, Price, and Collard, "Polygyny, Concubinage, and the Social Lives of Women in the Viking Age," 169.

96 Raffield, Price, and Collard, "Polygyny, Concubinage, and the Social Lives of Women," 169–177.

97 Ruth Mazo Karras, "Concubinage and Slavery in the Viking Age," *Scandinavian Studies* 62, no. 2 (1990), 141–143.

98 Raffield, Price, and Collard, "Polygyny, Concubinage, and the Social Lives of Women," 177. Auður Magnúsdóttir, "Frillor och fruar: politik och samlevnad på Island 1120–1400" (PhD Diss., Gothenburg University, 2001).

99 Gerald Stone, *Slav Outposts in Central European History* (London: Bloomsbury Academic, 2016), 5–44.

100 Olsson, *The Hostages of the Northmen*, 160–163.

101 Raffield, Price, and Collard, "Polygyny, Concubinage, and the Social Lives of Women."

102 Tschan, *History of the Archbishops of Hamburg-Bremen*, 203.

103 Finlay and Faulkes, "Óláfs saga Helga," 98.

104 Finlay and Faulkes, "Óláfs saga Helga," 84.

105 Elena Woodacre, *Queens and Queenship* (Leeds: ARC Humanities Press, 2021), 43–46.

106 Keith McMahon, *Celestial Women: Imperial Wives and Concubines in China from Song to Qing* (Lanham: Rowman and Littlefield, 2016). Woodacre, *Queens and Queenship*, 39–42.

107 Richard Frye, trans., *Ibn Fadlan's Journey to Russia: A Tenth-Century Traveler from Baghdad to the Volga River* (Princeton: Marjus Wiener Publishers, 2005), 64–71.

108 Raffield, Price, and Collard, "Polygyny, Concubinage, and the Social Lives of Women," 170.

109 Raffield, Price, and Collard, "Polygyny, Concubinage, and the Social Lives of Women," 170.

110 Raffield, Price, and Collard, "Polygyny, Concubinage, and the Social Lives of Women," 169.

111 Tschan, *History of the Archbishops of Hamburg-Bremen*, 123.

112 Raffield, Price, and Collard, "Polygyny, Concubinage, and the Social Lives of Women," 178–183.

113 David Herlihy, *Medieval Households* (Cambridge, MA: Harvard University Press, 1985), 61–62. Birgit Sawyer, "Marriage, Inheritance, and Property in Early Medieval Scandinavia" (unpublished paper, 2001), 4–8.

114 Jan Rüdiger, *All the King's Women: Polygyny and Politics in Europe, 900–1250* (Leiden: Brill, 2020), 386–388.

115 Huw Pryce, *Native Law and the Church in Medieval Wales* (Oxford: Oxford University Press, 1993), 96–100. Roger Turvey, *The Welsh Princes: The Native Rulers of Wales, 1063–1283* (reprint) (Abingdon: Routledge, 2013), 14–35.

116 Carl Frederik Bricka, *Dansk Biografisk Lexikon, vol. XVII* (Copenhagen: Gyldendalske Boghandels Forlag, 1905), 3–5.

117 Bricka, *Dansk Biografisk Lexikon*, 3–5.

118 Woodacre, *Queens and Queenship*, 1–22.

119 Woodacre, *Queens and Queenship*, 1–22.

120 Finlay and Faulkes, "Óláfs saga Helga," 84. About the Christianisation of Slavic and Baltic peoples, a few major works can provide a good overview. Nora Berend, ed., *Christianization and the Rise of Christian Monarchy: Scandinavia, Central Europe and Rus' c. 900–1200* (Cambridge: Cambridge University Press, 2007). Florin Curta, ed., *Eastern Europe in the Middle Ages (500–1300)* (Leiden: Brill, 2019). Eric Christiansen, *The Northern Crusades* (London: Penguin, 1997).

121 Rune Edberg, *Viking Princess, Christian Saint: Ingegerd, a woman in the 11th century*, 2nd edn, trans. Theodosia Tomkinson (Sigtuna: Sigtuna Museum, 2005).

122 Finlay and Faulkes, "Haralds saga Sigurðarsonar," in *Heimskringla III*, 72.

123 Irina Metzler, "Sex, Religion, and the Law," in *A Cultural History of Sexuality in the Middle Ages*, ed. Ruth Evans (London: Bloomsbury, 2012), 109–110.

124 Finlay and Faulkes, "Haralds saga Sigurðarsonar," 72.

125 Adam describes the circumstances of the union and its subsequent annulment in his *Gesta*. See Tschan, *History of the Archbishops of Hamburg-Bremen*, 123. Saxo gives his own version in Karsten Friis-Jensen, ed. and Peter Fisher, trans., Saxo Grammaticus. *Gesta Danorum: The History of the Danes, Volume II* (Oxford: Clarendon Press, 2015), 801–803.

126 Tschan, *History of the Archbishops of Hamburg-Bremen*, 126.

127 Friis-Jensen and Fisher, *Gesta Danorum II*, 801–803. Axelson, *Sverige i Utländsk Annalistik 900–1400* (Stockholm: Appelbergs, 1955), 34; 55–56.

128 Friis-Jensen and Fisher, *Gesta Danorum II*, 801–803.

129 Heinrich Wolter, "Chronica Bremensis," in *Rerum Germanicarum tomi II. Scriptores Germanicos*, ed. Heinrich Meibom (Rome: Collegio Romano, 1688), 39.

130 Tschan, *History of the Archbishops of Hamburg-Bremen*, 126.

131 Kurt Johannesson, trans., and Hans Helander, ed., *Göternas och svearnas historia* (Stockholm: Michaelisgillet and Kungl. Vitterhets Historie och Antikvitets Akademien, 2018), 502.

132 Tschan, *History of the Archbishops of Hamburg-Bremen*, 126.

133 Tolkien, *Saga of Heidrik*, 62.

134 Tschan, *History of the Archbishops of Hamburg-Bremen*, 126.

135 Hans Gillingstam, "Utomnordiskt och nordiskt i de äldsta svenska dynastiska förbindelserna," *Personhistorisk tidskrift* 77 (1981), 18.

136 He is said by Adam of Bremen to have neglected Christianity. The list of kings appended to *Västgötalagen* states that he was a bad king. The sagas portray him in much the same light.

137 Carl Henrik Martling, *En svensk helgonkrönika* (Skellefteå: Artos, 2001), 166–167.

138 Wilhelmina Stålberg and Per Gustaf Berg, *Anteckningar om svenska qvinnor* (Stockholm: P. G. Berg, 1864), 26.

139 Martling, *En svensk helgonkrönika*.

140 Tschan, *History of the Archbishops of Hamburg-Bremen*, 95.

141 Thomas Lindkvist, ed. and trans., *The Västgöta Laws* (Abingdon: Routledge, 2021), 196.

142 Sara Ellis Nilsson, "Creating Holy People and Places on the Periphery: A Study of the Emergence of Cults of Native Saints in the Ecclesiastical Provinces of Lund and Uppsala from the Eleventh to the Thirteenth Centuries" (PhD Diss., University of Gothenburg, 2015).

143 This is discussed by various contributors in Lars Boje Mortensen, ed., *The Making of Christian Myths in the Periphery of Latin Christendom* (Copenhagen: Museum Tusculanum Press, 2006).

144 Ellis Nilsson, "Creating Holy People and Places," 246.

145 Ellis Nilsson, "Creating Holy People and Places," 84–96.

146 Ellis Nilsson, "Creating Holy People and Places," 245. For older observations of the same phenomenon, see Tryggve Lundén, *Sveriges missionärer, helgon och kyrkogrundare. En bok om Sveriges kristnande* (Helsingborg: Artos, 1983), 132–133. The symbolic

implications of such characteristics are still debated. See Claire Sahlin, "Holy Women of Scandinavia," in *Medieval Holy Women in the Christian Tradition, c. 1100–1500*, ed. Alastair Minnis and Rosalynn Voaden (Turnhout: Brepols, 2010), 689–723.

147 The only primary source relating the struggle for the throne after Stenkil's reign is Adam's *Gesta* (Tschan, *History of the Archbishops of Hamburg-Bremen*, 159–160).

148 Ellis Nilsson, "Creating Holy People and Places," 251.

149 Ellis Nilsson, "Creating Holy People and Places," 37. She also discusses several specific saints and the circumstances surrounding their martyrdom throughout the dissertation. See 124–126 for an example of martyrdom (Knud the Holy) openly used for political purposes.

150 Ellis Nilsson, "Creating Holy People and Places," 67–69.

151 See the contributions to the first section of *Mystifying the Monarch: Studies on Discourse, Power, and History*, ed. Jeroen Deploige and Gita Deneckere (Amsterdam: Amsterdam University Press, 2006).

152 Numerous instances of "creative genealogies" can be found in Old Norse literature, not least in "Ynglinga saga" in *Heimskringla*, which presents the legendary Swedish kings' a particularly prestigious ancestry including gods and mythological figures. Specific examples have been identified by Triin Laidoner in *Ancestor Worship and the Elite in Late Iron Age Scandinavia: A Grave Matter* (Abingdon: Routledge, 2020), for instance, 1651–1666. For a case study showing the need to political manipulation of illustrious ancestors, see 121–125.

153 The symbolic relationship between Christianity and the monarchy has been studied at length in Europe, and the mechanisms through which God's grace was said to be channelled through monarchs has been explained by scholars such as Alain Boureau and Thomas Lindkvist, to whom I defer on this matter. See Alain Boureau, "How Christian was the Sacralization of Monarchy in Western Europe (Twelfth-Fifteenth Centuries)?," in *Mystifying the Monarch*, 25–34. In a Swedish context, see for instance, Thomas Lindkvist, "Kungamakt, kristnande, statsbildning," in *Kristnandet i Sverige. Gamla källor och nya perspektiv*, ed. Bertil Nilsson (Uppsala: Lunne Böcker, 1996), 217–241.

3

CHRISTIAN QUEENSHIP
1090–1210

The Christianisation of Sweden and its practical implications for daily life in the kingdom have been studied elsewhere, but it is useful to remind ourselves of the context within which the queens studied in this chapter lived and reigned.[1] The Church was an important factor in the process of state formation in Sweden – as it was in many other places in Europe. However, before it could expand its jurisdiction over Sweden – through territorial and institutional division such as dioceses and parishes – it first needed to penetrate local communities where pre-Christian beliefs and customs endured for centuries after the first missionaries landed in Sweden from Germany. This religious transition was not solely a question of shifting beliefs. The Church also introduced a new thought system, as well as a type of administration which dealt with all aspects of people's lives. Growing ecclesiastical influence, especially after the archdiocese of Uppsala was established in 1164 – thus making Sweden its own ecclesiastical province for the first time – brought with it new taxes, new laws, and an increasingly centrally controlled society.[2]

We know that the Church did not become omnipresent entirely thanks to itself. Its spread required the cooperation of elite families who allowed, and in many cases actively supported, the establishment of ecclesiastical institutions, and the necessary power-sharing that resulted from it. Monasticism played a significant role in the process of forging relationships between lay and ecclesiastical elites, not just in Sweden but elsewhere in Scandinavia too. As will be shown shortly, it was common

DOI: 10.4324/9781003392200-3

for rich landowners to give land to monastic orders to establish new foundations. In exchange, that house would lend its political support to its benefactor's family. This is a common pattern witnessed elsewhere in Europe as well. As mentioned previously in relation to local saints, having relatives publicly recognised as pious, generally decent people, was great for raising a family's profile. It was even more so for families with royal ambitions. Recognition from a monastic institution, or within one's parish, could quickly snowball into recognition at much higher levels. Elite families were thus usually keen to make friends with bishops, prelates, and ultimately, the Pope.[3]

As mentioned, missionaries (mostly German and English) had been preaching the new faith since the ninth century with more or less success depending on the area. Ansgar, who was the first missionary official sent to Sweden in the late 820s, actively preached in Uppland and is said to have established a church in Birka.[4] However, he had very little lasting influence and there is no evidence that the region widely embraced the new religion before the twelfth century. Indeed, Uppland was traditionally seen as the beating heart of Old Norse religions, and Old Uppsala as the religious capital city of pre-Christian Scandinavia. This is related by Adam of Bremen, but also in *Heimskringla*, and various other medieval sources. Archaeological evidence also shows that Old Uppsala was indeed an important religious centre, and excavations have unearthed a wealth of remains including the foundations of a temple, large buildings, numerous graves, stone ships, and of course the famous royal mounds.[5] As will be mentioned again later, rebellions took place in the region in the second half of the thirteenth century. These may have been partly because of a persistent religious and cultural divide between the Christian royal authorities which wanted to establish taxes and centralise power, and the population which still supported traditional modes of governance, including the landed men's right to elect the king, the assemblies' authority on choosing a bishop, and the provision of armed support instead of taxes.[6]

Götaland, on the contrary, saw the rapid adoption of Christianity and its administrative apparatus. Several dioceses were quickly established in the south of Sweden during the eleventh and twelfth centuries. Firstly, the diocese of Skara was formed as early as 990 and certainly by the mid-eleventh century. In the twelfth century, two other dioceses were established: one in Linköping by 1139 and one in Växjö in the 1170s.[7] For context, we should remember that Skåne and Blekinge belonged to Denmark until the seventeenth century. The archdiocese of Lund, originally established as a regular diocese in the 1060s, held authority over the entirety of Scandinavia, after taking over from the archdiocese of Hamburg-Bremen in 1104.[8] The quick adoption of Christianity in the south of Sweden may therefore have partly had to do with its proximity to important Christian centres such as Lund, but also Germany.

It is not to say that the Church had no presence in the northern parts of the realm, but the Church's establishment in Götaland was much less opposed than in Svealand, and papal letters show that the Holy See had a close collaborative relationship with the local kings from Götaland.[9] A diocese was established in Västerås by the second half of the twelfth century, although little is known about it, which points to its lack of influence. Another existed in Strängnäs by 1171, possibly having replaced an earlier one in nearby Eskilstuna, known in the 1120s. Further north still, there were bishops in Sigtuna already during the reign of Inge the Elder (son of Ingamoder, who reigned during the late eleventh century until his death in about 1120). Most importantly, an archdiocese was created specifically to cover Sweden in 1164 with its seat in Uppsala. The reason why the archdiocese was given to Uppsala and not Sigtuna has been discussed elsewhere, but this may have been an attempt to replace Old Norse religion symbolically and physically in Uppsala.[10] However, as mentioned above, tensions remained high between adopters of Christianity and those who favoured the old religion in Svealand, and there is evidence that pagan customs there were still observed well into the twelfth century.[11]

The details of the foundation of Sweden's earliest monastic institutions will be given shortly, as most had connections with royal women. In summary, most were also concentrated in the south and established within a hundred years of each other during the eleventh and twelfth centuries. They include some famous

houses such as Vreta and Alvastra, both in Östergötland, Gudhem, and Varnhem in Västergötland and Roma on Gotland.
A couple of outliers can be found in Småland, Södermanland, and
Närke, with the last two being ambiguously located (both geographically and culturally) in between Götaland and Svealand,
but still far enough from Uppland not to infringe on traditional
pagan territories. No monasteries were established in Uppland
prior to the thirteenth century with the exception of Viby near
Sigtuna which had to be quickly moved to Södermanland where it
became known as Julita.[12] As will become obvious in this chapter,
the development of Christianity and the establishment of important religious institutions in the south of Sweden led to a shift in
power dynamics. Throughout the Viking Age, Uppland had been
the political and religious centre of what is now Sweden. However, the new religion, to which kings were drawn for political,
economic, and personal reasons laid out below, led to the reloca-
tion of power, and a new geographical distribution of the elites.

Royal women played a very important role in the Church's
establishment in Sweden. As will be shown shortly, they were
some of the earliest recorded sponsors of new monasteries and
churches, donating land and money to budding institutions which
relied on the support of their wealthy patrons. Sweden's royal
women often maintained a close relationship with these institutions throughout their lives. These women's patronage legitimised and empowered these monastic institutions, which went
onto becoming powerful landowners and political actors. This
relationship was often a personal one as well, as several queens
became nuns in widowhood and died in nunneries. The rather
quick and ostentatious adoption of Christian values by Swedish
queens might be explained by two factors. Firstly, it was an act of
intercession. Women, who were idealised in Christian thought as
weak, gentle, and humble, were the perfect link between the king
and the Church, whose interests clashed regularly. This role also
mirrored that of the Virgin Mary, the Queen of Heaven, who was
seen as an intercessor between God and people.[13] While acting
in their own name, secular queens nevertheless represented the
monarchy and served a pivotal diplomatic role in the process of
state formation, which hinged on the relationship between the

Church and the Crown. Secondly, women in Sweden had long been closely associated with religion. As we saw earlier, women had traditionally been considered wiser and closer to the "occult" than men, again serving as a link between people and their deity. It is likely that such a traditionally Norse perception of women persisted well into the Christian period. Considering that many queens of Sweden came from regions where Christianity was already more widely adopted, it is no surprise that they came to play an important symbolic and performative role in this shifting religious landscape. The first queen studied in this chapter, Helena, illustrates this transitional phase.

3.1   Helena

Succession following Stenkil's death around 1066 was complicated. Stenkil and Ingamoder's sons were King Inge (known as the Elder) and King Halsten, but the royal list appended to *Västgötalagen* says that Stenkil was succeeded by Håkan the Red, about whom little is known.[14] Adam of Bremen also writes that Håkan was king of Sweden, although he places his reign after the two Eriks' rebellion, the short reign and deposition of Halsten, and that of another king called Anund Gårdske ("from Russia").[15] An old hypothesis suggests that this King Anund Gårdske, who otherwise does not appear anywhere else, may be identical with Inge the Elder, because the circumstances of their rise and fall (exiled due to their Christian faith) are similar.[16] However, more recent scholars such as Mats Roslund have argued that both men were distinct and that the accession of Anund Gårdske to power is an example of the Uppland elite calling on a Rus leader to fill a power vacuum. This might therefore illustrate the close ties between these two peoples of common ancestry.[17] This remains unclear. A papal letter from 1080 also shows that Inge and Halsten co-ruled until Halsten was deposed.[18] Why Inge was allowed to remain king is unknown, although, like Olof Skötkonung, it may be that he agreed to stay within Götaland. This murky period in Sweden's history, between 1066 and 1080, has sometimes been described as a civil war. While the extent of the conflict is unclear, it was certainly a time when several men claimed power, and it is possible that there were multiple self-declared kings at once. In any case, order was restored when Halsten's sons, Inge the Younger and Philip, later succeeded Inge the Elder.

In this context, the first woman to be discussed in the third chapter of this monograph is Helena, who was the wife of Inge the Elder – and therefore Ingamoder's daughter-in-law. Very little is known about her background. She might have been a pagan who, like many others during the same period, converted to Christianity. This is implicitly alluded to in "Hervarar saga ok Heiðreks" which tells us that her name was Maer and that she was the sister of a pagan man called Sveinn.[19] It is not said where they came from, but Sveinn is alleged to have usurped power and ruled Svealand following the local assembly's rejection of Inge on religious grounds. It can therefore be assumed that he and Maer must have at least come from within Sweden as it is extremely unlikely that the proud people of Uppland would have chosen a Danish or Norwegian king. It is however impossible to pinpoint whether they came from Svealand or Götaland, although the political climate of the eleventh century favours Svealand – this is detailed shortly.

A tricky point in the study of Inge the Elder's queen is that she is never called Helena in this saga. She is only known as Maer, which means "maiden," and is a very uncommon name. The saga was however written in the thirteenth century and, as with all sagas, it aimed to entertain the audience. It has therefore been suggested that "Maer" was just a nickname given to Helena to underline her supposed purity in comparison with her brother, Sveinn, whose name literally means "swain." The pair's existence is not necessarily to be doubted, but their names do allow for the possibility that a religious metaphor was sought.[20] The name Helena first appears in a twelfth-century Danish genealogy of the Danish royal family which has her as Inge the Younger's queen.[21] Because of this, Maer and Helena have been equated. The link is admittedly fragile, but Inge is not said to have had any known concubine, and both women are referred to as being his wife. This may then be a case – again – of a woman known by two different names. It was common for both men and women to adopt a Christian name upon baptism, or to have two names which they used in different contexts. The king Anund Jacob, whom we mentioned in the previous chapter, is a good illustration of this practice. Initially baptised Jacob, he adopted the name Anund to please the people of Svealand who wished for the king to have a traditional Norse name. He was thereafter widely known as Anund Jacob, possibly using one or the other as needed.[22] It is therefore possible that the queen had a pagan name before her marriage and was thereafter known as Helena, perhaps as a reference to Saint Helena.

Whether Maer/Helena converted by choice or by force is unclear, and the historicity of the saga is also unproven, but there is evidence that the queen was involved in the endowment of Sweden's first monastic institution. First, one misconception should be dispelled immediately. Because of an error in the reading of some medieval sources, a few early modern historians believed that Helena was the wife of Inge the Younger rather than the Elder, but this clashes with medieval sources which claim instead that she was indeed Inge the Elder's wife. A charter from 1194 names her as such.[23] "Hervarar saga ok Heiðreks" which, as mentioned previously, was written in the thirteenth century (which, although by no means contemporary, is still rather early compared to early modern sources) also makes this statement.[24]

As Inge the Elder's wife, she was probably involved in the establishment of the Benedictine nunnery at Vreta, which is also the earliest recorded monastic institution in Sweden and was founded during his reign. The nunnery, which was dedicated to the Virgin Mary and was most probably established as a Benedictine institution like others from that period, may have adopted Cistercian rule around 1162 (although it did not formally belong to the Cistercian Order, which did not accept women until the thirteenth century).[25] It is this date, 1162, which many later medieval sources retain as its foundation date.[26] However, historians from the sixteenth and seventeenth centuries such as Olaus Petri, who may have had access to sources which are now lost, were adamant that there was a nunnery in Vreta before the 1160s.[27] This claim is partly based on the existence of several chronicles, the oldest being the *Registrum Upsalense* from 1344, which state that Inge the Younger – his namesake nephew – was poisoned in Vreta in the early twelfth century.[28] Early modern writers need to be read with caution, however, as we know that they mixed up Inge the Elder and Inge the Younger, and therefore perpetuated an inaccurate chronology. However, archaeological excavations have confirmed that there was an earlier church on the site of the current nunnery in the eleventh century.[29] There is therefore no reason to doubt that the nunnery was established as early as 1099. Early modern writers are consistent when discussing Helena and systematically list her among the original sponsors of Vreta Abbey. Rasmus Ludvigsson, writing in 1579, says "Konung Inge i Swerige [...] sampt medh sin drötning Helena funderede först Wreta Clöster." Rasmus Ludvigsson goes on to give a detailed breakdown of all the lands and farms the royal couple are alleged to have donated to the Church which include "4 ottunger jord i lille Wreta."[30]

It has been suggested that the lands given to Vreta by the royal couple came from Helena's own personal inheritance. As much as this would be a great talking point in the context of this study of female power, it is unlikely. As stated previously, we do not know for certain whether Helena was originally a pagan, but it is possible. If she was, it is more probable that her family came from Svealand. There is indeed little chance that they could have been openly pagan while owning large swathes of land in a pre-dominantly Christian region. In addition, we may note the existence of a runestone which mentions the names of several siblings including a woman called Maer, and her brother, Sveinn. The content of this runestone has been long debated, but it was raised in the eleventh century, it is located in an area where one would expect to find traces of paganism during this period, and it also would have been a very uncanny coincidence for a woman called Maer – a name which otherwise virtually does not appear anywhere else – to also have a brother named Sveinn, just like Inge's wife from the sagas.[31] While it is engraved with a Christian cross, the stone itself was not commissioned by Maer and Sveinn, and it is therefore not evidence of their own religious beliefs.

Furthermore, it would have been politically smart for Inge to marry someone from outside his own region. Helena would have brought lands and resources with her, while this new alliance would have enabled the king to extend his influence and reach out to segments of the population with which he would have had little contact until then. Indeed, we know that Inge the Elder's family already had its roots in Götaland. We have mentioned that his father King Stenkil came from a prominent Geatish family while Ingamoder is associated with Götaland as well. Admittedly, the family is more closely associated with Västergötland, and it is where Inge fled during Sveinn's takeover according to "Hervarar saga ok Heiðreks."[32] However, large family estates were hardly ever confined to specific provincial boundaries, and the House of Stenkil certainly owned lands in Östergötland.[33] It is therefore much more likely that the lands given to Vreta came from Inge's possessions.

What is possible, however, is that these lands were given to her by Inge as a morning gift, and that she subsequently decided herself to use them to found a nunnery. The practice of a husband giving his newly wed wife a gift on the morning after their first night together is well documented in medieval Europe. Because of the scarcity of sources, evidence of it is missing in many of the cases studied in this book. We know that morning gifts were widespread in medieval Sweden, and even lower echelons of society such as peasants practiced the tradition. Nevertheless, we should note that it is less clear when exactly it became a normal custom in Sweden, and whether its rise in popularity was linked to Christianisation. Additionally, morning gifts varied depending on a husband's needs and circumstances, of course, and it was certainly not always land.[34] However, it is worth keeping the custom in mind when looking at land owned by women, as it often explains discrepancies between a woman's native region and her possessions elsewhere, which could seem unconnected to her background, as in Helena's case here.[35]

This does not diminish the importance of Helena's contribution to the foundation of the nunnery. Being named as one of the founders of the abbey – irrespective of whose family the lands came from – would have been important for political reasons. By converting to the new faith and publicly showing support for the Church, Helena could serve as a poster girl for the new religion, and hers could be used as an example of a success story by ecclesiastical authorities eager to convince the common people to switch beliefs. It is also interesting that Vreta should have been a nunnery rather than a monastery. We do not know why Sweden's first monastic institution was dedicated to women but it might have been a conscious choice. Monastic institutions needed to be populated, and in many early instances, monks and nuns came from areas where Christianity was more widespread (notably France, where the Cistercian order was founded).[36] Founding a new house therefore involved a recruitment process which had to be carefully planned, and the make-up of a monastery's population could send a powerful political message. Finally, Helena's sponsorship of Vreta, which was the first of a very long series of such foundations by later successive queens, proved a turning point in the definition of queenship in Sweden. It is unclear whether this was purposefully meant to serve as a template for future queens, but it certainly started the trend. From Helena onwards, royal women routinely engaged with outside institutions which did not solely revolve around their husband. Helena's role as founder of Vreta was not exclusively defined by her relationship to the king. This was a significant shift from late Viking Age women who, even though they might have played a political role, did so within a very constrained framework dominated by their husbands.

Sweden is quite exceptional in Europe in that at the end of the twelfth century, there were more nunneries than monasteries in the kingdom.[37] Several reasons have been suggested for this. Firstly, medieval Christian society made it more complicated for single women to live freely, without some sort of guardianship. There were therefore suddenly a lot of unmarried daughters and widows which had to be taken care of, and entering a convent could be a good alternative to married life. It is also possible that women were initially more openly accepted as religious actors. Indeed, the domination of men in a monastic context only developed at a later stage of the process of Christianisation, when Christian society became increasingly hierarchised and organised.[38] It may also be added that, as discussed in the first chapter, women in pre-Christian Norse society were more readily accepted as religious figures than in the later Middle Ages. Considering that early Christianity in Scandinavia was tinged with remnants of pagan practice, it is possible that the elites were naturally more open to the establishment of Christian institutions for women.

Inge and Helena's union provides us with an exemplary marriage by Christian standards. He did not have any known concubine, and the marriage ran its course naturally without annulment, dispensation, or scandal of any sort. It is therefore a useful illustration of what was increasingly becoming the ideal in Scandinavia and elsewhere in Europe in terms of matrimony. It is during the late eleventh and twelfth centuries (when the Gregorian reform movement took the Church by storm) that marriage became a sacrament, and that much of the theological and legal framework around it was established, including strict rules about who could marry, how a betrothal should take place, what constituted a valid marriage, and whether a union could be dissolved. Although a few decades after the death of Inge, it is notably during the papacy of Alexander III (1159–1181) that the prohibition on incest was increased from three degrees to seven, a ban which had significant political implications (and was in fact later reduced as it proved unworkable).[39] Marriage, which until then had not been thoroughly codified by ecclesiastical authorities, took on a much more important religious and symbolic meaning, and began to be seen as a contract which not only indissolubly tied two individuals but also directly involved a personal relationship with God.[40]

The consequences of breaching such a contract, notably through repudiating a wife or taking another, therefore became much more serious. Thus, marriage and its correct performance became an integral part of the legitimisation of kingship. Unlike in previous centuries, a man could not simply break off a union and very few situations could warrant the annulment of a marriage.[41] This ensured the rise of the married household as a stable economic and political unit, which profoundly reshaped Europe's economic and political landscape.[42] As scholars such as Georges Duby have shown, the elites were subjected to especially tight religious constraints and demands, not least because the economic and political stakes were so much higher than in lower-class marriages.[43] Nevertheless, while the rules of matrimony grew extremely complex in theologically sophisticated areas such as France, Sweden during the same period was comparatively very simplistic. None-theless, being aware of the developments witnessed elsewhere in Europe is useful for understanding some of the decisions made on its periphery.

Helena had four children with Inge. They had a son named Ragnvald, about whom little is known but who might have died before his father as he seemingly never reigned, nor does he explicitly appear in any sources dated to after Inge's death. Sven Tunberg has instead suggested that this Ragnvald might be the one who was killed during his *eriksgata* for disrespecting the hostage-taking tradition. This theory could explain why the people of Västergötland, following their rejection of Ragnvald, turned to Magnus Nielsen (Inge's grandson and Ragnvald's nephew) as their new king, as he would have then been a law-ful successor – more on this below.[44] This remains, however, only a theory and is yet to be proved beyond doubt, notably because all surviving sources were written long after the events that they allude to. The royal couple also had three daugh-ters: Margareta, Kristina, and Katarina. All three, it should be noted, were given Christian names, which represents a shift from earlier practices. Not all the queens who came after the Christianisation of Sweden had Christian names, as it was also extremely common to be named after a grandmother or other ancestor, but Helena and Inge's name choices are so untradi-tional that they must have been a political statement. However, it is unclear who they were named after, but it is possible that the royal couple drew inspiration from other royal families else-where in Europe – Saint Margaret of Scotland, for instance, was contemporary.

Kristina Ingesdotter flourished in Kievan Rus, where she became the wife of Grand Prince Mstislav I of Kiev of the Chernigov dynasty. She had several children with him, none of whom returned to Sweden. Her daughter Ingeborg was, however, married to the Danish prince Knud Lavard, and remained close to her aunt, the Danish queen Margareta Fredkulla (also one of Inge's three daughters, studied below). Kristina Ingesdotter is bet-ter studied in an eastern European context and therefore does not form part of the current study.[45] Extremely little is known about Katarina Ingesdotter. According to "Knýtlinga saga," she was married to a Danish prince called Bjørn Haraldsen Ironside with whom she had one child, named Kristina (probably after her aunt, whom we just mentioned), who later became Queen of Sweden and will be discussed at a later point of this chapter.[46] As it will be shown, the existence of Queen Kristina is proven beyond doubt, and we may therefore be able to trust the saga regarding her filiation. Margareta Ingesdotter, better known as Margareta Fredkulla, is presented in the next biography.

The rest of Helena's life following the death of Inge is unclear. According to the early modern Catholic historian Johannes Messenius, who had access to sources which have not survived, she finished her life in Vreta, which she had helped found. It is possible: the custom for queens to finish their lives in their favoured monastic institution became widespread in the following decades and centuries. In any case, there is nothing to suggest that she lived beyond 1120.[47]

3.2   Margareta Fredkulla

A lot more can be said about Margareta Fredkulla, who played an important political role both in Denmark and Sweden in the early twelfth century. She was first married to King Magnus III of Norway in 1101. According to Norwegian monk Theodoricus, writing in the twelfth century, this union was part of a peace treaty between Sweden and Norway. Icelandic sources further add that this is how she received her nickname, *Fredkulla*, which means "Peace Maiden."[48] Saxo adds that upon her marriage, she received large landholdings in Dalsland, just across from the border, in Östergötland.[49] However, the marriage only lasted two years as Magnus was killed in 1103, and was apparently childless. Margareta left Norway very quickly following the death of Magnus, which might have earned her the wrath of the Norwegian people. Indeed, it has been speculated that she may be the unnamed Norwegian queen who was accused of stealing the relics of Saint Olaf in the late twelfth-century *Passio Olavi*.[50] However, although it is chronologically accurate, this episode does not appear anywhere else, and is more likely just an attempt to discredit her.

Yet, Margareta was not Norwegian, and she had not had any children with Magnus, which means that she did not personally have very strong ties with Norway. The uproar that her departure caused is therefore a little intriguing. The people's reaction to her leaving the country is interesting in itself, as it shows that queens, even once their tenure came to an end (here because of the death of the king), could be seen as belonging to that kingdom, thus leaving it would amount to treason or betrayal. The expectation might have been that she would remarry within the kingdom and commit to it. It would be romantic to see this as the expression of people's affection for her, and the hurt that they felt when she left. It is more likely, however, that this had to do with Margareta's immense wealth and her landholdings in Dalsland, just across from the border in Östergötland, which she had received as part of the settlement between Norway and Sweden upon marrying Magnus. By leaving and thus taking her landholdings away with her, Margareta closed the door to Norwegian annexation of this region.

Although there is no surviving evidence that explains her movements, her quick remarriage may have been organised by her father, Inge the Elder, who was reigning at the time and may have wanted to use this opportunity to forge a new alliance with Denmark, which is what Saxo, writing just a few decades later, suggests as well.[51] She then married King Niels of Denmark shortly after he became king in 1104, and remained in Denmark until her death, sometime between 1117 and 1131. There is a wide range of possible dates for her death because medieval sources which mention it give conflicting information. The *Necrologium* of the cathedral of Lund says that she died on 4 November, but it does not precise the year.[52] The records of the monastery in Næstved in Denmark, which only exist in later copies, claim that she died in 1117.[53] However, this seems very early, as other near-contemporary sources such as Saxo and the *Slavic Chronicle of Helmold* tell us that she was politically active during the events that eventually led to the civil war that pit Knud Lavard and Henrik Skadelår against each other during the 1120s. We know that she had direct dealings with Knud Lavard during the 1120s. Saxo relates a conversation that they supposedly had on her deathbed whereby she urged him to try and appease the kingdom. Knud Lavard himself is known to have died in 1131, which suggests that she died before then.[54]

As Danish queen, Margareta yielded immense influence. This has been written about elsewhere and will not be dealt with in the present book, but it is clear that she governed Denmark alongside (and perhaps even instead of) her husband. Scholars have gone as far as stating that it is thanks to her, through her extensive social network, that King Niels was able to reign as long as he did (30 years).[55] Many sources describe Niels as a pleasant and quiet man who, to an extent, was not fit to rule as he clearly preferred a peaceful and private life to the grandeur and complexity that necessarily accompanies kingship.[56] In this context, everything points to Margareta having played a major political role as queen and *de facto* ruler. There is plenty of evidence of her political influence, not least the coins that bore her name alongside that of her husband. She is the only queen whose name appears on coins during this period in Europe.[57] These coins were minted in Lund (then part of the kingdom of Denmark), and were not only evidence of Margareta's personal influence but also may have served as a symbol of the new alliance between Sweden and Denmark. Coins, in the early Middle Ages, were an extremely important tool for propaganda and publicity, and essentially served as mass media. Having her name engraved on coins clearly shows that Margareta was publicly on equal footing with her husband, an extremely rare – if not unique – phenomenon in twelfth-century Europe.

Like many noble and royal women of her time, she was a generous sponsor of the Church. Saxo is particularly keen to emphasise this aspect of her reign by pointing out that she did not only donate riches and wealth to churches but also made vestments and chasubles for the use of priests and other clergymen so as to relieve their living conditions and visually promote the faith.[58] This is reminiscent of Saint Edith of Wilton, mentioned in the previous chapter, who was also renowned for making her vestments. This was certainly considered a show of true piety, as opposed to the less personal act of donating money or land, which by this point was essentially expected as part of the royal couple's duties. Margareta also sponsored churches abroad, however, in what is a display of her international outreach and activities abroad. A letter from 1117 written by the theologian Theobald of Étampes thanks her for her support of the Abbey of Saint-Étienne in Caen, Normandy.[59] This is significant as it places her reign in an international context, and evidences contacts with other Christian kingdoms at a personal level. There is no such clear evidence of active engagement outside Scandinavia by Swedish nobles during the same period. However, Margareta's support of the abbey in Normandy marks the beginning of bilateral exchanges, as opposed to continental Church actors providing personnel and money to Scandinavian houses in a one-way relationship. It underlines the growth of the Church and monasticism in Scandinavia.

In a strictly Swedish context, Margareta is important because she used her family ties to advance her only son Magnus' position, which eventually led him to being recognised as king in parts of Sweden. When Inge the Elder died, Margareta inherited land in Sweden. The detail of how much and where is not known, but it is probable that most of Margareta's lands were in Västergötland. This would be logical considering her previous marriage to Magnus of Norway (whereby she received parts of Dalsland as dower), and is also suggested by her son Magnus' later claim to kingship in Västergötland. In this case, she would have been subjected to the laws of this province. According to the thirteenth-century *Västgölagen*, there were rules governing gifts and the division of family estates. This was regardless of gender. The aim of these rules was to avoid splitting up family estates that had been passed on. Properties that were bought from another landowner could be sold again, but inherited lands had to be offered to legal heirs first.[60]

Margareta cannot have been Inge's and Helena's only heir, as she had siblings: Kristina and Katarina. The latter certainly inherited something, although Kristina, who lived in Kievan Rus, was possibly too far away to invoke her inheritance rights. Margareta did give lands to Kristina's daughter Ingeborg, however, who also lived in Denmark as the wife of Danish prince Knud Lavard (a marriage arranged by Margareta herself), which suggests that geographical proximity was required to inherit property. This is mentioned again in *Västgötalagen* in which an ancient clause explicitly forbids people living in "Greece" (the Byzantine Empire and surrounding regions) to inherit property in the province, possibly to avoid properties being left unattended and unprotected, and to encourage people to stay.[61] It was perhaps similar for those living elsewhere outside the region.

Saxo writes that she divided the lands that she inherited, kept some for herself, and distributed the rest to her nieces.[62] This is not just Margareta being generous. This was a shrewd political and diplomatic move. Land-giving as a tool for ensuring kinsmen's loyalty was not new, but it is mainly associated with kings and other powerful noblemen. It was a way of buying someone's support and obedience. It is very interesting to see a woman engage in the practice. It is particularly unusual here because there is no evidence that King Niels did the same. Although he may have used a similar strategy, it is not recorded as precisely as in Margareta's case. This further supports the idea that she was the one ruling and that it is her manoeuvring that lay at the foundation of Niels' power. It also illustrates how Scandinavian women could oversee their own assets and decide what to do with them without their husband's permission, and how such transactions had a tangible impact on political developments.

Following the death of King Inge the Younger (Margareta's cousin), there was a power vacuum in Sweden. As we mentioned, Ragnvald Knaphövde may have tried to get himself confirmed as king, but died in around the 1130s. It was then Margareta's son, Magnus Nielsen, that the people of Västergötland chose as king instead (his wife, Rikissa, is presented later in this chapter). This is despite Magnus being a problematic member of the family. According to Saxo, he "enacted a loathsome crime in murdering a relative and became a famous example of treachery."[63] It is unclear what this refers to, but Magnus was nevertheless a legitimate pretender to the throne, being a grandchild of Inge the Younger, and thus a member of the Stenkil dynasty on the maternal line. We also know that Margareta was a wealthy landowner, and Magnus' claim to Sweden's throne likely came after her death, which as we saw, has been dated to between 1117 and 1131. This means that by the time he was involved in Swedish politics, he probably owned large swathes of land that had once belonged to his mother, and before that to Inge the Elder.

What this episode also shows is the importance of land ownership in medieval Scandinavia in the context of kingship. Not unsurprisingly, owning a significant amount of land in an area lent extra weight to a pretender's claim to kingship over that area. It was particularly advantageous to own large estates in the most populated areas such as Uppland. Land ownership mattered as much, if not more, than ancestry – which becomes even more evident upon the accession of the commoner Sverker the Elder to the throne, shortly after Magnus' return to Denmark. Margareta's division of her inheritance had the direct result that entire chunks of Swedish land ended up in the hands of Danish and Norwegian nobles. We mentioned in relation to Sigrid Storråda that as late as the thirteenth century, Danish kings possessed land in southern Sweden. Margareta's case is one example of how this could happen.

3.3   Ingegerd Haraldsdatter

Inge the Elder's successors were Inge the Younger and Filip, his nephews. Icelandic sources claim that Inge the Younger co-ruled the kingdom alongside Filip from about 1105 until Filip's death in 1118.[64] This is not clear from older sources, which suggest instead that Filip was king before Inge.[65] In any case, very little is known about Filip and his wife. "Hervarar saga" tells us that he was married to a Norwegian princess called Ingegerd about whom not much can be said. In the saga she is purported to be King Harald Hardrada's daughter (presumably) with Queen Elisiv of Kiev.[66] While yet to be confirmed by further sources, this is entirely possible as Harald and Elisiv's marriage is well documented and took place in either 1045 or 1046.[67] As the eldest of two daughters born from this union, it is considered that Ingegerd was born around 1046. She may have been first married to King Olaf I of Denmark around 1066. The Danish king died in 1095 and it remains unclear whether they had issue.[68]

Nothing can be said about Ingegerd as Queen of Sweden in that there is no surviving evidence of her personality, popularity,

and reign in general. However, the circumstances of her coming
to the throne are worth commenting on. By the time she married
Filip shortly after the death of Olaf, she must have been 50 years
old. It is unclear how the union was arranged and whether it
came with any conditions, but by medieval standards, a 50-year
old was extremely old regardless of gender, and even more so
for a woman whose main role in society was to procreate. Even
for modern women, the chances of having children naturally
at that age are slim, and this royal marriage can therefore not
have been expected to produce an heir. That is very interesting, especially considering that Filip had no other known wife
or concubine, and is not recorded as having had any children
either. This suggests two things: either the saga is wrong and
Ingegerd was never Queen of Sweden, or the union was so dip-
lomatically beneficial that it was worth sacrificing any hope of
producing a lawful heir. A definite answer to this observation
cannot be given here, but marrying a former queen was usually
a smart diplomatic move. Filip and Inge the Younger had inherited the throne from their uncle who, as mentioned previously,
had faced many challenges to his own rule. Marrying a former
queen added an extra layer of legitimacy to his kingship. Having children with his queen was perhaps not a consideration for
Filip as concubines' children were still routinely recognised as
legitimate heirs during this period of Scandinavian history. He
might therefore have hoped to father children with other women
while enjoying the prestige stemming from his royal union. This
is, however, speculation and the exact motivations behind Filip
and Ingegerd's marriage remain unclear.

Following King Filip's death, Inge the Younger continued to
reign alone until his own death around 1123. There is conflicting
information about his marriage(s). There are two women who
are alleged to have been lawfully married to him: Ulvhild Håkonsdatter and Ragnhild of Tälje. It is unclear whether he married
one and then the other, or whether commentators mistakenly
identified the same wife as different women (who clearly were
well-documented, separate individuals). In any case, both women
played important roles in the spread of Christianity in Sweden, as
shown below.

3.4 Ragnhild of Tälje

It is completely unclear whether Ragnhild of Tälje belongs in this book. While this woman probably existed, her queenship is disputed. There are no surviving contemporary sources, and therefore nothing of what is known about Ragnhild can be confirmed beyond doubt. Biographical details such as the years of her birth and death, and her family background are completely unknown. Both the "Prosaiska krönikan" and "Lilla rimkrönikan," written in the fifteenth-century, claim that she was married to Inge the Younger and thus Queen of Sweden.[69] Her epitaph, supposedly found in the church of Södertälje and destroyed in the sixteenth or seventeenth century (but transcribed in the fifteenth century), also claims that she was a queen, although it does not give the name of her spouse.[70] To complicate matters, two versions of the original late medieval transcription exist, one of which tells us that she was Queen of Norway – something which scholars have not been able to explain yet, but is probably a mistake.[71] It is surprising, considering how important she seems to have been, that contemporary sources should be silent about her. This could be explained if she was married to Inge but the union ended, for whatever reason, before he became king.

Her family background is completely unknown, but has been the object of much speculation. Because her epitaph says that she was the daughter of a man called Halsten, it has been suggested that she was the daughter of King Halsten, whom we briefly mentioned previously. This is impossible, if one believes that she was married to Inge the Younger as per the chronicles, since it would mean that she had married her own brother. Others have instead suggested that the inscription refers to Alstan Folkesson, which would make her a member of the powerful Bjälbo family. This certainly would explain how she came to become queen, as the Bjälbo family was an illustrious clan which yielded significant political and economic influence.[72] Marrying into this family would have therefore brought Inge the Younger a lot of wealth and significant political support. There is, however, no concrete evidence for this claim and this instead relies on the dating of Ranghild's reign and the fact that little is known about Alstan

Folkesson's children. It could, quite frankly, be any other Halsten/ Alstan.

Ragnhild is certainly one of the most mysterious women studied in this monograph. Because she is such an elusive character, it is impossible to know what aspects of her biography have been fabricated. She is nevertheless interesting because she illustrates what was expected of high-status Christian women in the twelfth century, but also in the later Middle Ages. Indeed, she has clearly been idealised, and was known in the later medieval period as a saint. Her (now destroyed) epitaph in the church of Södertälje describes her as "ruler of the Swedes, a flower without thorn, a queen for a kingdom," an inscription which makes use of terms which were still highly contentious in the twelfth century, when she is alleged to have lived. This part of the epitaph, through the vocabulary it uses, therefore seems to reflect a later medieval understanding of the Swedish nation. The inscription goes on to mention her pilgrimage to Rome and Jerusalem, and credits her with building "the temple in Tälje" (the church) which she "enriched with money and adorned with donations." A last part praises her pious deeds, which includes caring for the sick, and ends with a prayer to her.[73] We do not know when this inscription was made. It does not survive and therefore it is impossible to date with precision. It is nevertheless interesting because it gives an overview of what was expected of high-status Christian women in medieval Sweden.

Church-building was similar to the founding of monasteries in that it was a public display of piety and could be used to secure the political support of the Church. A major difference between the sponsoring of a monastery and that of a church, however, is that regular people could more easily interact with a church than with a monastery. Monastic institutions were self-sufficient and mainly closed off. Churches, on the other hand, were always open. It was in church that people practiced their new faith, and it was in the priest that they could find moral comfort. Churches were the heart of the Christian community, and as such also served a range of non-religious purposes. For example, they could serve as shelter in case of conflict, and they were used as meeting places (we know, for instance, that churches in Norway could be used for administrative purposes).[74] Building a church was thus as much of a gift to the people as it was a gift to the ecclesiastical institutions.

It is not only royal figures who built churches and indeed, there is evidence that many of Sweden's earliest churches – which were often originally wooden and later rebuilt in stone – were built by local magnates. Gotland's medieval churches, of which over 90 survive, are prime examples of this trend, and the practice of privately funding churches is mentioned in the island's laws.[75] In the early days of Christianity, rites were not always conducted in churches. Indeed, they were expensive to build, they required staffing (at least one priest), and had to be built in locations where sufficient numbers of Christians could be found, so as to financially and politically support a new parish. There are very few regions in Sweden where all these conditions were met prior to the twelfth century. Birgit Sawyer has in fact suggested that the high number of Christian runestones in Uppland might have been caused by a lack of Christian facilities, such as churches and cemeteries, which forced Christian families to express their faith differently.[76] There was also an additional difficulty: that of access. Medieval Sweden was – and to an extent remains – an extremely rural kingdom with vast empty regions and many scattered communities, often separated by natural barriers such as thick forests. It was technically impossible for a lot of people to travel to a church, especially in the winter. As a result, masses and religious events could take place at designated sites which had been chosen for their convenience. Few of these sites had fully built churches but instead used makeshift altars. Several sites are known from the early modern period, and it is likely that the practice originated in the Middle Ages.[77]

Ragnhild's epitaph also mentions that she went on pilgrimage which makes her the first recorded (alleged) queen of Sweden to have personally gone on a pilgrimage. Pilgrimages were an important aspect of the religious lives of Christian people, both men and women. Despite the long distance, many went to the Holy Land, which was the most prestigious destination, but other sites were also the focal points of pilgrims such as Santiago de Compostella which was also a very popular destination for Scandinavians in the twelfth and thirteenth centuries.[78] A pilgrimage was therefore a common journey to undertake for whoever had the means to do so. There is plenty of evidence, from the Icelandic sagas to monastic records, that in the late Viking Age, when Christianity spread among Scandinavian seafarers, Viking leaders regularly went to Jerusalem and Rome. This was considered prestigious, and also gave Viking noblemen the chance to prove their ingenuity, physical endurance, strength of character, and other characteristics.[79] In *Orkneyinga saga*, for instance, Earl Ragnvald Kolsson's pilgrimage to the Holy Land is an important episode which is told over no less than five chapters. Ragnvald ruled Orkney between 1129 and 1158, which made him contemporary with Ragnhild. The tale of his travel, which includes stops at the court of Queen Ermingerd in southern France as well as in Byzantium, is clearly meant to underline his nobility of character, his religious devotion, and also his education.[80] No detail is given of what he actually did once he reached his destination. It is the initiative and the trip itself that are considered important. Most tales of pilgrimage in the sagas emphasise the importance of visiting royalty and elite friends along the way, with a customary meeting with the Byzantine emperor the usual climax of the story. Accounts of pilgrimage often served as literary motif.[81] While some were clearly fictional, many probably had some truth to it, and it is likely that people coming across Ragnhild's epitaph would have understood the implications of her going on pilgrimage.

It was especially important for elite individuals and royalty as a show of piety, and it may well have been part of the queen's job to serve as an example for the rest of the population by undertaking such a perilous journey out of devotion. As mentioned, it was also a social exercise, and it allowed elite individuals to meet the Pope and other high-ranking ecclesiastics, thus giving a diplomatic twist to what was otherwise a sign of Christian commitment. We have no further information about Ragnhild's pilgrimage, and therefore we do not know what she did there. In fact, we do not know whether she truly went, or whether this is a later claim aiming to enhance her Christian persona; but going on pilgrimage certainly helped cement someone's legacy as a good Christian, and brought them long-lasting prestige, as evidenced by the fact that this is mentioned on her epitaph. It is worth noting that Earl Ragnvald too was subsequently recognised as a saint, although like Ragnhild (and Ingamoder-Ingemo), there is no evidence that he ever underwent the proper canonisation process. As others have written elsewhere, however, canonisation was not strictly required for one to become a saint, and merely provided official recognition of that status. The rigid process dictated by Canon Law which is now commonly associated with canonisation did not become systematic until the thirteenth century.[82] Ragnvald's, Ragnhild's, and Ingemo's legacy as saints may therefore be a grassroots phenomenon, and reflect their popularity among the population, rather than their actual links to the Church and its institutions.

Such journeys may also have been motivated by genuine religious fervour.[83] These were difficult trips with no guarantee that one would come back alive. Several high-profile noblemen nearly contemporary with Ragnhild perished during such pilgrimages, including Svend Godwinson, the cousin of Svend Estridsen whom we discussed earlier, who died in 1052, and Lǫgmaðr Guðrøðarson, King of Man and the Isles who died in 1095.[84] Ragnhild, who lived around the same period, would have been aware of this risk. We know from documentary and non-fictional sources (as opposed to the sagas) that Scandinavian pilgrims embarked on long trips across Europe and the Middle East out of true faith. Lists of otherwise unknown pilgrims are also recorded in the registers of those monasteries where they stopped and other reliable sources. Such travellers may have had a range of motivations, from wanting adventure to truly seeking a religious experience (Figure 3.1).[85]

There are some traces of Ragnhild's veneration as a saint in the medieval period. She was never formally canonised and does not appear in the calendar of saints' feast days, but paintings dated to the fourteenth or fifteenth centuries which are thought to depict her in pilgrim attire can still be found in the churches of Börje, Viksta, and Enångers.[86] Börje and Viksta are both located in Uppland while Enångers is located in Hälsingland, further north than the other two. It is unlikely that Ragnhild would have been venerated in Hälsingland already in the twelfth century, as

FIGURE 3.1   Later painting of Saint Ragnhild in Börje Church. Photograph by Lennart Karlsson, SHM.

the region was barely Christianised then. However, it is possible that her cult spread there later in the medieval period, perhaps brought over by clergymen who had worked in Uppland. Like Ingamoder, Ragnhild's cult, which was evidently fairly localised, is known only from the fourteenth century onwards. This could be the result of the destruction of earlier sources, but it is more likely that something happened in Swedish society at some point in the later Middle Ages which led to local saints, including earlier ones, to gain in popularity or be revived.

It would be foolish to ignore the obvious: the immense popularity of Birgitta of Sweden both during her lifetime and after her canonisation. Saint Birgitta of Sweden lived between c. 1303 and 1373. She was a noblewoman who became an important religious figure following the death of her husband in 1344. From an early age she had had a reputation as a mystic and visionary, and is known for her *Revelations*, compiled by her followers to support her canonisation. She also founded the Order of the Most Holy Saviour, most commonly known as the Bridgettines, which was formally approved in 1370. She was canonised in 1391.[87] Saint Birgitta immensely influenced Christianity in medieval Sweden, and served as an important role model for Christian women not only in Scandinavia but elsewhere in Europe as well.[88]

There are clear common points between Birgitta, Ingamoder, and Ragnhild. All three were women of high status (although not necessarily of royal birth), had been married, and had lived a standard lay existence before their lives took a religious turn. This last aspect is particularly important as this means that ordinary women could easily identify with these three saints. It is possible that as Birgitta's popularity soared in the fourteenth century, it became trendy to venerate female saints. This also means that it is also impossible to tell whether their alleged personal history and deeds reflect contemporary expectations, or later medieval ones. Further research into the possible connection between the cult of Birgitta and the revival of earlier female saints such as Ragnhild of Tälje may shed light on this question.

We should also note that the current use of Ragnhild's image on the seal of the city of Södertälje and the local places named after her are the result of early modern efforts to popularise her as a symbolic Christian figure.[89] They do not stem at all from her medieval cult, thus further blurring the line between myth and historical reality. In this context, it will come as no surprise that we have no reliable information about Ragnhild's life or her death, except for the fact that she was evidently buried in the church of Södertälje, which she is said to have founded.

3.5 Ulvhild Håkonsdatter

Ulvhild Håkonsdatter was a Norwegian noblewoman. The Icelandic saga *Fagrskinna*, which records the history of some of the kings of Norway, claims that she was the daughter of Håkon Finnsson, a powerful magnate himself descended from the powerful Thjotta family. The identity of her mother is unknown. According to the same saga, Ulvhild was first married to Inge the Younger and upon his death, subsequently became the queen of Denmark through her marriage to King Niels.[90] She eventually married King Sverker the Elder of Sweden whose power base was in Östergötland although, as will be detailed shortly, the circumstances of the end to her marriage to King Niels remain unclear. Saxo suggests that she may have left the union while Niels was still alive, but he died shortly after, killed by some of his displeased subjects in Schweslig in 1134, after which Ulvhild was free to live as Sverker's queen.[91]

Ulvhild is one of the queens about whom we know the most for this period, but all our knowledge of her relies on later sources, mainly consisting of Icelandic sagas which are often unreliable. Until her marriage to Sverker, no details of her life can be confirmed by way of non-fictional, contemporary sources. It is therefore important to remember that large parts of her reconstructed biography have not been confirmed beyond doubt. Apart from the basic genealogical information gleaned from "Fagrskinna," we do not know anything about her early life and how she ended up marrying Inge the Younger. One can only speculate on the circumstances of their meeting and the reasons for their marriage, although it is likely that her family's wealth, fame, and likely political influence must have been enticing for the Swedish king. According to Snorri Sturluson, the Thjotta clan had an illustrious military heritage, having participated in the Battle of Helgeå in 1025 as well as at the Battle of Stiklestad in 1030. Much of the family's prestige seems to have derived from a wealthy landowner named Hårek, who was Ulvhild's grandfather according to "Fagrskinna." He lived in the late tenth century and eleventh century, and had close ties to both King Olaf Haraldsson of Norway and King Cnut the Great of England and Denmark. The writer further explains, without giving details, that Hårek derived from "high lineage," and that his paternal grandmother was a Norwegian princess, daughter of Harald Fairhair.[92] It is difficult to confirm, and there are some chronological inconsistencies in the saga.[93] It is unlikely, for instance, that Ulvhild was the granddaughter (rather than the great-granddaughter) of a man born in the tenth century, but such a prestigious background would certainly justify Ulvhild's standing in Scandinavian society. *Heimskringla*'s account, as usual, is difficult to confirm too, but it suggests that the family had considerable political influence in the eleventh century, and had strong ties to both Danish and Norwegian Crowns. It may well have remained similarly powerful later on as well, which might have played a role in Inge's decision to marry a woman hailing from this family.

Indeed, Inge's lifetime and that of his successors were heavily impacted by recurring conflicts with the Danish Crown, and it is possible that a marriage with Ulvhild aimed to ensure support from the Thjotta family. There is also, of course, the issue of her mother's unknown identity, which has attracted much speculation. Her mother's lineage could also explain Ulvhild's social status. Adolf Schück suggested that she was an illegitimate daughter of Margareta Fredkulla, as this would explain the unopposed dissolution of Ulvhild's marriage to King Niels, her stepfather (more on this below).[94] However, this seems to be impossible, because of the short time that seems to have lapsed between Margareta's marriages to Magnus and then to Niels. The possibility that Margareta birthed Ulvhild out of wedlock exists, but this would have probably been recorded by authors such as Saxo, who make no mention of a link between Margareta and Ulvhild. This matter therefore remains unresolved.

Very little is known about Inge's reign in general, and even less so about his relationship with Ulvhild. The royal couple is not recorded as having had children. This marriage, however, may have propelled the queen to the forefront of Scandinavian diplomacy, and she derived much of her later power and influence from being the wife of the last king of the Stenkil dynasty. Inge died poisoned in obscure circumstances, a deed for which Ulvhild has been blamed in later scholarship despite a lack of evidence. The exact date for this event is unknown, although it may have taken place around 1123, when King Sigurd I of Norway invaded Småland, without any mention of a reigning Swedish king at the time.[95] Following Inge's death, Ulvhild moved to Denmark rather than returning to Norway, as evidenced by her marriage to Niels. The reasons for this are unknown, although she may simply have spotted an opportunity in becoming the Danish king's new wife following the death of Margareta Fredkulla, whom we mentioned previously.

Of Ulvhild's marriage to Niels, little is known as well. By the time she married him, Niels was an old man – at least in his sixties – and most of his reign was well behind him. As mentioned in connection with Margareta Fredkulla, it is likely that Niels gradually lost much of his influence following her death. This union did not produce any children either and, as will be explained shortly, it is possible that Ulvhild simply deserted Niels before moving to Sweden to marry Sverker. It is unclear how long she remained in Denmark, although she probably left in the early 1130s, as Niels died, now single, in 1134.[96]

The reasons behind her marriage to Sverker are more easily identified. He had no royal blood, and instead hailed from a wealthy landowning family. His father is named as Kornuba (or Korn Ubbe) in *Västgötalagen*.[97] It is unclear why the Swedes chose Sverker as king, although there was clearly a power vacuum following the extinction of the House of Stenkil following the death of Inge the Younger, Ulvhild's first husband, and the last representative of that dynasty in direct line. Sverker's two predecessors, Magnus and Ragnvald, were also both out of the question. Indeed, Ragnvald was swiftly murdered for disrespecting traditions, whereas Magnus Nielsen, who was the son of King

Niels and Margareta Fredkulla and therefore Ulvhild's stepson (and perhaps her brother, if she was Margareta's daughter), was only recognised in parts of Götaland, and spent much of his royal career as co-king of Denmark. Sverker therefore seized an opportunity, and Saxo writes that the Swedes chose him because they refused to be ruled by another foreigner.[98]

As with many of Sweden's early kings, Sverker needed a prestigious match to legitimise his authority. Ulvhild was such a match. As the widow of Inge, she represented the House of Stenkil, and most probably had inherited lands and wealth in Götaland. As former queen of Denmark, she was also a diplomatic asset, opening up the possibility of further alliances, and consolidating economic links between the two kingdoms. Indeed, as Magnus' stepmother, there was a chance that his followers would embrace her and rally behind Sverker, thus healing the rift between the Geats and the Swedes after a turbulent succession. From this point of view, Sverker needed Ulvhild more than she needed him, and Saxo writes that the king actively sought Ulvhild who was then still married to the king of Denmark. Saxo was critical of this union, which he did not regard as lawful. It is unclear whether his version of Ulvhild and Sverker's elopement is true, but he writes that

> Ulvild, whom Niels had married after Margrete's death, was first inveigled by this Sverker through mediators bearing love-tokens, and soon afterwards stealthily abducted by the man himself, who brought her to the point of sleeping with him. Treating this union as wedlock, he made her the mother of Karl, a later successor of his to the Swedish crown.[99]

This may be vastly exaggerated. Such abductions must have happened as they are routinely depicted in the sagas as well as non-fictional medieval sources, but it is difficult to see how such an event could result in anything less than war between the two kingdoms. Yet, there is no evidence of such a conflict between Sverker and Niels, nor is there any evidence that Ulvhild was not considered a legitimate spouse of Sverker. Saxo's suggestion that she was his concubine first before marrying him is nevertheless interesting, as this would be a case where the concubine, who was really just a queen-in-waiting, may have been treated as such even before the union was finalised.

There is, however, also no evidence of a divorce between Ulvhild and Niels, nor is there any surviving paperwork documenting the annulment of their union. This is surprising considering that this process, which required lengthy justification, was usually well-documented. For Ulvhild to be allowed to marry Sverker, there must have certainly been an agreement of sorts and the marriage must have been terminated, but it is unclear how. The hypothesis that Ulvhild's mother was in fact Margareta Fredkulla has been mentioned previously. This would have made Niels her stepfather, and such a marriage would have been easy to annul as the spouses would have been too closely related.[100] For the reasons discussed above, this is chronologically unlikely. However, this is an example of how a royal marriage could quickly be terminated, and we know that spouses who regretted their union could sometimes try and prove that they were too closely related to be married.[101] Unfortunately, the lack of sources to confirm any of these theories remains a significant obstacle. Instead, Sverker and his betrothed may have simply waited for Niels to die, which happened in 1134. It is also unclear why Ulvhild left, although I posit that King Niels was simply too old. We know that he was several decades older than Ulvhild, and that their union did not produce children. It might well be that a conclusion was reached that this union was no longer beneficial to either spouse, and to the kingdom in general. This is pure speculation, however, but could explain why Ulvhild was able to switch husbands without causing a diplomatic incident.

With Sverker, Ulvhild had several children. The first to be born was Karl, possibly when King Niels was still alive (as we saw, Saxo suggested the illicit affair took place before his death). They most certainly also had a son called Jon, who became infamous for being a violent bully.[102] They may also have had two daughters, although this is less clear. As usual in medieval sources, daughters were not given as much attention. We know that Karl had a sister, Ingegerd, who became the abbess of Vreta Abbey. She is studied further in this chapter. It is unclear whether this was a uterine sister, or a half-sister. Another daughter of Sverker, called Helena, is known to have reigned as Queen of Denmark, but the identity of her own mother is also unknown. She is discussed later on as well.

As the wife of King Sverker the Elder, Ulvhild is credited with having invited the Cistercians to establish themselves in Sweden. Thus, the abbey of Alvastra was founded sometime between 1142 and 1144. This time, there is evidence for her direct intervention in reliable sources. It is related in *Exordium magnum cisterciense*, a collection of stories about the Cistercian Order compiled by the abbot Conrad of Eberbach from the 1180s to the 1220s.[103] The thirteenth-century *Narratiancula de fundatione monasterii Vitae-scholæ*, which describes the foundation of Sweden's first Cistercian monasteries, also names her (alongside Sverker) as founder of Alvastra.[104] In a sixteenth-century document, Bishop Hans Brask tells us that Alvastra was built on land that belonged to Ulvhild, which she had received as a morning gift from Sverker.[105] The writer probably had access to sources which are now lost, and it is impossible to independently confirm this claim at present. It would, however, be in line with what seems to have been a common practice not only among royal women but also noble-women, as evidenced by the numerous charters witnessing the giving of land received as wedding gifts to monastic institutions throughout the Middle Ages. Even more interestingly, perhaps, Brask points out that the abbey never belonged to the Crown, but rather was a private foundation (Figure 3.2).

The foundation of this abbey was a momentous event in Swedish history. Indeed, the Cistercians' influence on medieval Swedish society cannot be overstated. They were not the first monastic order to establish themselves in Sweden, but they were the first to be successful and spread across multiple regions. The Cistercian model was particularly productive. Wherever they established a house, the Cistercians developed agriculture, architecture, building techniques, and other such practical inventions. They were also well organised, and their monasteries formed a network within which economic activity was fostered notably through the employment of lay brothers. The Cistercians were much more efficient than the regular clergy at spreading

FIGURE 3.2 Aerial view of Alvastra Abbey © Jeppe Gustafsson/ Alamy Stock Photo.

across the realm. They relied on sympathetic landowners to give them the land necessary to build their communities, but were otherwise fairly closed off.[106] It also needs to be noted that the Church and the monastic orders were in fact separate entities, with religious orders following their own rules. The Cistercians, in particular, were allowed in 1119 by Pope Calixtus II to rule themselves independently.[107] Additionally, many early medieval monks were not ordained priests (and nuns never were), and therefore members of monastic houses were not direct agents of the Church, or closely involved with the bishop.[108] Monks were essentially autonomous. It may be, therefore, that in the eyes of the population, monks, who were less directly involved with the public, were considered less of a threat than priests and missionaries who actively preached the new faith, and most irritatingly for people, enforced its rules. Monasticism neverthe-less had a long-lasting impact in Sweden as elsewhere in Europe, with the development of education, for example, being closely tied to monasteries which could school local children, especially those of high-status families.[109]

As a woman from Norway, where Christianity was more developed than in Sweden, Ulvhild must have been aware of the importance of supporting monastic institutions to establish influence in a particular region. Furthermore, as a former queen of Denmark, she was certainly well acquainted with the politics and alliances necessary to impose one's dynasty. Both Denmark and Norway had more, and older monastic institutions than Sweden in the first half of the twelfth century. However, the Cistercians had not established themselves anywhere in Scandinavia until Ulvhild invited them. The abbey that they founded at her request was thus the very first Cistercian institution in Scandinavia. The order went on to become the most successful across Europe until their progressive decline in the fourteenth century.[110] Inviting the Cistercians was not simply a private endeavour but an intensely political undertaking, perhaps best evidenced by the fact that the creation of a royal foundation (Alvastra) was immediately countered by the creation of an abbey under direct ecclesiastical control, Nydala, which was probably on the initiative of Bishop Gisle of Linköping and Archbishop Eskil of Lund, who may have wanted to fund a monastic house without direct ties to the Crown. This may have been to ensure that at least one abbey followed Church policy, including the Christianisation of the remaining pagan populations as a matter of urgency.[111] In turn, this suggests that the ecclesiastical authorities did not necessarily consider Alvastra as a serious or reliable foundation from a religious perspective, but primarily as a political tool in the hands of Ulvhild and Sverker.

Another noteworthy aspect of Ulvhild's life is that she was married to no fewer than three kings, at least one of whom she chose for herself (Sverker), rather than the other way around. If there is any truth to Saxo's version of events, Ulvhild must have chosen to leave Denmark to return to Sweden. She certainly chose not to return to her native Norway. As mentioned, there is no evidence that she had any recent royal blood, but instead climbed up the social ladder through her political manoeuvrings. There is a lingering image among the general public that things such as virginity and innocence were very important female attributes. This is true to an extent. Indeed, the ideal woman in medieval

Christian thought was weak. Virginity was important to establish clear filiation, but it was also a hugely symbolic characteristic.[112] Chastity represented the rejection of earthen pleasures and considerations, was thought to elevate one's soul, and to bring one closer to God. It showed that a woman was able to transcend her evil nature and resist the temptations of her flesh. For women across the medieval world, the image of the Virgin Mary was an obvious ideal sometimes reflected directly in women's seals and iconography, but that of a more complex character such as Mary Magdalene who through penance and good deeds restored her reputation following her sinning, was an important (and more accessible) role model too.[113]

However, all these feminine traits were an ideal, and not always the practical solution. What the clergy and theologians expected of women differed from what regular men did. Widowhood was extremely common in the medieval period, especially in times of war. In lay society, it was perfectly acceptable, and even expected, that women would remarry. Swedish provincial laws planned for it, Icelandic sagas show us that it was common in medieval Scandinavia, and indeed all the biographies given in the present book confirm that this was normal practice.[114] It was more problematic on many fronts – not least economic – to be a single woman than to be a remarried one. This is tied to the fact that the household was the most important economic unit in medieval Europe, and ideologically, this had to consist of a man and a woman.[115] In high-status families, where striking the right alliance and finding a good match was of utmost importance, little consideration was given to whether a woman had been married before or not. It has been pointed out that while the religious feminine ideal was that of a virgin or chaste woman, thus not producing children, noblemen and royalty actively sought women who had had children before as this proved their ability to procreate.[116]

Furthermore, as Swedish noblemen sought foreign women of royal pedigree to shore up their claim to power, having an experienced consort was an advantage. It is only towards the end of the period studied in this book that queens started being married off at a very young age, when political dynamics required quicker decisions and careful planning of long-term alliances sometimes as soon as a girl was born. The main obstacle to remarrying in the twelfth century was thus the risk of committing incest, which as we saw previously, had a much broader definition in the Middle Ages. It is therefore not surprising to see women enter their third union or more, and queens marrying multiple kings or high-ranking noblemen in different countries was also a common development. Crucially, most women were considered worthy of marriage as long as they could produce heirs. It was therefore possible for a queen to get married late in life, and their alleged years of birth suggest that Ulvhild might have been older than Sverker.

From that point of view, queenship could be understood as a job more than a passive status. On a personal level, Ulvhild probably loved, and wanted power. She could have easily entered a nunnery after the end of her first royal marriage had she not been interested in staying within the centre of power. She must also have been a valuable consort, especially for Sverker, as by the time she married him, she had much experience of politics, diplomacy, and courtly culture. In fact, the question of courtly culture really should become part of our focus from Ulvhild's reign onwards. As mentioned earlier, we have very little information about how and where Sweden's earliest queens lived. Unlike elsewhere in medieval Europe, courtly culture was not yet developed in the kingdom, but this may have started to change with Sverker's reign.

Sverker is often credited with building the royal fortress of Näs on Visingsö, an island near the southern shore of Lake Vättern, which is Sweden's oldest recorded castle explicitly associated with the monarchy. It is unclear, however, who exactly built it. There have been suggestions that it might have been Sverker's son instead, King Karl Sverkersson who, according to *Västgötalagen*, was also assassinated there.[117] Karl's wife, Kristina Hvide (studied shortly), was also a member of the court in Denmark, and would have thus also been familiar with its workings and advantages. As mentioned, the exact construction dates of the castle are unknown. It is possible that the castle was started by Sverker and Ulvhild, and finished by Karl and Kristina. Ulvhild died around 1148, and Sverker died about ten years later. It is therefore conceivable that the project spanned two reigns, but it cannot be confirmed. The main reason for thinking that Ulvhild

FIGURE 3.3 View of Näs Castle © Thomas Males/Alamy Stock Photo.

was behind the castle's inception is because she was so demonstrably influential in Swedish politics during her reign, notably through her invitation of the Cistercians, that it simply makes sense that she would also have had a hand in revolutionising the monarchy (Figure 3.3).

Indeed, this castle is the earliest recorded purpose-built royal residence in Sweden. Its location was highly symbolic: it is roughly located at the crossroad between Svealand, Västergötland, and Östergötland. This cannot have been a coincidence and is instead a powerful metaphor for the consolidation of the realm. By medieval standards, it was not very well-built for a fortress, and would not have resisted a sustained assault. It was, in fact, burned down within a hundred years of its erection.[118] Instead, the structure may have served as a physical representation of the Crown's power, and was a first attempt by a king to physically establish himself at the crossroads of the realm's main provinces. This must also mean that other people occupied the castle because it is obvious that the king and queen cannot have lived alone. As mentioned previously, it is highly likely that a king was always accompanied by a retinue to ensure his constant protection. These people must have therefore lived in the castle as well. Although nearly never recorded in the earlier part of the Middle Ages in Sweden, we know from elsewhere in medieval Europe that queens and noblewomen also had maids and companions around them to help them dress, wash, and keep them company. While initially practical, the social and political role of maids and servants has long been recognised as an important part of the royal household, although the question of female servants in particular remains understudied. Yet, studies across high-status households elsewhere in Europe show that through her maids, a queen or noblewoman could extend her power base.[119]

As discussed previously, the end of Ulvhild's marriage to King Niels must have been rather amicable as there is no evidence that any conflict ensued. Her transfer from the Danish court to Sweden must have been smooth, and in this context, it is extremely likely that she brought with her HER own group of maids and servants. There must have therefore been a significant female presence in the castle, too. Sadly, there is no surviving evidence concerning the court's organisation during Sverker's reign, and it remains, at this stage, educated guesswork. It is nevertheless tempting to see Ulvhild as the driving force behind the construction of this castle. As a former queen of Denmark, she would have been familiar and comfortable with the concept of court. The Danish and Norwegian courts were much more developed than that of Sweden, as with many other aspects of state apparatus. It is especially true in Norway, which was the most centralised of the three Scandinavian kingdoms, and where a well-rounded courtly culture, including courtly literature and art, flourished from the late twelfth century onwards.[120] While courtly culture in general was still at a very early stage during Ulvhild's lifetime, as a Norwegian noblewoman, she would have understood that investing in courtly culture was important not just as a way of crystallising the Crown's standing and prestige in people's minds, but also to keep one's friends (and enemies) close. Sverker, as a newcomer onto the royal stage, would not have been able to appreciate this, which is why it is likely that he acted on his wife's advice. Nevertheless, it took much longer for the court in Sweden to develop, and it only truly reached maturity in the last quarter of the thirteenth century – something which will be detailed in the next chapter.

A last interesting aspect of Ulvhild's life is the fact that it is claimed in some secondary literature that she murdered her former husband, King Inge the Younger. This would be an astonishing development for a character that otherwise presented herself as a pious woman and great sponsor of the Church. Of course, the story of Inge's murder is just that: an unverifiable story like many others about early medieval queens. It is not related in any medieval source and is instead the product of pure speculation. It is also an example of a so-called "fact" which has found its way into much secondary literature, when all that is known from near-contemporary sources is that Inge was poisoned, without a perpetrator being named. The story is nevertheless fascinating. Indeed, Ulvhild (as a character in this story) is a perfect example of how one's public image could clash with one's behaviour in private. It is a good reminder that religion was a political tool and not merely a spiritual aid. Showing oneself as pious did not mean that one actually was, and an individual's support for ecclesiastical institutions does not mean that they privately subscribed to their teachings. Ulvhild also showcases women's political ambitions and their initiative. Of all the women studied so far, she may be the first example of a woman who was known to have intrigued at the same level as the men in their political entourage.

It should be noted, however, that royal sponsorship of ecclesiastical institutions may not always have been motivated by power. Philip Line has pointed out that kings and noblemen were well aware that many of their deeds were morally dubious, not least murders. Sponsoring the Church may have therefore been an attempt at redemption.[121] It may well be the same with women like Ulvhild. Her devotion in later life is not evidence of a past crime, but it could nevertheless have been the result of remorse, or a desire to embrace a different lifestyle after a life of political intrigue. She certainly became a much quieter character in the last few years of her life, about which nothing is known. Her cause of death is also unknown, as is its precise date. 1148 is usually considered a good approximation, because Sverker had remarried, taking Rikissa of Poland as his new wife by 1150 (see below).

It has also been suggested that Ulvhild might have been buried in Alvastra Abbey, like other queens such as Helena and Brigida Haraldsdatter who may also have been buried in the monastic institutions that they founded.

3.6   Rikissa of Poland

Following the death of Queen Ulvhild, Sverker remarried with Rikissa of Poland. Rikissa was a member of the prestigious House of Piast in Poland. She was the daughter of Bolesław III Wrymouth, the powerful high duke of Poland. Her mother's identity is less certain but she was probably Bolesław's second wife Salomea of Berg, daughter of a Swabian count and herself a shrewd and influential political actor.[122] Depending on different Slavic sources, Rikissa's date of birth is given as 12 April 1106, or 1116, but we do not know when she died.[123]

There were several advantages to marrying Rikissa for Sverker. Firstly, she had been the wife of Magnus Nielsen, who we saw had been chosen as king by the people of Västergötland. Sverker was from Östergötland, as evidenced by his family landholdings.[124] They had thus been rivals, and it is probable that by marrying his widow, Sverker aimed to appease Magnus' remaining followers to consolidate his realm. Furthermore, the Piast dynasty was also a lot more stable than any other royal family of early medieval Sweden. It had continuously reigned since the tenth century and carried on until the late fourteenth century. The very first queen that we studied in this book, Sigrid Storråda, presumably came from Poland and was probably the daughter of Mieszko of Poland, who was an early member of the Piast dynasty. With stability also came wealth, and it is evident that such a match would have been advantageous for Sverker who, we must remember, had no royal blood at all. His marriage to Rikissa also shows that even though contacts between Sweden and the Slavic kingdoms were not as intense as they had been 200 years prior, it could nevertheless still be considered advantageous to maintain good relations with the east.

However, twelfth-century Poland was very different from tenth-century Poland. When Erik Segersäll married Sigrid, Poland was undergoing Christianisation and pagan elements were still an important part of Slavic culture. By the twelfth century, however, state formation and the consolidation of the monarchy in Poland had significantly advanced. Leadership, or at least its hierarchy, was better defined than in Sweden, with the Polish aristocracy being significantly more developed than that of Sweden, which did not really come about for another century. This might be due to Poland's long ties with the Holy German Empire, to which the Polish dukes and kings had been somewhat subordinate since the tenth century.[125] German influence on social classes in Poland was thus felt earlier than in Sweden. Creating ties of kinship through marriage with this powerful Polish dynasty was therefore a smart political move on Sverker's part. It guaranteed support from his in-laws if need be, and allowed him to establish some influence in the east through his children, who automatically inherited a high social status in their mother's land as well.

To an extent, Poland and Sweden were similar during this period in that they were both located (geographically and politically) on the periphery of Europe. Both kingdoms were still fragile concepts with Sweden being particularly prone to sudden changes in the definition of its borders, and Boleslaw III's realm being divided upon his death in 1138.[126] Polish historians have pointed out that the Piast dynasty, despite its longevity and importance in eastern Europe, was not seen as particularly attractive elsewhere in more prestigious kingdoms such as Germany.[127] This is certainly true of Sweden too, and it is not surprising either that Sverker should choose Rikissa as a second queen rather than as a first choice (and likewise, as Rikissa's marriage with Sverker was her third). This union could be read as an alliance between two marginal families trying to strengthen each other.

Rikissa had been married twice before her union with Sverker. Firstly, we know from *Gesta Danorum* that she married Magnus Nielsen, also known as Magnus I, in the late 1120s. Magnus, son of Margareta Fredkulla and grandson of Inge the Elder whom we discussed previously, was briefly recognised as king in Västergötland following the murder of Ragnvald Knaphövde.[128] While Saxo does not name her, we know her name from other genealogies, including that given in "Knýtlinga saga."[129] As Magnus' wife,

Rikissa was therefore technically Queen of Sweden for a while. However, Magnus' authority was weak, and his reign short as he focused on his claim to the Danish throne. During this union, she was possibly based in Denmark, and following Magnus' death in 1134, she returned to Poland. With Magnus, she had at least one son, Knud, who later became King of Denmark in 1146, and married Helena Sverkersdotter, his stepsister, who will be discussed shortly.

In Poland, her father arranged another marriage, although the identity of her second husband is disputed. The most accepted theory is that she married a prince of the Rurikid dynasty – the Rus royal dynasty founded by Swedish Vikings a few centuries prior – Volodar of Minsk. With Volodar, she may have had three children including a daughter, Sophia of Minsk, mentioned in "Fagrskinna," who herself will be mentioned again in this book as the mother of a later queen of Sweden.[130] However, for reasons which are unclear, her marriage to Volodar may have been dissolved and she once again returned to Poland. It must be noted, however, that the details of Rikissa's life in Poland remain the subject of intense debate among historians of medieval Poland. Much about it can be read elsewhere, although most of the scholarship remains to be translated into English.[131] In any case, it is in this troubled context that she married Sverker the Elder soon after Ulvhild's death, sometime between 1148 and 1150. We know that she was certainly Sverker's wife in 1150 or 1151, which is when her son Knud V of Denmark fled to Sweden following a civil war. Writing about the event, Saxo describes Knud as "being initially welcome to his stepfather in Sweden," whom he explicitly identifies as Sverker.[132]

With Sverker, she had a son named Boleslaw, who was named after her father, as was customary in both Swedish and Polish families during that period. His properties are said in Valdemar II's *jordebog* to have been inherited by his sister *Sophia regina*, his half-sister Sophia of Minsk.[133] This may be the same Boleslaw who contested the Swedish throne in the 1160s and died in battle around 1172. It is also unclear whether the royal couple had another child. Later medieval sources, chiefly Olaus Petri's chronicle, claim that Sune Sik was the younger son of Sverker and

Rikissa. According to the same source, Sune Sik was the father of Ingrid Ylva, the powerful matriarch of the Bjälbo branch of the Folkung family which produced several kings of Sweden as well as bishops, dukes, and a king of Denmark.[134] This information remains, however, uncertain.

Apart from that, little is known about Rikissa during her tenure as Queen of Sweden. It is especially interesting to note that she is not explicitly associated with any donation, although these may be hidden behind Sverker's name. As can be expected, nothing is known about Rikissa following the death of Sverker. Yet, her dynastic legacy in Scandinavia was particularly rich. Through her daughter Sophia of Minsk, Rikissa was a grandmother to no fewer than two kings of Denmark, one queen of France, one German Countess as well as one German Duchess, but also nuns, and another Rikissa, also Queen of Sweden as the wife of Erik Knutsson who is presented in the next chapter. There is no evidence that she remarried and instead disappears from the historical record. Her resting place is unknown as well, although we know that several members of Sverker's immediate family and descendants were buried in Alvastra Abbey. It is therefore possible that she was buried there.[135]

3.7   Kristina Bjørnsdatter

Following Sverker the Elder's murder, succession again became complicated. The circumstances surrounding Erik's accession to the throne are completely unclear. Historians do not yet know why Karl Sverkersson, Sverker's son and heir, was initially bypassed in the succession. Some scholars suspect that both kings may have eventually reigned at the same time, with Karl having authority over Östergötland, as evidenced by a charter from 1159,[136] and Erik presumably over Västergötland and Svealand, where he owned an estate. This is yet another reminder that the kingdom was still fragmented and loosely defined, and that the power of a "king" could be fractured. Erik's identity is somewhat unclear, however his family name, Jedvardsson, suggests that he had an English background. All that we know, in fact, is that he claimed power in the 1150s either just before or following

Sverker's assassination, and reigned for a few years, possibly taking part in the Baltic Crusades.[137]

His wife Kristina was a Danish and Swedish princess who, according to "Knýtlinga saga," was a daughter of Bjørn Haraldsen Ironside and, conveniently, Inge the Elder's granddaughter through her possible mother Katarina Ingesdotter, mentioned previously.[138] While the latter filiation is less clear, it would nevertheless make complete sense both from a chronological and political perspective. A familiar pattern is thus discernible, whereby Erik, a powerful individual whose blood links to royalty nevertheless remain unclear, strengthened his claim to the throne by marrying a woman of royal descent. The date of their marriage is unknown although it must have taken place long before Erik's ascent to power in the 1150s. Indeed, their son, the future King Knut, reigned for over 20 years from 1167, which suggests that he may have been born in the 1140s or before.

The chronology is unclear but Kristina, as Erik's wife, may have been queen at the same time as another Kristina, who was the wife of the rival king Karl Sverkersson. This is an interesting situation, although the scarcity of sources makes it impossible to know how this arrangement worked. Both women may never have interacted, as they probably lived in different regions and belonged to different factions, and yet they were related through a common ancestor, Kristina Ingesdotter, to whom they both owed their name. Erik's wife, studied here, as the likely daughter of Katarina Ingesdotter, may have been the niece of Kristina Ingesdotter. Karl's wife, studied later in this chapter, was her great-granddaughter. Through their respective marriages, both kings could thus claim to continue the line of Inge the Elder. In addition, Kristina, of course, was an openly Christian name. During a period when Scandinavian names were still extremely commonplace due to traditional naming patterns underlining ancestry, the giving of such unambiguously Christian names was also a powerful statement.

The reign of Erik and Kristina was a tumultuous period in Sweden's religious history, and it shows a much darker aspect to the Christianisation process. Indeed, Erik is most famous for his alleged involvement in the Baltic Crusades, a series of campaigns which aimed to Christianise Finland and the Baltic regions which now correspond to Estonia, Latvia, and Lithuania.[139] These were brutal raids on the pagan coastal communities of the eastern Baltic region. Several crusades occurred over a period stretching several centuries, and Erik's crusade may have been the first.[140] Some scholars such as Thomas Lindkvist have cast doubt on the veracity of the scarce sources which mention it, but if it did happen, it was probably not a very large enterprise. Nevertheless, Erik's crusading activities cemented his reputation as a pious king. Murdered in 1160, he began being venerated as early as 1198. His bones were formally enshrined in 1257 and their move to the new cathedral in Uppsala in 1273 is well documented. While never formally canonised, he was already known as a saint in the thirteenth century, as evidenced by several papal letters, and 18 May is still observed as his feast day by both the Catholic Church and the Church of Sweden.[141]

Erik and Kristina's reign also highlights the more complex aspect of the relationship and power struggles between lay and ecclesiastical elites. Indeed, while all the Christian monarchs and their wives discussed so far seemed to entertain positive relationships with the nascent Church administration, there is evidence of disagreements between the monks of Varnhem Abbey and the royal couple. The thirteenth-century *Narratiuncula de fundatione monasterii Vitaescholae* tells how Erik and Kristina harassed the monks at Varnhem, to the point of some of them leaving for Denmark where they founded Vitskøl Abbey in April 1158.[142] Kristina is specifically accused of sending women to dance naked and taunt the monks at the abbey. As the incident is known from the very monastery that the monks of Varnhem are credited with founding, however, it is also possibly biased, and is clearly in favour of the monks involved in this conflict. The chronicle tells us that the dispute arose because of some land used by the abbey which Kristina considered hers, as per her inheritance from a woman called Sigrid, mentioned in the previous chapter, whose identity, relationship to the queen, and extent of her wealth remain debated.[143]

We know from other cases that land disputes between benefactors and the ecclesiastical institutions that they supported were fairly common. Others have written about the fact that "given" land was in fact only ever borrowed, and many benefactors did expect to get their land back at some point. This also explains the number of charters renewing or confirming the grant of lands, as continued use in perpetuity was not actually taken for granted.[144] The reason this particular dispute is well-known is of course because it involved the highest echelon of society – the king and queen – and because the harassment depicted was particularly crude. It might seem surprising that Kristina opposed the monks rather than tolerating them on her land, and the manner in which she is said to have driven them away is less than elegant. From what we have seen of other leading women so far, this was not very queenly behaviour. Instead, it shows Kristina as a property owner who, despite her royal status, also had personal interests to foster. It is perhaps judicious to see this not as a dispute between the king and the monks, but between the landlady and her tenants.

While Kristina's example is unique in this study, there are other known instances of overzealous queens elsewhere in Europe. In England, Eleanor of Castile, who reigned a few decades later, was notorious for her harsh estate management which included arbitrarily restricting her tenants' rights, imprisoning those who protested, and seizing their homes. In one particularly gruesome case, Eleanor's officials dumped a baby on the road.[145] The amount and nature of complaints was such that an official inquiry was opened to investigate the situation (albeit after her death).[146] In comparison, Kristina seems very tame indeed. Yet, male landlords probably employed similarly harsh methods. The main reasons why Kristina's behaviour seems particularly shocking is because we are not used to seeing women as powerful landlords, and because queenship is tightly connected to Christian ideals of gentleness, peacemaking and humility, which are completely at odds with these women's reputations.

There is, however, also plenty of evidence of the Swedish royal couple's pro-clerical stance in their donations to the abbey of Nydala in Småland, for instance, recorded in 1208 when King Erik Knutsson confirmed the arrangement.[147] There is also evidence that the king had a good relationship with the abbot of Alvastra Abbey, mother-house to Varnhem, and Erik's general behaviour towards religious matters, including his work to improve the collection of the tithe, shows that he was amiable to the Church.[148] Erik's devotion to the advancement of Christianity certainly cannot be put in doubt, considering his alleged involvement in the Crusades, which was not simply political manoeuvring but had tangible consequences. It might therefore not be a case of actual opposition to the Church, but it sheds light on the grittier detail of the relationship between monastic institutions and the lay people who enabled them in the first place.

Saint Erik had two sons and two daughters of whom we know and whose mother was presumably Kristina. They were Knut, who reigned in the last quarter of the twelfth century, and his brother Filip, who is mentioned in a charter but about whom little is known.[149] Their daughters were Katarina, and Margareta, who notably became Queen of Norway. According to "Knýtlinga saga," Katarina married a nobleman called Nils Blake.[150] Little else is known about her. Margareta, on the other hand, had an eventful and well-documented life as Queen of Norway through her marriage to King Sverre Sigurdsson.[151] She is better studied in a Norwegian context and is therefore not part of this study. According to his legend, Erik was murdered while attending mass in the old cathedral of Uppsala on 18 May 1160 by Magnus Henriksson who briefly succeeded him as Magnus II.[152] There is no suggestion that the queen was targeted in this attack, and she must have fled, but her whereabouts after this event are unknown, as is the year of her death.

3.8   Brigida Haraldsdatter

Brigida Haraldsdatter was a short-lived queen of Sweden who reigned for about a year around 1160. She was the daughter, albeit illegitimate, of King Harald Gille of Norway, and may have been born shortly after his accession to the throne, around 1131. Her mother's identity is unknown, which suggests that she may have been a concubine. It has been suggested that this may have been Tora Guttormsdotter, who had a long-lasting relationship with King Harald and also gave birth to King Sigurd II of Norway.[153] In any case, Brigida's royal pedigree cannot be dismissed, and she was certainly considered a legitimate princess of Norway.

Brigida is thought to have been married before her union to Magnus II, although the identity of her first husband remains unclear. "Haraldssona saga" in *Heimskringla* says that she was first married to Inge the Younger, then the Swedish jarl Karl Suneson, and only after him Magnus.[154] The marriage with Inge is clearly impossible, as she was certainly born after his death. Indeed, considering that she was the wife of Magnus II until his death in 1161, and only then remarried the jarl Birger Brosa with whom she went on to have numerous children, she cannot have been born before the late 1120s. A marriage to the jarl Karl Suneson is slightly more plausible, although she would have been extremely young, as we know that Karl Suneson was active as late as 1137. The year of his death is not known.[155] There are no non-fictional sources to confirm this information and it is therefore best taken with caution. This union would have made sense, however, as Karl Suneson is said in "Haraldssona saga" to have been of Norwegian ancestry, while Brigida was Norwegian herself. Karl was of high status, being descended from Norwegian jarls on his mother's side.[156] It is possible that the two families knew each other, and therefore arranged for a match, which would have been balanced in terms of social standing. Nevertheless, nothing is known of this alleged marriage and as mentioned, not even Karl's year of death is known. What is sure, however, is that Brigida then married Magnus Henriksson, also known as Magnus II.

While Brigida was considered a worthy and legitimate princess despite being a love child, this is not true of her husband, Magnus II. He is a disputed king, and some historians argue that he should not be part of the official list of Swedish monarchs. This is because, in order to claim the throne of Sweden for himself, he may have committed no less than two regicides, and planned a third. Magnus was a Danish lord whose status and legitimacy were unclear. He was a great-grandson of the Swedish king Inge the Younger through his mother, Ingrid Ragnvaldsdotter, whose father (whom we mentioned briefly earlier), either died before he could inherit the throne, or is identical with the infamous Ragnvald Knaphövde who was killed during his *eriksgata*. Magnus' father was a grandson of King Svend Estridsen of Denmark through his father, Henrik Skatelår, one of Svend's numerous illegitimate sons. In addition, through his mother's successive marriages, he also had ties with royalty in Norway.[157] Thus, Magnus had distant links with all three Scandinavian royal families, without himself being sufficiently important to truly have a role to play. To gain the throne of Sweden, which as we have seen so far was hotly contested in the mid-twelfth century, he had to carve a path to it.

Therefore, he first commissioned the murder of Sverker the Elder on Christmas Day in 1156, mentioned in an early thirteenth-century charter. *Västgötalagen* states that Sverker was murdered by a trusted servant on that date, which is also confirmed in a papal letter. The letter, however, suggests that Saint Erik was behind the deed, while Saxo indicates that it is Magnus who ordered the killing.[158] In any case, Magnus subsequently ordered the murder of Sverker's successor, Saint Erik, on 18 May 1160. This is related in "Erikslegenden," a hagiography written in the thirteenth century and possibly based on an earlier text. The legend tells us that Erik was murdered while attending Mass, a particularly deviant offence by Christian standards.[159]

Magnus, perhaps surprisingly, earned few followers with this strategy, and his conduct was widely considered unacceptable. While murdering one's way to the throne might have been acceptable in pre-Christian times, it was less so in the wake of Christianisation, which emphasised the God-given nature of royal power, and obviously condemned murder, one of the capital sins. Saxo also writes that in a last attempt at ridding himself of any competition, Magnus plotted the murder of Karl Sverkersson, who succeeded Erik, although this failed, leading to Magnus' death in battle against his foe.[160] "Erikslegenden" claims instead that it is a peasant rebellion, spurred by allies of the late superfluous Erik, which led to Magnus' downfall. Regardless of the exact details and chronology of the events, Magnus was quickly punished for his behaviour, and had no time nor any authority to perform royal duties. In this context, little can be written about his wife's royal career, not least because the couple's time in power – if it can even be described as such – was so short. The fact that her husband was considered illegitimate by so many suggests that she must have automatically been considered an illegitimate queen as well. Rather, it is what she did after the death of Magnus which cemented her place in Swedish history.

Brigida remarried with Birger Brosa who was to become jarl in 1174. The date of their marriage is unclear although it preceded his election as jarl.[161] Birger Brosa was a member of the Bjälbo family, and as such, he was a safe prospect for Brigida, bringing with him land, wealth, and high status, without the turbulent happenings of royal life. For him, this was an unparalleled opportunity to cement his political ambitions because although Magnus' reign was problematic, disputed, and short, Brigida remained a former queen and was still the daughter of a legitimate king. A familiar pattern can be distinguished here again, whereby a Swedish nobleman with no royal connections married a foreign woman of royal pedigree to advance his own position. It is quite telling, in fact, that the first fact we know for certain about Birger Brosa is his marriage to Brigida, told in "Haraldssona saga" and "Sverris saga" among others, which seems to kickstart his political career.[162] Birger Brosa is not said in any other source to have married anyone else but Brigida. With him, she had several children. "Haraldssona saga" names their sons as Jarl Filip, Jarl Folke, Jarl Knut and Magnus. Their daughters were: Ingegerd who later became Queen of Sweden, as well as Margareta and Kristina about whom nothing else is known.[163]

Brigida's story highlights the volatility of legitimate power in medieval Sweden. While she herself was not a legitimate queen, and was not given the space to do much during her short reign, she nevertheless had a royal legacy in that her daughter, Ingegerd, whom she had with a man of non-royal descent but high social standing, the jarl Birger Brosa, became Queen of Sweden by marrying King Sverker the Younger (she is presented at the end of this chapter). In this case, it is not Brigida's tenure as queen which directly legitimised her line, but her marriage to the much-respected Birger Brosa, who was an important statesman and belonged to the illustrious Bjälbo family, whom we have mentioned previously. Her royal pedigree on her father's side must have helped her be accepted into the high levels of Swedish society, but her daughter's case shows how different avenues could lead one to

royal status. It also shows that some particularly powerful noblemen could yield more influence than people of royal descent,
thus underlining the elective nature of the monarchy in medieval
Sweden, and the lack of linearity in the succession process.

Unlike many queens, we know roughly what happened to
Brigida after the death of her husbands. She finished her life in
Riseberga Abbey, a Cistercian monastery in Närke, where she
died in October 1209.[164] We know this thanks to the *Liber Daticus vetustior*, a martyrology from Lund started in the late twelfth
century as an update to the *Necrologium Lundense*. This choice
of abbey was not accidental. It is the same abbey to which Birger
Brosa had bestowed large tracts of land as early as the 1180s.[165]
We do not know why this particular abbey attracted Birger's and
Brigida's favour. Birger Brosa owned land in this region, and so
it may have simply been convenient to support this institution. It
has also been noted that the wording of one of Birger's donation
charters to Riserberga suggests that it might in fact have been
founded on his initiative, although this is unclear.[166] It would nevertheless fit within the pattern of power couples with royal ties
founding nunneries and monasteries, and it is indeed uncanny
that Riseberga should have profited so much from its association
with Birger Brosa and his wife, and she ended her life as a nun
there. This mirrors the relationship between Queen Helena and
Vreta Abbey which, as mentioned previously, might have served
as a template for future queens.

3.9   Kristina Stigsdatter Hvide

Little is known about Kristina Stigsdatter Hvide except for some
basic genealogical information. Her father is given in "Knýtlinga
saga" as the Danish nobleman Stig Hvide, and her mother the
Danish princess Margareta Knudsdotter, daughter of Knud
Lavard and Ingeborg of Kiev, herself a daughter of Kristina Ingesdotter of Sweden.[167] However, the official genealogy of the Hvide
family, compiled in the medieval period in the Danish abbey of
Sorø (which was founded by members of the family) and later
copied in the early modern period, does not mention any children
of Stig Hvide.[168] It is therefore unclear whether this identification

is completely correct. This also makes it impossible to determine the motivation behind this union. She must have been wealthy, and her being the granddaughter of Knud Lavard, who was the legitimate son of a Danish king and a hugely popular figure (he was canonised in 1169) may have played a role in shoring up support for Karl's reign. This is, however, speculative.

She married Karl Sverkersson around 1164 when he acceded to the throne. We know thanks to Saxo that she was taken from Skåne by Jarl Guttorm and brought to the king in 1163 a little earlier than her wedding, which took place after a new archbishop was installed in 1164.[169] This timing was highly symbolic. Indeed, until 1164, Sweden had been part of the archdiocese of Lund. The creation of a Swedish province, spearheaded by the archbishop based in Uppsala, was an important step in the formation of a Swedish state.[170] Karl Sverkersson and Kristina's wedding was therefore the first royal union to take place under the auspices of an archbishop of Sweden. Nevertheless, the earliest recorded charter which mentions Karl Sverkersson only recognises him as king of the Geats, which confirms what is by now a common pattern of Christian kings having little influence in Svealand.[171] It is therefore likely that Kristina was also limited in her outreach, and the fact that so little information survives about her suggests that she may not have played much of a public role. This may have been exacerbated by the fact that she did not remain queen very long as her husband Karl Sverkersson was murdered in 1167.[172] Only one child is known without doubt to have been born from Kristina and Karl's union: a son named Sverker, who later reigned as King Sverker the Younger. *Västgötalagen* claims that following the death of his father, the young Sverker was taken to Denmark for protection. He clearly must have been taken to his maternal relatives.[173] However, nothing is known of the rest of Kristina's life and her year of death is unknown.

3.10   Ingegerd Sverkersdotter

Although Ingegerd was the daughter of a king, she was never queen; but she is one of a handful of non-regal women studied in this monograph because her life sheds light on the sort of immense power that women of high birth could exert behind the scenes. It is unclear who Ingegerd's mother was. It may have been Ulvhild, but it is not said explicitly anywhere. She could also have been an unknown concubine or mistress of Sverker the Elder. She is clearly named in relatively few sources, but we know that she was the abbess of Vreta Abbey throughout the second half of the twelfth century until her death in 1204. This is related in the medieval register of the cathedral of Linköping.[174] This was a prestigious position to hold, at least as powerful as the office of queen, and she did so for over 40 years, which is remarkable by any standard. The usual pathway to becoming an abbess was to start as a nun and, through impeccable conduct, devotion, charisma – and often some intrigue – climb up the hierarchical ladder. Abbesses, like abbots, were elected by the monastic community that they went on to lead.[175] It is unclear whether Ingegerd went through the entire process or whether she was fast-tracked as the daughter of the king. Nevertheless, the fact that she led the abbey for so long suggests that she was probably appreciated and competent.

Ingegerd is the first known abbess of Vreta, although this is not to say that she was the very first. Indeed, the abbey was founded in the early twelfth century, well before Ingegerd was born. The exact date of foundation is debated, but the abbey was sanctioned by Paschal II, who became Pope in 1099, and was sponsored by Inge the Elder, who died before 1110.[176] A later medieval list of abbesses also suggests that Ingegerd may have been the fourth, although nothing is known of her predecessors.[177] She may have been, however, the first Cistercian abbess of the nunnery, as Vreta was initially founded as a Benedictine institution like several others in Sweden.

There is plenty of evidence that the abbey thrived under her leadership. The list of donations to Vreta surviving from a couple of sixteenth-century manuscripts, which we mentioned earlier, shows that the nunnery received numerous donations during her tenure, and that the abbey's economic activity, especially in terms of land transactions, was particularly dynamic. The list of transactions, which includes the jarl Guttorm transferring ownership of a property in Småland to the abbey (located in Östergötland, over 200 kilometres away), shows that Ingegerd was able to considerably expand the abbey's geographical sphere of influence.[178] Unsurprisingly, this period saw Vreta become closely associated with royal power, becoming the main educational institution for royal girls, as well as the burial place of several members of the royal family. This is much like the priory in Amesbury in England which, during the same time period, fulfilled a similar function by housing a significant number of aristocratic and royal women.[179] This underlines again the parallels between the development of Sweden's monastic houses and that of other institutions across Europe; and there is no doubt that Vreta's powerful royal abbess, Ingegerd, was the reason for its continued association with the Crown throughout the twelfth century.[180]

Abbesses could have significant political influence and economic power in the Middle Ages. This is an aspect of cloistered life which is only now starting to garner attention in scholarship. Becoming a nun, and progressing through the hierarchy, gave women a precious alternative to domestic life. It was not solely an honorific position to recognise one's pious life. As the leader of their monastic community, they managed the nuns, the lay people associated with the house, but also the abbey's properties and economy.[181] This, in fact, gave a tremendous amount of power to the women who took on the position. It is no coincidence that many of Europe's most influential medieval women were religious figures. Celibacy gave them agency as they were not submitted to a husband. Abbesses were theoretically still subordinate to their male counterparts, but we know that abbesses in some regions were given extraordinary powers approaching those of a bishop. Some monastic institutions also housed both men and women, who were of course kept separate and, in many cases, it is the abbess who led the whole community. Not all regions within Christendom afforded as much authority to abbesses, but in western Europe, a complex mixture of economic factors as well as an abbess' own personal prestige and competence could trump institutional hierarchy, and many abbesses were significant political actors in their own right.[182]

Ingegerd was the abbess when her sister Helena, discussed below, entered the community as a nun following the death of her husband, King Knud V of Denmark. Unfortunately, nothing is known about their relationship either inside or outside the nunnery. Ingegerd died in 1204, probably many years after her sister, and both were presumably buried in the abbey.

3.11   Helena Sverkersdotter of Denmark

Helena is an enigmatic figure because her name is uncertain. She was the daughter of Sverker the Elder and Queen Ulvhild, in which case she was probably known as Helena Sverkersdotter. However, she is not to be confused with another Helena Sverkersdotter, born at the end of the twelfth century as the daughter of Sverker the Younger and who is presented at the end of this chapter. The present Helena's date of birth is unknown but based on the known elements of her life such as her (likely) marriage to Knud V of Denmark in 1157, she must have been born sometime in the 1130s or 1140s.

As mentioned, she was probably the wife of Knud V of Denmark who reigned between 1146 and 1157. This is not explicitly mentioned anywhere but cannot be otherwise. Indeed, we know that after the death of his first queen, Knud married an unnamed daughter of Sverker the Elder in 1156. This is related in "Knýtlinga saga."[183] The *Necrologium Lundense*, which compiles a twelfth-century necrology of eminent figures of the time, mentions an *Elena Regina*.[184] There was no other Queen Helena anywhere in Scandinavia during this period and it has therefore been widely assumed among scholars that this must be the same woman. Due to Knud's untimely death a year into the marriage, it is unclear whether Helena had any children by him. Knud had at least three known children, at least two of which are known to have been born to concubines before their father's marriage, but it is unclear whether any was born of his union with Helena.[185] There is no evidence of it, and no later mention of her children.

A sixteenth-century donation list to Vreta Abbey mentions that a queen named Helena donated land to the house, and thereafter entered it, where she finished her life. Nils Ahnlund thought that this referred to Inge the Elder's wife Helena, whom we presented earlier and who was said by Messenius to have entered Vreta too, but the donation list seems to suggest that this other

Helena reigned around the time of Karl Sverkersson, which points to Helena Sverkersdotter.[186] This is not related in any surviving medieval document and the source is problematic because of its date. However, it is entirely possible because it was common for medieval noblewomen and former queens to become nuns after the death of their husbands, or sometimes as a sole career choice like Ingegerd. As mentioned above, Helena's sister Ingegerd was the abbess of Vreta Abbey for 40 years between c. 1162 and 1204, and during this period, the abbey had established itself as a prominent institution for the education of royal children, and as the burial ground for several members of the royal family. This house would have therefore been a natural choice for Helena. Not much is known about her activities in the monastery and, according to the *Necrologium Lundense*, she died on 12 December although no year is given.

3.12 The Unnamed Wife of Knut I – Cecilia?

King Knut I of Sweden was the son of Saint Erik and his wife Kristina, whom we encountered earlier. He reigned as sole king from 1173 to his death around 1195, although he had been contesting the Crown for a few years prior to 1173, having notably killed Karl Sverkersson in 1167.[187] We know that Knut was married. What we do not know, however, is his wife's name, or the details of their marriage. She has usually been associated by scholars with a noblewoman named Cecilia Johansdotter, who was possibly the daughter of Sverker the Elder's infamous son, Jon. This is based on a rather complicated, and contested, reconstruction of her biography.

A fourteenth-century genealogy claims that the mother of Saint Erik (erroneously known as Erik IX) was named Cecilia, and that she was the daughter of King Sven.[188] This may refer to the pagan King Sven who briefly reigned after the devout Christian King Inge the Elder, whom we have previously discussed several times. However, this is widely interpreted as a mistake and understood as meaning that Cecilia was instead the mother of Erik X, whose father was Knut I. Indeed, Cecilia being Sven's daughter is chronologically unlikely, as Sven is thought to have died sometime in the 1080s, whereas Cecilia was queen in the 1160s. Furthermore, the same genealogy also makes her the sister of Ulf Jarl and Kol. These two men are known from other sources and certainly were contemporary, however they are said in another genealogy to have been Sverker the Elder's grandsons through his infamous son Jon Sverkersson.[189] Cecilia would thus have been their sister, which works better chronologically.

This family tree nevertheless remains completely hypothetical as both sources are unreliable. An additional question regarding Cecilia's filiation is that of alliances. Knut I belonged to the House of Erik, his father. If Cecilia was Jon's daughter, that made her a member of the House of Sverker, and a niece of Karl Sverkersson, who was killed by Knut himself shortly before his marriage to Cecilia in 1167.[190] It is unclear whether this was in battle or a premeditated murder but, in any case, these two families were rivals, which makes it less likely that such a union could be organised. However, it may precisely be because they were rivals that Cecilia married Knut, to join forces in the context of growing tensions in the Baltic region. Indeed, Knut's reign was characterised by widespread struggles against pagans from the east Baltic region (modern-day Estonia and Karelia).[191] The conflicts culminated in 1187, when there is some evidence that eastern pagans invaded Uppland, attacked Sigtuna, and murdered the archbishop Johannes.[192] The severity of the attack has been debated, but in this turbulent context, it may have made sense for the Houses of Erik and that of Sverker to ally. Following the death of Knut I in 1195 or 1196, it is Sverker Karlsson (Sverker the Younger), the son of Karl Sverkersson whom Knut had killed in 1167, who inherited the throne without dispute. This peaceful transition is certainly less surprising if Cecilia was indeed Karl's niece and therefore Sverker's first cousin.

With Knut, Cecilia had at least four children about whom a reasonable amount of information is known. Firstly, they had several sons whose names are mostly not recorded but whose fate is known. Nearly all were slain at the Battle of Älgarås in November 1205.[193] The only survivor, Erik, went on to become king in 1208.[194] They might also have had a daughter together, although this is less clear and is not found explicitly in any surviving sources. It is suggested in some later Icelandic narratives such as "Hákonar saga Hákonarsonar." Her name may have been Sigrid Knutsdotter but considering that she is not mentioned in any contemporary sources, her existence should be considered carefully.[195]

Despite the scarcity of information about Cecilia, some details of the queen's personal life are known without doubt. She is mentioned in a papal letter written by Celestine III from 1193. It reveals that she was betrothed to Knut as a young girl when he was young as well, but that she had to spend a few years in a convent as a protective measure because of serious threats to her safety due to unrest within the kingdom. The letter tells us that she was considered to be the only woman in the realm of sufficiently high birth to be queen. She then married Knut lawfully and had children with him, who are not named, but one of whom was designated heir to the throne. We also learn that she then fell seriously ill, promised to observe chastity in the hope that this would attract God's favour, but eventually recovered. Her husband Knut then asked the Pope to resume married life with her to counter his political opponents who committed slander against him for not having a queen.[196] This letter mentions previous correspondence with the Pope's predecessor, Clement III, confirming that the queen's illness lasted several years.

The outcome of the royal couple's request was positive, and the Pope allowed the couple to be reunited, but the queen disappears from the historical record after this. While we know from *Västgötalagen* that Knut died in 1195 or 1196 after reigning for 23 years, we know nothing of her whereabouts nor the year of her death.[197] This letter, which is uncommon for never naming either the queen nor king, nevertheless shows that the king *needed* her to govern, again showing that a queen was not merely an accessory to her husband's kingship but could play an important role in legitimising it. This request also sheds light on one of the more uncommon reasons for women to enter a convent. All the women discussed so far who spent a significant amount of time in a convent did so following the death of their husband, presumably because they did not want to remarry. As will be shown shortly, others were placed in convents for their education, and could spend several years cloistered for this reason. Yet, this queen's experience is very different. She willingly entered a nunnery in order to seek healing, which she thought could only be achieved by pleasing God. This is in line with the medieval belief that some diseases were a punishment from God. Therefore, her service as a nun and subsequent rejection of earthly considerations were seen as penance. This evidences her piousness and illustrates how royal figures sometimes supported ecclesiastical institutions out of genuine faith.

3.13   Ingegerd Birgersdotter

Little can be said about the two recorded wives of King Sverker the Younger, who reigned from the late twelfth century until 1208. It is not even clear which woman was queen first although for reasons detailed below, it is likely that it may have been Ingegerd first, and then Benedicta. In all cases, Sverker reigned from about 1195 or 1196 to 1208 before he was exiled following the Battle of Lena in 1208, and finally killed at the Battle of Gestilren in 1210. This is confirmed by multiple medieval chronicles.[198] These two women must have therefore been queens during this short period.

Ingegerd was a member of the powerful Bjälbo family, which regularly features in Sweden's royal biographies. According to multiple Icelandic sagas, including "Haraldssona saga" and "Sverris saga," both from the early thirteenth century and possibly contemporary, her father was Birger Brosa.[199] Her mother was Brigida Haraldsdatter, presented previously. Ingegerd gave birth around 1201 to a son named Johan who succeeded his grandfather as jarl when he was just a baby, and subsequently became king in 1216 as Johan I.[200] He was crowned in 1219 but died just three years later, unmarried and childless.[201] It remains unclear why Ingegerd's union with Sverker ended, although there is no mention of a divorce or any issue of this sort. Therefore, she must have died, but we do not know when, although this must have happened before 1203 for reasons given below. She might have died of complications following childbirth, as the birth of her son is the last event with which she is associated.

3.14   Benedicta Ebbesdatter Hvide

Benedicta came from the important Danish Hvide clan, like Sverker II's own mother, Kristina. This is confirmed by the same aforementioned medieval Danish genealogy (and copied in the early modern period), which also tells us that Benedicta's father was Ebbe Sunesson, and that she was a niece of the famed archbishop Andreas of Lund.[202] Thanks to the list of kings appended to *Västgötalagen*, we know that Sverker II was taken to Denmark following the murder of his father Karl Sverkersson around 1167.[203] It has therefore been assumed that he got to know Benedicta during his time at the Danish court, which is indeed the most natural explanation for this royal match. This union was very important strategically speaking. Sverker's marriage to Ingegerd had already given him precious economic resources in Östergötland as well as some political support thanks to his father-in-law the jarl Birger Brosa. The second half of Sverker's reign was nevertheless more turbulent as the adult sons of Sverker's predecessor, Knut I, challenged him for the throne, starting in 1203. This challenge culminated in the Battle of Älgarås in 1205. Knut's sons may have had Norwegian support, as evidenced by the only survivor Erik's flight to Norway after the battle.[204] It would therefore have been quite a natural progression, considering Sverker's Danish links, that he would in turn seek support in Denmark. This would date Sverker and Benedicta's marriage to around 1203. Sverker certainly earned military support from his new wife's family, and her father Ebbe, uncle Lars, as well as other close relatives, died fighting for Sverker at the Battle of Lena in 1208.[205] Together, they had a daughter named Helena Sverkersdotter who is studied in the next chapter. Little else is known about Benedicta, however, and we do not know when and where she died.

3.15   Concluding Remarks

In conclusion, queenship in Sweden significantly developed during the twelfth century as a queen's function within the monarchy became much better defined than in previous centuries. The family structure itself became more stable, hinging on the newly established requirement to be lawfully married, and monogamous. Monogamy in particular elevated royal women's status as they were now the key to dynastic continuity, as illegitimate children progressively lost access to power. As the gatekeepers of a king's posterity, queens thus began serving as communication agents and figureheads for the royal dynasty to which they belonged. This was a crucial role at a time when good relations with the Church majorly influenced a king's ability to exert power. A Swedish queen's most important function during the twelfth century was thus the fostering of positive relations with ecclesiastical institutions in order to secure political support for their family. It became the norm for queens to found and/or fund monasteries, commission churches, and ensure that the royal family had a stable and permanent relationship with a given house or diocese. This close association between queens and the Church also led to the introduction of new ideals. Twelfth-century queens all had to display similar traits, drawing on Christian teachings: piety, humility, and charity being the most essential. This greatly influenced their behaviour but also their representation, and the manner in which they were remembered by successive generations.

What is also noticeable in this chapter is the sheer number of royal women who lived during the twelfth century. This is a reflection of the tumultuous political landscape of the time. The twelfth century was an extremely violent period, not just in Sweden but elsewhere in Scandinavia too, as state formation led prominent families to fight over land and internal resources in the process of consolidating their estates. The question of legitimacy thus became particularly important as multiple kings could claim the throne at the same time. Marrying women of foreign and royal origin therefore became a common strategy to support one's claim to power, and increase a dynasty's prestige. Unrest within Scandinavia also required strategic alliances across borders. As a result, most women studied in this chapter were of Norwegian and Danish origin, as both kingdoms were noticeably more advanced in their state formation process than Sweden. Ultimately, however, it is a family's approval by the Church and its representatives that could differentiate between a legitimate sovereign and an usurper, further underlining the importance of the queen's role as intercessor. It is therefore clear that royal women of this period exerted considerable political influence in the shadow of their husbands. The next chapter will illustrate how this influence became increasingly publicly acknowledged in the thirteenth and fourteenth centuries.

Notes

1 For a concise, but comprehensive overview, see Bertil Nilsson, *Sveriges Kyrkohistoria. Missionstid och Tidig Medeltid* (Stockholm: Verbum, 1998). Also edited by Nilsson, *Kristnandet i Sverige: gamla källor och nya perspektiv* (Lund: Lunne, 1996).
2 Nilsson, *Sveriges Kyrkohistoria*, 98–114.
3 Philp Line, *Kingship and State Formation in Sweden: c. 1130–1290* (Leiden: Brill, 2007), 347–349.
4 Nilsson, *Sveriges Kyrkohistoria*, 42–50.
5 John Ljungkvist and Per Frölund, "Gamla Uppsala – The Emergence of a Centre and a Magnate Complex," *Journal of Archaeology and Ancient History* 16 (2015), 14–21.
6 Lars Gahrn, in: *Kärnhuset i riksäpplet*, ed. Karin Blent, Elisabeth Svalin, and Iréne Andersson Flygare (Uppsala: Upplands fornminnesförening och hembygdsförbund, 1993), 81–82.
7 Nilsson, *Sveriges Kyrkohistoria*, 73–84.
8 Nilsson, *Sveriges Kyrkohistoria*, 73–84.
9 Nils Blomkvist, Stefan Brink, and Thomas Lindkvist, "The Kingdom of Sweden," in *Christianization and the Rise of Christian Monarchy Scandinavia, Central Europe and Rus' C.900–1200*, ed. Nora Berend (Cambridge: Cambridge University Press, 2007), 185–187.
10 Nilsson, *Sveriges Kyrkohistoria*, 73–84.
11 Blomkvist, Brink, and Lindkvist, "The Kingdom of Sweden," 185–187. Line, *Kingship and State Formation*, 340–341.
12 Catharina Andersson, "Cistercian Monasteries in Medieval Sweden. Foundations and Recruitments, 1143–1420," *Religions* 12, no. 8: 582 (2021), 2–3.
13 John Carmi Parsons, "The Queen's Intercession," in *Power of the Weak: Studies on Medieval Women*, ed. Jennifer Carpenter and Selly-Beth MacLean (Chicago: University of Illinois Press, 1995), 154–162. The biblical Queen Esther, while not as relatable for women expected to produce an heir as she is not said to have had children, was also an important role model for high-status medieval women in Europe. See Lois Huynecutt, "Intercession and the High-Medieval Queen: The Esther Topos," in *Power of the Weak*.
14 Thomas Lindkvist, ed. and trans., *The Västgöta Laws* (Abingdon: Routledge, 2021), 196.

15 Tschan, trans., *The History of the Archbishops of Hamburg-Bremen*, 159.

16 "Inge," in *Nordisk Familjebok, bd. 12*, ed. Theodor Westrin (Stockholm: Nordisk Familjeboks förlags aktiebolag, 1910).

17 Mats Roslund, *Guests in the House: Cultural Transmission between Slavs and Scandinavians 900 to 1300 AD* (Leiden: Brill, 2007), 34.

18 SDHK nr 169.

19 Tolkien, ed. and trans., *Saga of King Heidrik*, 62–63.

20 Lars Lönnroth, *Isländska mytsagor* (Stockholm: Atlantis, 1995), 131–132.

21 Martin Clarentius Gertz, ed., "Wilhelmi Abbatis Genealogica Regum Danorum," in *Scriptores minores historiæ Danicæ medii ævi ex codicibus denuo*, ed. Martin Clarentius Gertz (Copenhagen: I Kommission hos G. E. C. Gad, 1917), 182.

22 Tschan, *History of the Archbishops of Hamburg-Bremen*, 81; 95–96. For another example, see Knut/Lambert, son of King Svend of Denmark, 91.

23 SDHK nr 270.

24 Tolkien, *Saga of Heidrik*, 62.

25 Brian Patrick McGuire, "Vretas nonner i europæisk perspektiv," in *Fokus Vreta kloster. 17 nya rön om Sveriges äldsta kloster*, ed. Göran Tagesson (Stockholm: Historiska Museet, 2010), 244.

26 Nils Ahnlund, "Vreta Klosters Äldsta Donatorer," *Historisk Tidskrift 65* (1945), 301–302.

27 Ahnlund, "Vreta Klosters Äldsta Donatorer," 303–305.

28 Ahnlund, "Vreta Klosters Äldsta Donatorer," 303–305.

29 Göran Tagesson, *Vreta Klosters Kyrka* (Linköping: Svenska Kyrkan, 2007), 4–5.

30 Rasmus Ludvigsson, "Brevis historica narration" as quoted by Ahnlund, 319–320.

31 U 861 which according to Rundata reads *sihikþurn ' ... [risa * stin] ' uk ' bru ' kera : at : aterf : sun : uk ' a(t) ' mai : tutor : sin : eþorn : uk : suen : uk ' (u)ikþu-... ' sikb--... ...(ʀ) ' isi*. This is translated as "Sigþorn ... the stone raised and the bridge made in memory of Ádjarfr, (his) son, and in memory of Mey, his daughter; Eiþorn and Sveinn and Vígþorn ... Sig-... ..." Erik Brate translated the woman's name as "Mö" and was one of the first to link her to Helena. See *Sveriges Runinskrifter III. Runinskrifter från 1000-talet* (Stockholm: Natur och Kultur, 1922), 82.

32 Tolkien, *Saga of Heidrik*, 63.

33 Tagesson, *Vreta Klosters Kyrka*, 4–5.

34 Mia Korpiola, *Between Betrothal and Bedding: Marriage Formation in Sweden 1200–1600* (Leiden: Brill, 2009), 78–86.

35 Outside Sweden, work is ongoing in this area of queenship studies. "Examining the Resources & Revenues of Royal Women in Premodern Europe" is a project which investigates the question of queens' economic agency, and the different manners in which they could acquire wealth and possessions in different European courts.

A similar approach applied to Sweden would elucidate some of the questions posed in this monograph.

36 Brian Patrick Maguire, "Cistercian Origins in Denmark and Sweden: The Twelfth Century Founders," in *Itinéraires du savoir de l'Italie à la Scandinavie (Xe-XVIe Siècle)*, ed. Corinne Péneau (Paris: Editions Sorbonne, 2009), 85–97.

37 Andersson, "Cistercian Monasteries," 3–4.

38 Andersson, "Cistercian Monasteries," 3–4.

39 Philip Reynolds gives a thorough presentation of the development of marriage and all that it entailed from the twelfth century onwards in *How Marriage Became One of the Sacraments: The Sacramental Theology of Marriage from Its Medieval Origins to the Council of Trent* (Cambridge: Cambridge University Press, 2016).

40 Reynolds, *How Marriage Became One of the Sacraments*, 12–21. John Witte, *From Sacrament to Contract: Marriage, Religion, and Law in the Western Tradition*, 2nd edn (Louisville: Westminster John Knox Press, 2012), 46–52; 87–96.

41 Else Mundal, "The Double Impact of Christianization for Women in Old Norse Culture," in *Gender and Religion*, ed. Kari E. Børresen (Rome: Carocci, 2001), 245–248.

42 Duby briefly compares the early model based on Roman practices with the Church's later medieval (and much more rigid) notion of marriage in *Love and Marriage in the Middle Ages*, trans. Jane Dunnett (Chicago: University of Chicago Press, 1994), 7–23.

43 Duby, *Love and Marriage*, 105–129.

44 Sven Tunberg, "Ragnvald Knapphövde: Ett bidrag till diskussionen om Sveriges medeltida konungalängd," *Svensk Tidskrift* 41 (1954), 35–40.

45 Martin Dimnik, *The Dynasty of Chernigov, 1146–1246* (Cambridge: Cambridge University Press, 2003), 113.

46 Hermann Pálsson and Paul Edwards, trans., *Knýtlinga saga: The History of the Kings of Denmark* (Odense: Odense University Press, 1986), 123–124.

47 Johannes Messenius, "Chronologiæ Scondianæ," in *Johannes Messenius Scondia Illustrata vol. I–X*, ed. Johann Peringskiöld (Stockholm: Olavi Enæi, 1700–1703), 95.

48 Gustav Storm, ed., "Historia de antiquitate regum norwagiensium," in *Monumenta Historica Norvegiae*, ed. Gustav Storm (Copenhagen: A.W. Brøgger, 1880), 60–62. Alison Finlay and Anthony Faulkes, trans, "Magnúss saga berfœtts," in *Snorri Sturluson. Heimskringla Volume III. Magnús Óláfsson to Magnús Erlingsson* (London: Viking Society for Northern Research, 2015), 139.

49 Storm, "Historia de antiquitate regum," 62.

50 Devra Kunin, trans., and Carl Phelpstead, ed., *A History of Norway and the Passion and Miracles of the Blessed Óláfr* (London: Viking Society for Northern Research, 2001), 61.

51 Friis-Jensen, ed., and Fisher, trans., *Saxo Grammaticus. Gesta Danorum*, 897–899.

52 Erik Kroman, ed., *Corpus codicum Danicorum medii aevi vol. I: Necrologium Lundense* (Copenhagen: Ejnar Munksgaard, 1960), 333 (fol. 166r).

53 Ellen Jørgensen, ed., "Annales Nestvedienses 821–1300," in *Annales Danici Medii Ævi: Editionem Nouam Curauit*, ed. Ellen Jørgensen (Copenhagen: I Kommission Hos G. E. C. Gad, 1920), 19; 71.

54 Thomas Riis, "The Significance of 25 June, 1170," in *Of Chronicles and Kings: National Saints and the Emergence of Nation States in the High Middle Ages*, ed. John Bergsagel, David Hiley and Thomas Riis (Copenhagen: Museum Tusculanum Press, 2015), 93–94.

55 Helle Vogt, *The Function of Kinship in Medieval Nordic Legislation* (Leiden: Brill, 2010), 13.

56 Friis-Jensen and Fisher, *Gesta Danorum II*, 897.

57 Peter Christian Hauberg, *Myntforhold og udmyntninger i Danmark indtil 1146* (Copenhagen: B. Lunos, 1900), 59.

58 Friis-Jensen and Fisher, *Gesta Danorum II*, 899.

59 Bernard Gineste, "Thibaud d'Étampes," *Les Cahiers d'Étampes-Histoire* 10 (2009), 43–58.

60 Lindkvist, *The Västgöta Laws*, 52–53; 117–118.

61 Lindkvist, *The Västgöta Laws*, 41.

62 Friis-Jensen and Fisher, *Gesta Danorum II*, 899.

63 Friis-Jensen and Fisher, *Gesta Danorum II*, 899.

64 Siân Grønlie, ed., *The Book of the Icelanders — The Story of the Conversion* (London: Viking Society for Nothern Research, 2006), 53.

65 Lindkvist, *The Västgöta Laws*, 197.

66 Tolkien, *Saga of Heidrik*, 63.

67 T. N. Dzhakson, "Elizaveta Iaroslavna, koroleva norvezhskaia," in *Vostochnaia Evropa v istoricheskoi retrospektive: K 80-letiiu V.T. Pashuto* (Moscow: Iazyki russkoi kul'tury, 1999), 63–71.

68 Michael H. Gelting, "Scandinavian and the North Sea World," in *The Cambridge Companion to the Age of William the Conqueror*, ed. Benjamin Pohl (Cambridge: Cambridge University Press, 2022), 56.

69 Gustaf Edvard Klemming, ed., "Prosaiska krönikan," in *Småstycken på forn Svenska*, ed. Gustaf Edvard Klemming (Stockholm: Kungl. Boktryckeriet, 1881), 235. The "Lilla Rimkrönikan" is based entirely off it.

70 The epitaph is reproduced in full by Carl Henrik Martling in *En svensk helgonkrönika* (Skellefteå: Artos, 2001), 114. See also Henrik Alm, *Drottning Ragnhild och hennes gravskrift i Tälje* (Strängnäs: Tidnings Tryckeri, 1931). A list of early modern transcriptions of the epitaph can be found in Hans Gillingstam "Ragnhild," in *Svenskt biografiskt lexicon band 29*, ed. Göran Nilzén (Stockholm: Riksarkivet, 1995–1997), 613.

71 Gillingstam, "Ragnhild," 613.

72 Hans Gillingstam, "Folkungaätten," in *Svenskt biografiskt lexikon band 16*, ed. Bertil Boëthius (Stockholm: Bonnier, 1964–1966), 260.

73 Martling, *En svensk helgonkrönika*, 114.
74 Sarah Semple, Alex Sanmark, Frode Iversen, and Natascha Mehler, *Negotiating the North: Meeting-Places in the Middle Ages in the North Sea Zone* (Abingdon: Routledge, 2021), 149–150.
75 Christine Peel, ed. and trans., *Guta Lag and Guta Saga: The Law and History of the Gotlanders* (Abingdon: Routledge, 2015), 308.
76 Birgit and Peter Sawyer, *Medieval Scandinavia: From Conversion to Reformation circa 800–1500* (Minneapolis: University of Minnesota Press, 1993), 13.
77 Terese Zachrisson, "The Saint in the Woods: Semi-Domestic Shrines in Rural Sweden, c. 1500–1800," *Religions* 10, no. 6: 386 (2019), 2–3.
78 Denys Pringle, "Scandinavian Pilgrims and the Churches of the Holy Land in the Twelfth and Thirteenth Centuries," in *Tracing the Jerusalem Code Volume 1: The Holy City Christian Cultures in Medieval Scandinavia (ca. 1100–1536)*, ed. Kristin B. Aavitsland and M. Bonde (Berlin: De Gruyter, 2021), 199–213.
79 Joyce Hill, "Pilgrimage and Prestige in the Icelandic Sagas," *Saga-Book* 23 (1990–1993), 433–453.
80 Hermann Pálsson and Paul Edwards, trans., *Orkneyinga saga: The History of the Earls of Orkney* (London: Penguin Books, 1978), 164–184.
81 Hill, "Pilgrimage and Prestige," 434–447.
82 Roberto Paciocco, "The Canonization of Saints in the Middle Ages: Procedure, Documentation, Meanings," in *A Companion to Medieval Miracle Collections*, ed. Sari Katajala-Peltomaa, Jenni Kuuliala and Iona McCleery (Leiden: Brill, 2021), 60–65.
83 Hill, "Pilgrimage and Prestige," 433.
84 Pringle, "Scandinavian Pilgrims," 199.
85 Pringle, "Scandinavian Pilgrims," 202–212.
86 Åke Nisbeth, *Enångers Kyrkor* (Stockholm: Riksantikvarieämbetet, 1994), 16–17. Information about the Viksta and Börje paintings can be found in the archives of the Riksantikvarieämbetet, serial numbers 14066 and 14065 respectively.
87 Maria H. Oen, "Birgitta Birgersdotter and the *Liber celestis revelacionum*," in *A Companion to Birgitta of Sweden and Her Legacy in the Later Middle Ages*, ed. Maria H. Oen (Leiden: Brill, 2019), 1–4.
88 Päivi Salmesvuori, *Power and Sainthood: The Case of Birgitta of Sweden* (New York: Palgrave Macmillan, 2014), 41–61.
89 Sven Ingemar Olofsson, "Sankt Olofs stad," in *Södertälje stads historia del. 1*, ed. Alf Nordström (Stockholm: Södertälje stads drätselkammare, 1968), 142–144.
90 Alison Finlay, trans., *Fagrskinna: A Catalogue of the Kings of Norway* (Leiden: Brill, 2004), 236.
91 Friis-Jensen and Fischer, *Gesta Danorum*, 961; 969–671.
92 Alison Finlay and Anthony Faulkes, trans, "Óláfs saga Helga," in *Snorri Sturluson. Heimskringla Volume II. Óláfr Haraldsson*

(The Saint) (London: Viking Society for Northern Research, 2014), 114; 196.

93 Adolf Schük, "Drottning Ulvhilds härkomst," *Personhistorisk tidskrift* 51 (1953), 28.

94 Schük, "Drottning Ulvhilds härkomst," 30.

95 Tore Nyberg, *Monasticism in North-Western Europe, 800–1200* (Aldershot: Ashgate, 2000), 120–121.

96 Schük, "Drottning Ulvhilds härkomst," 30.

97 Lindkvist, *The Västgöta Laws*, 197.

98 Friis-Jensen and Fisher, *Gesta Danorum*, 959–961.

99 Friis-Jensen and Fisher, *Gesta Danorum*, 961.

100 Schück, "Ulvhilds härkomst," 30.

101 Aline G. Hornaday, "Early Medieval Kinship Structures as Social and Political Controls," in *Medieval Family Roles: A Book of Essays*, ed. Cathy Jorgensen Itnyre (Abingdon: Routledge, 1996), 32.

102 Friis-Jensen and Fisher, *Gesta Danorum*, 1017; 1041.

103 Bruno Griesser, ed., *Exordium magnum Cisterciense, sive, Narratio de initio Cisterciensis Ordinis* (Rome: Editiones Cistercienses, 1961), 258–260.

104 Martin Clarentius Gertz, ed., "De fundatione monasterii Vitæscholæ," in *Scriptores minores historiæ Danicæ vol. II*, 134–142.

105 Hedda Gunneng, ed., *Biskop Hans Brasks registratur* (Uppsala: Svenska fornskriftsällsk, 2003), 55.

106 For overviews of the Cistercian Order and its presence in Scandinavia, see Janet Burton and Julie Kerr, *The Cistercians in the Middle Ages* (Woodbridge: The Boydell Press, 2011) and James France, *The Cistercians in Scandinavia* (Kalamazoo: Cistercian Publications, 1992).

107 Alfred Haverkamp, *Medieval Germany 1056–1273*, 2nd edn (Oxford: Oxford University Press, 1992), 57.

108 Fiona Griffiths, "The Mass in Monastic Practice: Nuns and Ordained Monks, c. 400–1200," in *The Cambridge History of Medieval Monasticism in the Latin West, vol. 1 and 2*, ed. Alison I. Beach and Isabelle Cochelin (Cambridge: Cambridge University Press, 2020), 730–733.

109 Andersson, "Cistercian Monasteries," 14.

110 France, *Cistercians in Scandinavia*, 359–393.

111 Line, *Kingship and State Formation*, 84.

112 Ana Maria S. A. Rodrigues, "Gender and Feminine Identity in the Middle Ages," in *Identity in the Middle Ages: Approaches from Southwestern Europe*, ed. Flocel Sabaté (Leeds: ARC Humanities Press, 2021), 125–126.

113 Rodrigues, "Gender and Feminine Identity," 125–126.

114 For some clauses relating to women entering their second or even third marriage, see Lindkvist, *The Västgöta Laws*, 39–40.

115 David Herlihy, *Medieval Households* (Cambridge, MA: Harvard University Press, 1985), 132–134.

116 Rodrigues, "Gender and Feminine Identity," 130.

117 Linkdvist, *The Västgöta Laws*, 197.

118 Line, *Kingship and State Formation*, 316–317. Birgitta Johansen and Ing-Marie Pettersson, *Från borg till bunker: Befästa anläggningar från förhistorisk och historisk tid* (Stockholm: Riksantikvarieämbetet, 1993), 20–21.

119 Caroline Dunn, "Serving Isabella of France: From Queen Consort to Dowager Queen," in *Royal and Elite Households in Medieval and Early Modern Europe: More Than Just a Castle*, ed. Theresa Earenfight (Leiden: Brill, 2018), 170–191.

120 Marlen Ferrer, "State Formation and Courtly Culture in the Scandinavian Kingdoms in the High Middle Ages," *Scandinavian Journal of History* 37, no. 1 (2012), 1–22.

121 Line, *Kingship and State Formation*, 82.

122 Grzegorz Pac, *Women in the Piast Dynasty: A Comparative Study of Piast Wives and Daughters (c. 965–c. 1144)*, trans. Anna Kijak (Leiden: Brill, 2022), 417–4718. Pac also discusses Salome at length. See also Hans-Otto Gaethke, *Die Eheschließung Herzog Bolesławs III. von Polen mit der Grafentochter Salome von Berg in Schwaben* (Hamburg: Verlag Dr. Kovač, 2022).

123 Polish historian Kazimierz Jasiński has worked on Piast genealogy and Rikissa's background is presented in *Rodowód pierwszych Piastów* (Krakow: Avalon, 2007), initially published in three parts in the 1970s.

124 Line, *Kingship and State Formation*, 78.

125 Jean W. Sedlar, *East Central Europe in the Middle Ages, 1000–1500* (Seattle: University of Washington Press, 2013), 368.

126 Nora Berend, Przemysław Urbańczyk, and Przemysław Wiszewski, *Central Europe in the High Middle Ages: Bohemia, Hungary and Poland, c. 900–c.1300* (Cambridge: Cambridge University Press, 2013), 74–178.

127 Pac, *Women in the Piast Dynasty*, 466–467.

128 Friis-Jensen and Fischer, *Gesta Danorum vol. II*, 919–921.

129 Hermann Pálsson and Edwards, trans., *Knýtlinga saga*, 130; 145–149; 151–152.

130 Rikissa's descendants are introduced in the roughly correct the royal genealogy presented in *Fagrskinna: A Catalogue of the Kings of Norway: A Translation with Introduction and Notes*, trans. by Alison Finlay (Leiden: Brill, 2003), 236. Although we note that Ulvhild's first husband was probably Inge and not Niels.

131 A thorough review of the scholarship about Rikissa has recently been compiled as part of the project "The Court of Russian princesses of the XI-XVI centuries," hosted by the Saint Petersburg State University. See "Rikissa/Ryksa of Poland," https://medievalprincesses.spbu.ru/en/articles/Rikissaryksa-of-poland, accessed 23 April 2024.

132 Friis-Jensen and Fischer, *Gesta Danorum vol. II*, 1017.

133 Nielsen, *Jordebog*, 122.

134 G. E. Klemming, ed., *Svenska Krönika* (Stockholm: H. Klemming, 1860), 59.

135 Erika Räf, *Alvastra Kloster* (Stockholm: Riksantikvarieämbetet, 2000), 10.

136 SDHK nr 44724.

137 Line, *Kingship and State Formation*, 89–91.

138 Hermann Pálsson and Edwards, *Knýtlinga saga*, 123.

139 Eric Christiansen, *The Northern Crusades*, 2nd edn (London: Penguin, 1998).

140 John H. Lind, "Consequences of the Crusades in Target Areas: The Case of Karelia," in *Crusade and Conversion on the Baltic Frontier, 1150–1500*, ed. Alan Murray (Aldershot: Ashgate, 2001), 142. In the same volume, Thomas Lindkvist, "Crusades and Crusading Ideology in the Political History of Sweden, 1140–1500," 120–123.

141 Anna Kjellström, "From Saint to Anthropological Specimen: The Transformation of the Alleged Skeletal Remains of Saint Erik," in *Interdisciplinary Explorations of Postmortem Interaction. Dead Bodies, Funerary Objects, and Burial Spaces Through Texts and Time*, ed. Estella Weiss-Krejci, Sebastian Becker and Philip Schwyzer (Cham: Springer, 2022), 168–170.

142 Jakob Landebek, ed., "Narratiuncula de fundatione monasterii Vitaescholae in Cimbria," in *Scriptores rerum danicarum medii ævi tomus IV*, ed. Jacob Landebek (Copenhagen: Godiche, 1776), 460. For a discussion of the event, see Nyberg, *Monasticism*, 133–134.

143 Christian Lovén, "Sigridlev och godsrikedomen i Stenkilsätten," in *Medeltida storgårdar. 15 uppsatser om ett tvärvetenskapligt forskningsproblem*, ed. Olof Karsvall and Kristofer Jupiter (Uppsala: Kungl. Gustav Adolfs Akademien, 2014), 145–154.

144 Ilana F. Silber, "Gift-Giving in the Great Traditions: The Case of Donations to Monasteries in the Medieval West," *European Journal of Sociology* 36, no. 2 (1995), 222–223. John Arnold, *What Is Medieval History?* (Hoboken: Wiley, 2008), 43–44.

145 Michael Prestwich, *Edward I* (New Haven: Yale University Press, 2008), 124–125.

146 John Carmi Parsons, "The Queen's Intercessor," in *Power of the Weak: Studies on Medieval Women*, ed. Jennifer Carpentier and Sally-Beth MacLean (Chicago: University of Illinois Press, 1995), 157.

147 SDHK nr 317.

148 Otto Janse, "Erik den helige såsom historisk person: några synpunkter," *Fornvännen* 49 (1954), 91–115.

149 SDHK nr 268.

150 Hermann Pálsson and Edwards, *Knýtlinga saga*, 123–124.

151 Narve Bjørgo, "Margrete Eriksdotter," *Store Norske Leksikon*, https://snl.no/Margrete_Eriksdotter, accessed 23 April 2024.

152 Hans Aili, trans., "Vita sancti Erici regis et martyris," in *Röster från svensk medeltid: Latinska Texter i Original och Översättning*, ed.

Hans Aili, Olle Ferm, and Helmer Gustavson (Stockholm: Natur och Kultur, 1990), 103.

153 Agneta Conradi Mattson, *Riseberga Kloster. Birger Brosa och Filipssönerna* (Örebro: Örebro Läns Museum, 1998), 168.

154 Finlay and Faulkes, "Haraldssona saga," in *Heimskringla III*, 204.

155 Conradi Mattson, *Riseberga Kloster*, 169,

156 Finlay and Faulkes, "Haraldssona saga," in *Heimskringla III*, 204, 187–188.

157 Hans Gillingstam, "Magnus Henriksson," in *Svenskt Biografiskt Lexicon bd 24*, ed. Birgitta Lager-Kromnow (Stockholm: Bonnier, 1986), 646.

158 SDHK nr 320. Lindkvist, *The Västgöta Laws*, 197. Friis-Jensen and Fischer, *Gesta Danorum vol. II*, 1075–1077.

159 Hans Aili, "Vita sancti Erici regis et martyris," 103.

160 Aili, "Vita sancti Erici regis et martyris," 103.

161 Conradi Mattson provides a chronology based on various political events in *Riseberga Kloster*, 174–175.

162 Karl Jónsson, *Konung Sverre Sigurdssons saga efter Flatöboken* ("Sverris saga"), trans. Hermann Vendell (Helsinki: Xylografiska atelierns tryckpräss, 1885), 7. Finlay and Faulkes, "Haraldssona saga," 204.

163 Karl Jónsson, "Sverris saga," 204.

164 Eva Nilsson Nylander, ed., *Mellan Evighet och Vardag. Lunds domkyrkas martyrologium Liber daticus vestustior: Studier och faksimilutgåva* (Lund: Universitetsbiblioteket, 2015), 192 (fol. 110r).

165 SDHK nr 245; 246.

166 Conradi Mattson, *Riseberga Kloster*, 208.

167 Hermann Pálsson and Edwards, *Knýtlinga saga*, 135.

168 Jakob Langebek, ed., "Monumenta Sorana Varia," in *Scriptores rerum danicarum medii ævi tomus IV*, 547–548.

169 Friis-Jensen and Fischer, *Gesta Danorum II*, 1213.

170 Line, *Kingship and State Formation*, 86–93.

171 SDHK nr 44724.

172 Langebek, ed., "Incerti Scriptoris Sveci Chronicon Rerum Sveo-Gothicarum," in *Scriptores IV*, 590. Jørgensen, ed., "Ex Annalibus Dano-Suecanis 826–1415," in *Annales Danici*, 138.

173 Lindkvist, *The Västgöta Laws*, 198.

174 Reproduced in Sigurd Curman and Erik Lundberg, *Sveriges Kyrkor. Östergötland, vol. II* (Stockholm: Esselte AB, 1935), 5.

175 Katrinette Bordawé, "Abbesses," in *Women and Gender in Medieval Europe: An Encyclopedia*, ed. Margaret Schaus (London: Taylor & Francis, 2006), 1–4.

176 Andersson, "Cistercian Monasteries in Sweden," 6–8.

177 A thorough reconstruction of the list of confirmed abbesses, and the sources which mention them, can be found in Frans Oscar Wågman, *Vreta kloster. Historik jämte vägledning vid besök i Vreta klosters kyrka och dess omgifningar* (Stockholm: Norstedt, 1904).

178 Salomon Kraft, "Vreta klosters äldre historia," *Kyrkohistorisk årsskrift* 45 (1945), 243–245.
179 Berenice M. Kerr, *Religious Life for Women c.1100–c.1350: Fontevraud in England* (Oxford: Oxford University Press, 1999), 240–241.
180 Kraft, "Vreta klosters äldre historia," 246–248.
181 Bordawé, "Abbess," 1–4.
182 Bordawé, "Abbess," 1–4.
183 Hermann Pálsson and Edwards, *Knýtlinga saga*, 152.
184 Kroman, *Necrologium Lundense*, 348 (fol. 173v).
185 Hans Olrik, "Knud Magnussen," in *Dansk Biografisk Lexicon, vol. IX*, ed. Carl Frederick Bricka (Copenhagen: Gyldendalske Boghandels Forlag, 1895), 263–264.
186 Ahnlund, "Vreta Klosters Äldsta Donatorer," 320.
187 Lindkvist, *The Västgöta Laws*, 198.
188 Langebek, "Incerti Scriptoris," 589.
189 Ahnlund, "Vreta klosters äldsta donatorer," 341.
190 Lindkvist, *The Västgöta Laws*, 198.
191 Anti Selart, *Livonia, Rus' and the Baltic Crusades in the Thirteenth Century* (Leiden: Brill, 2015), 49–52.
192 Mägi, *In Austrvegr*, 362–364,
193 Göta Paulsson, ed., "Annales 916–1263," in *Annales Suecici Medi Ævii*, ed. Göta Paulsson (Lund: Gleerup, 1974), 255. Also "Annales 1160–1336," 267 and "Annales 916–1430," 294.
194 Line, *Kingship and State Formation*, 107–109. SDHK nr 320.
195 George Webbe Dasent, trans., "The Saga of Hacon, Hacon's Son," in *Icelandic Sagas and Other Historical Documents Relating to the Settlements and Descents of the Northmen of the British Isles, vol. 4*, ed. George Webbe Dasent (Cambridge: Cambridge University Press, 2012), 151.
196 SDHK nr 269.
197 Lindkvist, *The Västgöta Laws*, 198.
198 Lindkvist, *The Västgöta Laws*, 198. Also, Langebek, "Incerti Scriptoris," 593.
199 Finlay and Faulkes, "Haraldssona saga," 204.
200 Karl Jónsson, *Sverris saga*, 275. Gustav Storm, "Den 'buxelöse Jarl' i Sverige," *Historisk tidskrift*, 23 (1903).
201 SDHK 349; 372. Lindkvist, *The Västgöta Laws*, 198.
202 Langebek, "Monumenta Sorana Varia," 548.
203 Lindkvist, *The Västgöta Laws*, 198.
204 Line, *Kingship and State Formation*, 104–105.
205 This is related in several sources including the *Skänningeannalerna* translated by Karl Fredrik Wasén and available through Foteviken Museum (http://wadbring.com/historia/sidor/skanninge2.htm); Gertz, "Continuatio Compendii Saxonis sive Chronica Jutensis," in *Scriptores minores historiæ Danicæ medii ævi ex codicibus denuo vol. I*, 441. Jakob Langebek, ed., "Anonymi veteris Rerum Danicarum & Svevicarum Chronologia," in *Scriptores rerum danicarum medii ævi tomus I*, ed. by Jacob Langebek (Copenhagen: Godiche, 1772), 390.

4

WOMEN AS INDEPENDENT POLITICAL ACTORS 1210–1330

This last chapter will present the royal women who lived in the thirteenth and early fourteenth centuries. Unlike the previous chapter, there are remarkably fewer women to study during this later period. This is to a large extent the result of the streamlining of inheritance practices and the adoption of canonical rules, whereby patrilineal succession became more prominent, thus reducing the pool of eligible monarchs (and consorts). While patrilineal succession did not become systematic before the late medieval period, most Swedish kings from the early thirteenth century forward inherited their power from their father, or from a brother. This is in contrast with the earlier centuries where power could shift from one dynasty to another, as political circumstances changed. Consequently, this also reduced the number of potential queens and matriarchs.

The royal women of thirteenth- and fourteenth-century Sweden are characterised by their increased visibility in the sources, and their growing influence within the political and economic life of the nascent kingdom. Not all these biographies are about queens. One for instance, presents Ingrid Ylva, who was a powerful landowner who steered a large estate in her own name. She was the mother of Birger Jarl, one of the most prominent statesmen in Swedish history, and two of her grandsons became kings. Another introduces a couple of princesses who were abducted by their suitors. While similar to Viking Age practices, it is the reaction to these events that is notable. As Christian values took hold in Swedish society, these abductions provoked outrage

DOI: 10.4324/9781003392200-4

and were condemned in medieval popular culture through songs and legends. However, it is what they tell us about the strategic importance of marrying girls of royal pedigree which is interesting. This reveals the struggle between aristocracy and monarchy, as the royal family increasingly monopolised power and resources, thus consolidating kingship to an extent never witnessed before.

The last biographies exclusively focus on queens and regents, most of whom were active in politics, publicly exerted influence, tended to their own financial affairs, and helped their husband (and sons) steer the kingdom. Their economic agency, and the power they derived from it, will become obvious – and again will reflect similar trends seen elsewhere in Europe.[1] It is in the context of the centralisation of power that courtly culture emerged in earnest in Sweden and that customs such as a coronation ceremony for the queen were introduced following continental examples. This chapter – and indeed this monograph – culminates with Ingeborg Håkonsdatter, whose regency saw Sweden gain its first *de jure* and *de facto* female leader.

4.1 Helena Sverkersdotter of Sweden (and Her Daughters)

Helena Sverkersdotter and her daughters were never queens and did not hold positions of authority in the royal government. They are nevertheless considered here because they illustrate the changing attitudes towards women in the context of matrimony, the power struggles that impacted the royal family's relations with other nobles, and the role of Vreta Abbey as a centre of education for high-status girls. Helena was the daughter of Sverker the Younger and Benedicta Hvide. She is directly mentioned in two charters dated to 1237 and 1240 in connection with donations made to Vreta Abbey by herself and her husband Sune Folkesson.[2] She married Sune Folkesson, who is identified in the 1237 charter as the son of a jarl named Folke, after he supposedly abducted her from Vreta Abbey where she was being educated in the first quarter of the thirteenth century. This is related in late medieval folksongs, the earliest of which, "Elinvisan," can be traced back to the fourteenth century.[3] It is also related in Messenius'

Scondia Illustrata but is not explicitly mentioned in contemporary sources.[4] However, it formed a part of a series of similar events which took place during this period and is therefore likely to have taken place – this will be discussed shortly. Little else is known about Helena, and the date of her death is unknown. Her seal survives and represents a stylised dragon enclosed within a star.[5]

Both of her daughters, Katarina and Bengta (named after her grandmother Benedicta Hvide), are mentioned, although only their initials are given in the charter from 1240. Katarina became queen as the wife of Erik Eriksson and will be presented in depth shortly, while Bengta's own abduction, also from Vreta, is the subject of another famous folksong, "Junker Lars klosterrov." According to the song, which also originates in the medieval period, Bengta was abducted by Lars Petersson, a high-ranking administrator from Östergötland, and taken to Norway.[6] Scholars have tentatively dated the event to around 1244. She was later released and is named in a charter from 1251 alongside her sister Katarina.[7] After Lars Petersson's death, she married Svantepolk Knutsson at some point before 1253.[8] Svantepolk was a wealthy knight, with whom she had several children. Little else is known about her life, but a charter from 1261 in which she gives most of her estates to the monks in Alvastra survives.[9] As she disappears from the historical records after this, and considering the significance of the gift described in the charter, it is likely that she died in 1261 or shortly after.

It is perhaps a little odd to start a chapter about women as "independent actors" with multiple examples of them being abducted. The "Vreta Maiden Abductions," as they are known in English, refer to a series of at least three abductions which took place during the thirteenth century. As we mentioned in relation to the earliest queens studied in this book, kidnapping women in order to marry them was common practice in medieval Scandinavia, as it was elsewhere in the Germanic world. This series of abductions from Vreta Abbey is nevertheless an outlier for two reasons. Firstly, these are said to have happened well into the Christian period, at a time when such a custom was on the way out, if not even unheard of in large sections of society. Secondly, something

which distinguishes these abductions from their Viking Age counterparts mentioned earlier, is the reaction to them. There is no evidence that Edla and Estrid's families fought to get them back after
Olof Skötkonung allegedly kidnapped them. That evidence might
have been lost, but considering that both women are relatively
well documented in later sources, one might expect any conflict to
have been documented too. As we saw, Adam of Bremen suggests
that these kidnappings served a diplomatic purpose as well. That
is not to say that Viking Age kidnappings were readily tolerated,
and there are plenty of examples in the Icelandic sagas – as well
as throughout historical sources outside of Scandinavia – of male
relatives setting out on expeditions to retrieve women. Nevertheless, it may have been more commonly accepted as a way of finding suitable women to marry, and the prospect of one's female
relatives becoming a sex slave or being forced to marry abroad
was just part of the culture. Well into the Christian period, however, mores had changed, and this was certainly not considered
acceptable to the same extent anymore. When Jon Sverkersson,
son of Sverker the Elder, kidnapped two Danish noblewomen
and raped them repeatedly in the 1140s, his actions caused an
uproar in Sweden and were used as a pretext for an armed conflict with Denmark. This was postponed, however, and eventually became unnecessary as Jon was killed at the hands of local
farmers who were horrified by his conduct.[10] Yet, in the three
cases studied here, it is not obvious that any of these kidnappings
took place without the girls' consent. Unsurprisingly, nothing is
said of the victim's feelings in any of the sources which mention
these events.

It is entirely possible that these kidnappings were in fact
planned, concerted efforts to escape an oppressive environment;
or simply to elope. One cannot trust the surviving evidence,
exclusively written down by ecclesiastical hands, to portray these
events objectively. The men's character might well have been
tarnished to protect the reputation of the royal girls involved.
Indeed, there are discrepancies in the way the Vreta abductions
were said to have been handled. Helena's abduction, described
by Johannes Messenius as violent, is not related anywhere in contemporary sources.[11] The two surviving charters which mention

Helena and her husband project the image of a legitimate couple who were popular enough for their donations to be accepted. Bengta's abduction ended with her being released and getting married to a new husband, Svantepolk Knutsson, although we do not know whether she had lived with Lars as his partner before that.[12] The circumstances of her release are unclear as well, and Lars may have simply died rather than be forced to let her go. In the case of Ingrid Svantepolkesdotter, supposedly abducted in 1287 or 1288 by Folke Algotsson, several of the men involved were jailed, whereas others had to flee to Norway.[13] However, there is no evidence that Ingrid was kept against her will. In fact, Folke and Ingrid married in Norway and she did not return to Sweden before c. 1310, after his death.[14]

However, the fact that three generations of the same family witnessed similar events nevertheless suggests that other factors than love or boredom were at play. In addition to the possibility that these were consented events portrayed as crimes, Agneta Conradi Mattsson has offered a thorough analysis of the various economic relationships which tied the families of the abductors and their victims, and concluded that these events were tightly associated with economic interests and disputes.[15] In this case, the kidnappings might have served as crude ways to settle feuds, much like in the Viking Age, although by the thirteenth century this method (and the lack of consent it engendered, both from the girl and her family), posed problems in the legitimisation of such unions.

Caroline Dunn's research has uncovered similar cases of abductions and forced marriages in England, where most kidnaps targeted noble and/or wealthy women. Thus, while the phenomenon did not solely target royal ladies, most kidnappers were clearly in search of wealth and prestige. A significant minority of cases involved commoners, however, which proves that women at all levels of society could be victims, and that men of all social classes were involved.[16] There is at least one lower-profile case in Vreta Abbey in the thirteenth century, whereby a young girl was taken to be married off to the servant of a man called Karl Bengtsson.[17] Dunn further writes that such unconsented unions could end in several ways. The woman might be forced to give in and stay with

her captor, especially if she had been raped and the union had
therefore been consummated. In some cases, she could consider
the vows invalid and ignore the situation (this is particularly true
of widows who were wealthy and powerful enough to ensure
their own protection). Others managed to return to their families.
Some high-profile cases made it to the courts.[18]

The picture in medieval Sweden is less clear not least because
the evidence is lacking, but contemporary examples from England
suggest that such abductions, while frowned upon by the authorities, might have been a rather common phenomenon elsewhere in
Europe, too. Birger Jarl's introduction of a law against the kid-
nap of women in the 1250s certainly suggests that the practice
was widespread enough to warrant legislation.[19] In addition, the
fact that these similar events all took place in Vreta underlines
the nunnery's importance as an educational centre for high-status
girls who were kept there for many years while waiting for a suitable match.

4.2   Ingrid Ylva

Of all the women discussed here, Ingrid Ylva is the one with the
most distant link to royalty, and the last non-queen to be studied in this monograph. While she might have been descended
from the Sverker dynasty, she did not marry a king, and none
of her children became royals – on paper. However, she was the
mother of Birger Jarl, who profoundly altered the trajectory of
Sweden's history, founded Stockholm, and strengthened the monarchy to such an extent that by his death in 1266, the Crown
had nearly caught up with other European monarchies in terms
of centralisation of power, border definition, institutionalisation, and legitimacy in the eyes of foreign powers.[20] Birger Jarl
himself was never officially king, although he was one in all but
name. Upon his becoming jarl in 1247 (a title which made him
the second most powerful man in the kingdom after the king), he
quickly manoeuvred to get his sons onto the throne.[21] However,
Birger Jarl did not come out of nowhere. He was a member of
the powerful noble family of Bjälbo which had already produced
several leading political figures from the twelfth century onwards.

As mentioned previously, Bjälbo was the name of an estate (which still exists) in Östergötland which belonged to his mother, and it therefore seems appropriate to look into her life.

Ingrid Ylva is the perfect starting point to investigate how women became increasingly powerful in public life. We have seen in the previous chapter that women could certainly have power and accumulate wealth, but this was often done away from the public eye. From the thirteenth century onwards, it became more common for some women to display their personal power publicly, and for them to become public figures in their own name. In fact, Viking Age women could be openly powerful and independently wealthy, as has been discussed before. It is with the acceleration of Christianisation in the twelfth century that there was a regression in women's agency, possibly caused by a very aggressive and dogmatic expansion of Christianity and its rigid laws in its first few decades in Sweden.

Most of what is known about Ingrid also comes from later sources and might therefore not be entirely accurate. The sixteenth-century chronicler Olaus Petri wrote that she was the daughter of Sune Sik (also known as Simon Sik), himself a son of Sverker the Elder and Rikissa of Poland, although no contemporary source confirms this.[22] This piece of information about Ingrid is unique in that it is neither corroborated nor denied in any other sources about her (except for Johannes Bureus, writing even later than Olaus Petri). There are several problems with this theory, however. Firstly, there is no contemporary mention of a son of Sverker and Rikissa named Sune Sik. Secondly, the only historical Sune Sik recorded in medieval charters was a nobleman who lived at the very end of the thirteenth century.[23] It is therefore possible that the early modern authors who wrote about this mixed together several characters. It is not implausible, however, that she was descended from a royal dynasty, and this would explain her wealth. Petri's chronicle explains that she was married to Magnus Minniskiöld, with whom she had Birger Jarl.[24] Magnus was a member of the powerful Bjälbo (or Folkung) dynasty and was a brother of the twelfth-century jarl Birger Brosa, as recorded in contemporary charters.[25] For Magnus to marry a woman of royal descent would thus fit with the usual pattern witnessed so far and supports the idea that Ingrid descended from a minor branch of some royal dynasty, possibly Sverker's.

According to the surviving documentation, she did not play a publicly political role, and does not appear in any charters concerning her son's political activities. Despite this, she was certainly very active in her local area. She personally commissioned and funded the bell tower in Bjälbo. An inscription on the medieval bell specifically dates its installation to 1240 and gives Ingrid as the commissioner.[26] The dating of the rest of the surviving structures is unclear, although architectural analysis suggests a construction date for the church itself in the mid-twelfth century, while dendrochronology has established that the tower was erected around 1220.[27] The jarl Birger Brosa, Ingrid's brother-in-law and head of the Bjälbo family, died in 1202.[28] It is unclear when her husband Magnus Minniskiöld died, although he also disappears from the historical record after 1202.[29] Birger Jarl, her son, can only have been a young child considering his death in 1266 around the age of 50, which only leaves Ingrid as a possible patron.[30] The tower, consisting originally of six floors – of which four survive – remains one of the tallest in Östergötland.[31]

Intriguingly, Ingrid Ylva is the only woman in this book who was said to be a witch. Like elsewhere in medieval Europe, witchcraft had long been part of folk culture, and had become increasingly documented and scrutinised in thirteenth-century Scandinavia.[32] Legends passed down the generations (the origins of which could not be identified for the purpose of this study) made Ingrid a white witch, an ambivalent status in the Middle Ages. White witches, unlike the witches routinely tortured and executed for their alleged crimes, were said to use their powers to benefit people, but their alleged powers were still met with suspicion from Church fathers.[33] The detail of what she is meant to have done has not made it to us, and it is therefore unclear why she was considered a witch and whether this was already the case while she was alive. However, her status as a white (and therefore benevolent) witch could suggest that she was popular among the population. It is quite uncommon for a noble and wealthy woman to be known as a witch. In Sweden as elsewhere in medieval Europe, witches were usually people living on the margins of society either by choice, or because of disability or poverty. For an elite woman of royal descent to be known as a witch is therefore quite exceptional. It is even more so in the thirteenth century, when Sweden was nearly entirely Christianised and certainly fully so in Östergötland, where the Bjälbo estate lies. Popular tradition claims that she requested to be buried upright in the tower that she commissioned, and that as long as she remained standing, the Bjälbo dynasty would reign over Sweden.[34]

There is no suggestion in the historical record that she had pagan tendencies. As we saw, she is in fact remembered as a church sponsor,[35] and her identification as a witch therefore clashes with what she is known to have done. Scholars such as Grant Loomis, however, have pointed out that the miracles supposedly performed by the saints can be understood as a sort of white witchcraft, and the place of "white magic" within Christianity has long been discussed.[36] This is a rather accurate comparison, as the main difference between a saint and a white witch is that the saint is said to derive their power from God, whereas a white witch somehow derives theirs from nature and supernatural forces, and/or from pagan gods.[37] Furthermore, like Ingamoder whom we discussed in the second chapter, the legends about Ingrid possibly emerged several decades after her death. It is unclear at which point she was first identified as a witch, but one cannot help but posit that it might have been a way for the general population – which it is known mixed Christian and pre-Christian beliefs well after Christianisation – to express the type of admiration and reverence that such community leaders often inspired. According to *Gråbrödradiariet*, she died in 1251, while Messenius tells us that she was buried (upright) in 1252.[38]

4.3   Rikissa Valdemarsdatter

Rikissa was the daughter of Sophia of Minsk and King Valdemar I of Denmark. Through her mother, she was the granddaughter of Sverker the Elder's queen, Rikissa of Poland, after whom she is named. Her date of birth is not known but she was her mother's last child with Valdemar, who died in 1182.[39] It is therefore usually estimated that she was born sometime around 1180.

She married Erik Knutsson in 1210, the same year when his predecessor, Sverker the Younger, died.[40] Rikissa is the first Swedish queen whose activities and attitude about courtly culture are partly known. A later medieval folksong about her claims that upon arriving in Sweden for her marriage, she expressed surprise at having to ride rather than being transported in a carriage, as she had been allegedly used to in Denmark. In response, her new ladies-in-waiting encouraged her to take up the Swedish way and forget her Danish manners.[41] It is impossible to verify the veracity of the song but there is also no reason to doubt it. Indeed, we know that courtly culture was more advanced in Denmark than in Sweden during this period, and it would therefore be quite normal for the princess, who had grown up at the Danish court and whose mother was of royal descent on both her father's and mother's sides, to notice Sweden's comparatively less sophisticated customs. This anecdote would therefore confirm that Sweden was not quite on a par with its Scandinavian neighbours in terms of courtly culture, and was still rather rudimentary. It is also very tempting to see in the Swedish way a more egalitarian approach, whereby women rode like men, rather than being confined to a passive role. There is a symbolic aspect to the idea of a queen proudly riding into her new kingdom, as opposed to being taken to it.

It also confirms that Swedish queens did have ladies-in-waiting and other noblewomen surrounding them. This has been discussed before in relation to earlier queens; but while we know that having female companions has most probably always been a component of royal life, the evidence until Rikissa had been extremely scarce. In her case, it is interesting to note that she is said to have received Swedish ladies-in-waiting rather than being accompanied by her own. The song may just have omitted some details, and it is still likely that Rikissa was allowed to bring with her some of her Danish entourage, but it is extremely interesting that she was expected to adopt her new country's customs. It may not sound surprising, but it is still a significant departure from the earliest queens presented in the first chapter who may have brought with them foreign influences to the nascent Swedish monarchy. By the early thirteenth century, Swedish royal culture was established enough that foreigners were now expected to adapt to it.

It is worth noting that while Erik was not the first Swedish king to be represented with a crown on his head – this is Anund Jacob, on his coins – Erik is the first for which there is evidence of a coronation ceremony similar to those witnessed elsewhere in Europe. This took place in 1210 according to *Skänningean-nalerna*, compiled by a Dominican nun in the last years of the thirteenth century. His wedding to Rikissa is said to have taken place the same year.[42] There is no evidence for a similar ceremony for her, and the first documented coronation of a queen is that of Helvig in 1281,[43] but Erik's ceremony is nevertheless evidence that the Swedish monarchy had started to adopt continental practices as well as courtly culture. There is not enough surviving material to know how the differences between Danish and Swedish courtly cultures affected Rikissa, but the context within which she lived is worth bearing in mind.

Rikissa and Erik Knutsson had two well documented daughters, and possibly two more whose identities are debated. Firstly, Ingeborg Eriksdotter will be later discussed in detail as the first wife of the highly powerful Birger Jarl. Secondly, Sofia Eriksdatter became Lady of Mecklenburg in 1237 through her marriage to Henrik Burwin III. As she has left few traces in Swedish sources, she is better studied in a German context.[44] The wife of Barnim I, Duke of Pomerania, Marianne, whom he married around 1240, is sometimes presented in scholarship as the daughter of Rikissa and Erik. However, the evidence is inconclusive and her genealogy remains debated.[45] A last hypothetical daughter, known only from the highly politicised fifteenth-century "Karlskrönikan", is not thought to have existed. Rikissa's only son, Erik Eriksson, who was born after his father's death, became king in 1222 and his wife is discussed below.

Because Rikissa's son Erik Eriksson was only born after the death of his father, another man was elected king in his stead: Johan Sverkersson, who only reigned a few years and died unmarried and childless. This election was opposed by the Pope and the King of Denmark who, naturally, preferred to see his nephew, Rikissa's son, on the throne.[46] Rikissa then fled back to Denmark, where she died on 8 May 1220, years before her son's accession to the throne, and her daughters' marriages. She is buried in Ringsted.[47]

4.4 Katarina Sunesdotter

Katarina was the daughter of Helena Sverkersdotter, whom we have discussed earlier, and her husband Sune Folkesson.[48] Through her double ancestry as a member of both the House of Sverker and the Bjälbo family, Katarina was poised to enjoy a very high status in society. It is therefore not surprising that she was seen as suitable for queenship. Her date of birth is unknown but she married King Erik Eriksson in 1244 near Uppsala.[49] Upon her wedding, she received an unusually large morning gift notably consisting of both Nyköping and Söderköping among other possessions, which gave her immense personal fortune.[50] Yet, her queenship was neither remarkable, nor lasted long.

Indeed, Erik Eriksson was a fairly weak king both politically and personally. As mentioned previously, he was born after his father's death, and was initially bypassed in the succession, with Johan Sverkersson elected instead. Erik had thus spent part of his childhood in exile in Denmark with his mother Rikissa. "Erik-skrönikan" tells that he spoke with a lisp and walked with a limp, which prevented him from taking part in tournaments.[51] Eventually allowed the throne around 1222 when he was still a young child, Erik's reign was essentially dependent on regents, councils, and other strongmen. He had to face local feuds and a rebellion against the Crown which had little to do with himself but rather with institutional conflicts. At the end of the 1220s, he once again had to flee to Denmark, only returning a few years later – although the exact chronology is not known.[52] He was then king until his death, which happened only a few years after his marriage to Katarina, in 1250.[53] No known children were born from this union. In this context, Katarina probably had little power as queen, and in spite of her considerable personal wealth, was one of the more passive queens to reign during the thirteenth century.

Nevertheless, we cannot discount the possibility that she may have been very economically active as owner of Nyköping and Söderköping among other manors. Indeed, Katarina is the first queen to appear in multiple charters. This might simply be because hers survived, and that earlier examples have been lost, but the fact that she was such an important landowner in her own right probably made her more politically and publicly active as well. This would be in line with other European kingdoms where women's economic agency was intrinsically linked to their public authority.[54] The most significant documents which mentioned her consist of her two wills, which she drew up in 1250. In them, she bequeathed many of her lands and possessions to Gudhem Abbey as well as other, unspecified monastic orders. She also left properties to the children of two noblemen and to her uncle, as well as the whole of Söderköping to her sister, with the rest of her assets going to charity. These two wills are interesting in several ways. They confirm, first of all, that women could dispose of their properties as they saw fit – although she does admit to listening to the advice of Birger Jarl and her uncle. It also gives us an idea of the type and amount of properties that a queen could person-ally hold. Indeed, she makes a clear distinction between what is hers by birth, including properties bought by her father, and what is due to her as the king's wife. She does not detail the latter possessions, which she simply allocates to charity, and instead focuses on her own assets.[55] This document, therefore, only gives us a truncated view of the true number of Katarina's possessions (Figure 4.1).

The surviving charters that mention her show that Katarina was still formally known as *drottning* even following the death of her husband, which is evidence that a dowager queen did not lose her status and prestige. This is an important detail which will later help us elucidate the role of some of these royal women who survived their husbands, sometimes by decades. The fact that no mention is made of any children confirms the widely held assumption that Katarina and Erik did not have any chil-dren, or that none survived infancy. We know the rough outline of Katarina's last years. Following her testament, she entered Gudhem Abbey – to whom she had just donated a significant part of her land assets – where she finished her life. The *Skän-ningeannalerna* state that Sweden's "K. drottning" died in 1252.[56]

FIGURE 4.1 Effigy of Katarina Sunesdotter from Gudhem Abbey, now in Stockholm. Photograph by Christer Åhlin, Historiska Museet, SHM.

Her contemporary effigy, which represents her with a crown, has survived and has been transferred from Gudhem to the Historical Museum in Stockholm.[57]

4.5   Ingeborg Eriksdotter

It is impossible to discuss medieval Sweden without mentioning Ingrid Ylva's most famous offspring, Birger Jarl (Birger Magnusson). As jarl, he was king in all but name, and careful manoeuvring ensured that no less than two of his sons inherited the Swedish throne, which makes him an important character in Sweden's royal history and justifies presenting his two wives, Ingeborg and Mechtild. What will quickly become noticeable is that Ingeborg and Mechtild are largely absent from Swedish sources, which is most probably linked to the immense power that their husband yielded. As a result, unlike most other women studied in this chapter, there is no evidence that they had any significant power and instead might have lurked in his shadow.

Birger Jarl was first married to Ingeborg Eriksdotter, daughter of Queen Rikissa and King Erik X of Sweden. Through her mother, Ingeborg was also the great-granddaughter of Sverker the Elder and a great-granddaughter of Saint Erik on her father's side. Last but not least, she was also the sister of King Erik Eriksson. She was thus very high-born, and an excellent match for Sweden's *de facto* ruler. Their marriage took place sometime in the 1230s, and certainly before 1240, as Valdemar was ten years old when he was chosen king in 1250. "Erikskrönikan" further tells us that she got married as soon as she came of age, which suggests that she was born in the 1220s.[58] Little can be said about Ingeborg during her time as the jarl's wife. She rarely appears in sources, and they do not allow us to build a picture of her character and her tenure as the jarl's wife. A passage in the chronicle suggests that Birger Jarl sometimes did ask for her opinion, and the chronicle claims that she is the one he turned to for advice about finding a wife for their son Valdemar. The narrator then writes that Ingeborg knew well how to "speak sweet words," a reference to her diplomatic talents which, in this case, involved advising her husband to ask someone else. This is an example of the type of mediating role that queens were expected to play. Medieval wives were expected to be able to soften their husbands' hearts through persuasion, even sometimes seduction, and help address their flawed instincts – brutality, cowardice, and greed, among others. Ironically, this was partly due to the association between women and spoken language, rooted in the story of Eve talking Adam into sinning; but language was here to be used by royal wives as a diplomatic tool.[59] This type of intercession was tightly associated with gender ideals whereby women were seen as peacemakers, but it also conferred them with genuine political agency at a time when theological developments elsewhere in Europe aimed to increasingly restrict women's influence.[60]

However, not much else is known about her personality. We do not even know where she lived although we know that the

Bjälbo family kept a private residence on their ancestral lands in Östergötland.[61] What we do know is that her ancestry lent considerable prestige to her husband and was probably a key factor in his coming to power. Her seal reflects this by representing her with a headdress stylised to look like a crown with a castle in the background.[62] Like many other men before him, Birger Jarl chose a woman of royal descent to position himself as a leading man in the realm. This certainly worked as he put their son Valdemar on the throne following King Erik Eriksson's death in 1250. We also know about Ingeborg's legacy through her children. Ingeborg gave birth to no fewer than eight children, all of whom not only survived childhood but also became important historical figures. They are King Valdemar, King Magnus Ladulås – often hailed as the first king of Sweden with real political power, international influence, and nearly uncontested authority – Queen Rikissa of Norway, Duke Bengt of Finland, Duke Erik of Småland, Duchess Ingeborg of Saxony, Princess Katarina of Anhalt, and Kristina Birgersdotter who married several noblemen. Unfortunately, Ingeborg did not live to see the destinies of her children. The *Skänningeannalerna* state that "Fru Ingeborg, hertiginna av Sverige," died on 17 June 1254. The same entry also tells us that her son Bengt, who later became Duke of Finland, was born the same year. This suggests that she died of childbirth complications.[63]

4.5.1   Comments about "Germany"

As will become clear shortly, the terms "German/Germany" are used in this book to refer to these areas which belong to present-day. However, its medieval realm was not as unified as these terms suggest, and it instead consisted of multiple principalities, dukedoms, and other polities which were independent. The modern terminology is used for clarity. By the mid-thirteenth century, as Sweden developed as a fully fledged and recognised kingdom, German immigration became an important component of society. Indeed, as the kingdom's role on the international stage expanded, so did its contacts with neighbouring powers outside of Scandinavia. Trade was a significant new asset for the kingdom, and the thirteenth century saw the frantic expansion, as well as the creation, of new cities and ports. Stockholm, for instance, was first built in the mid-thirteenth century, probably on the initiative of Birger Jarl, and quickly became an important trading place.[64] Visby, on Gotland, which had been part of the German-born and German-led Hanseatic League since the twelfth century, emerged as Sweden's richest and most dynamic town, and a significant part of its population was German. Much the same is true of Kalmar, which was also an important trading port.[65] Trading privileges had been in place between the citizens of some German regions and cities (such as the independent city of Lübeck) and Gotland since at least the second half of the twelfth century, as evidenced by two charters from 1163 and 1189.[66] By the time the impact that German citizens had on Sweden's development became clear, such exchanges had therefore been taking place for decades.

Indeed, we know that German citizens were responsible for many of the economic developments witnessed in cities across Sweden in the late thirteenth century. The records of town councils, themselves partly modelled on German examples, show that German citizens played a political role already in the thirteenth century. By the mid-fourteenth century, town councils were forced by law to be split evenly among Germans, and Swedes.[67] This shows the level of influence that they had on all aspects of city life. This was reflected in fourteenth-century urban and maritime laws as well, some of which show German influence. Multiple cities including Visby also simply adopted the Lübeck law, which spread among the Hanseatic League, rather than indigenous laws.[68]

As will be shown in connection with Magnus Ladulås, the kingdom moulded itself on the example of German society. The nascent aristocracy established by Magnus Ladulås in 1279 was clearly inspired by the German equivalent and many noblemen were, in fact, Germans (chiefly coming from Hanseatic cities, Saxony, and Holstein) who had settled in Sweden. Old Swedish, in its incarnation which emerged from the thirteenth-century onwards, was heavily influenced by German vocabulary and grammar.[69] In this context, it is unsurprising that powerful Swedish men sought to marry German noblewomen, and all the women studied below had at least one German parent. Such marriages gave Swedish men access to precious social and economic networks, not least through connections to the Hanseatic League.

4.6   Mechtild of Holstein

Mechtild of Holstein was the daughter of the earl Adolf IV of Holstein and his wife Helvig of Lippe who also came from a prestigious German noble family. She was probably born in the 1220s, although her exact date of birth is unknown. Before her arrival in Sweden in the 1260s, Mechtild had already had an illustrious royal career. She was a former queen consort of Denmark, having been married to Abel of Denmark between 1237 (or 1236, according to some annals) and 1252 when he died. She was crowned in Roskilde alongside him in 1250, an important event which, as will be discussed further in this chapter, may have influenced all later female coronations in Sweden.[70] Mechtild's life in Denmark makes it clear that she was a strong and politically savvy woman. Upon Abel's death in 1252, her son Valdemar was bypassed for succession and she subsequently had to flee and enter a convent, possibly in the diocese of Odense.[71] Nonetheless, this event did not stop her being politically active. On the contrary, she spent the next few years working behind the scenes to get her eldest son Valdemar, by now held captive by the archbishop of Cologne, his inheritance.[72] She eventually managed to get him released and consequently secured the Duchy of Sønderjylland for him in 1253. When Valdemar died around 1260, she positioned her younger son Erik as the new duke, while a third son, Abel, received some fiefs as compensation. With King Abel she also had a daughter, Sophie, who married Bernhard I, Prince of Anhalt-Bernburg in 1258.[73]

Mechtild's role in manoeuvring her children's political careers is mainly implicit, but no one else could have been the driving force behind their fates. The few surviving sources show that she played a decisive role in the history of Schleswig-Holstein: she is for instance accused in the *Annales Ripenses* and *Annales Ryenses* to have destroyed papal and imperial letters initially issued to King Valdemar I in the twelfth century which proved his right to the lands north of the River Elbe.[74] Additionally, in 1260, she distributed previously Danish regions to her sons.[75] This further enraged the Danish people and cemented her dynasty's claim to the southern part of Denmark, which eventually became permanently German.[76] Because of that important – but precarious – political situation, she had to seek support outside of Denmark. There was a generally strong anti-German sentiment in the kingdom at the time, with Mechtild the particular target of much criticism – the *Annales Ripenses* and *Annales Ryenses* called her *filia dyaboli*, "daughter of the Devil."[77] This sentiment did not spread to Sweden, which had no territorial claims against the Germans, and that is how she married Birger Jarl, who was one of the few men in Scandinavia powerful enough to protect her interests. She planned her marriage to Birger Jarl, who had been one of her husband's fiercest enemies, while still a nun.[78]

After breaking her religious vows, Mechtild became the second wife of Birger Jarl after Ingeborg Eriksdotter's death. They married in 1261.[79] The marriage was quite the political statement, considering the bitter feud which had embroiled King Abel and Birger Jarl. It also made clear that Mechtild sought to remain close to power and had recognised Birger Jarl's undeniable authority within Sweden. The union enabled her to secure a powerful ally after years of fighting to maintain hers and her sons' status and inheritance. It was purely political, and the couple did not have any more children. She was, however, stepmother to Birger's children from his marriage to Ingeborg, including the future kings Magnus, Valdemar, the future queen of Norway Rikissa Birgersdotter, and five other children who went onto become dukes and countesses (Figure 4.2).

As with her predecessor, Ingeborg, not much can be said either about her time as Birger's wife in Sweden. She does not appear in many sources and it is therefore not possible to judge her popularity in a Swedish context. Birger was a strongman, and a domineering personality in Swedish politics. It is possible that she had no leeway to exercise power within this marriage. If she ever influenced him or took part in his decisions, this was not documented. Following the death of Birger Jarl in 1266, Mechtild retreated from public life and little is known about that period

FIGURE 4.2   Effigies of Mechtild of Holstein, Birger Jarl, and Erik Birgersson in Varnhem Abbey. © Jeppe Gustafsson/ Alamy Stock Photo

of her life. She may have returned to Germany, although it is unclear. She survived all her children. She died in 1288 and was buried in Varnhem Abbey next to Birger Jarl and his son Erik, whose remains show was disabled.[80] All three share a grave and tombstone. Interestingly, Mechtild is given the central position on the monument, being represented much more prominently than the men, and she is shown with a crown on her head, thus emphasising her queenly status, even long after her queenship ended. The monument makes it clear that she was of much higher social status than her husband, despite him being the dominant political actor in medieval Sweden.[81]

4.7   Sofia Eriksdatter

Sofia was the daughter of King Erik IV Plogpenning of Denmark, and his wife, a Saxon princess named Jutta whom he had married in 1239, as related in multiple Danish chronicles.[82] Her date of birth is unknown, but her father was murdered in 1250, and Sofia married Valdemar Birgersson in 1260. She may therefore have been born in the late 1240s. Losing her father at such a young age also made Sofia very rich, and an attractive bride. For Birger Jarl, it was the perfect opportunity to create a strong, and profitable alliance between Denmark and Sweden, by marrying his son to Sofia. Upon learning that she would marry Valdemar, she is said in "Erikskrönikan" to have prayed to the Virgin Mary and uttered these words: "Give me happiness together with him, and him with me." Whether this happened cannot be verified, but this short sentence nevertheless tells us much about the future queen. It portrays her as pious and as holding Mary in high regard. It also presents her as a humble, devoted future bride, for whom the success of her marriage was paramount. Whether this is an accurate description is unknown. The author further describes how "she travelled in great joy and without difficulty, with great honour and much courtliness." The chronicle also claims that she received the towns of Malmö and Trelleborg as gifts from her father, making her independently wealthy. This is a textbook depiction of the perfect medieval royal bride.[83] Her seal represents her as such, sitting on a throne, wearing a luxurious dress, with a crown on her head.[84] While she is not the only medieval queen of Sweden represented with a crown, she is the only one shown in such a typically kingly position of power. This is unique both in Sweden and Denmark during this period.

This image of Sofia as an idealised bride is even more interesting that it stands in sharp contrast with what the chronicle subsequently tells us about her behaviour as queen. Indeed, she was known for her strong temperament and less-than-regal insults, notably aimed at her brothers-in-law. Valdemar had been elected king while still a child and crowned in Linköping in 1251. It is his father, Birger Jarl, who truly exerted power. Therefore, by marrying Valdemar, Sofia technically became queen but it is only after 1266, when Birger Jarl died, that she enjoyed a higher status. Furthermore, upon Birger Jarl's marriage to Mecthild of Holstein, Sofia became the stepdaughter of the former Queen of Denmark, whose previous husband, King Abel of Denmark, is said to have murdered Sofia's father. This was an uncomfortable position which might have diminished her own authority.[85] There is no evidence that she was ever crowned, despite being represented on her personal seal with a crown on her head.[86] This may be because her husband had already been crowned years prior, and a stand-alone female coronation might not have been considered necessary. Indeed, most queens in Scandinavia and elsewhere in Europe who were formally crowned were so alongside their husbands, and not independently of them. A notable exception is Helvig of Holstein, studied shortly.

After becoming *de facto* king, Valdemar and his younger brothers, Magnus (Ladulås) and Erik, were embroiled in regular conflicts. Siding with her husband, Sofia quickly gained a reputation for her sharp tongue. She is said to have called Magnus *ketlaböther* ("the tinker," owing to his reputedly dark and slender appearance), and Erik *Erik alls intet* ("nothing-at-all Erik," possibly due to his disability).[87] As with some of the earlier queens who also had the reputation for being strong-willed, and perhaps even unruly, it is unclear whether there is any truth to it. Erik's nickname is for example also known from "Magnúss saga lagabœtis," where it is claimed that he called himself that because of his lack of noble title.[88] It is therefore not clear that the cruel taunt should be attributed to Sofia. Most of what we know of these episodes comes from "Erikskrönikan," a fourteenth-century chronicle, parts of which are considered biased, exaggerated, or unreliable.[89]

Sofia and Valdemar had at least five daughters whose lives are known. Most became prominent noblewomen outside of Sweden and therefore are only briefly mentioned here. Ingeborg became Countess of Holstein through her marriage to Gerhard of Holstein who was an important ally for the Swedish Crown as the brother of Queen Helvig, discussed below. Marina became Countess of Diepholz through her marriage to Rudolf of Diepholz, again a powerful German ally, and Rikissa became Queen of Poland by marrying King Przemyslaw II.[90] Two more daughters, Katarina and Margareta, are recorded although little can be written about them. Katarina died in 1283. Margareta became a nun in Skänninge in 1288, possibly after a failed engagement.[91] Sofia's sons were Erik, who died an infant in 1261,[92] and another Erik who became a prominent nobleman and is a recurrent character of "Erikskrönikan."

Despite the success of their children, Sofia and Valdemar's marriage was not a happy one. Valdemar's many infidelities proved a stain on his kingship and on his wife's reputation. One such event put Sofia directly at the centre of a controversy, through no fault of her own, when her sister Jutta (named after their mother) visited Sweden in 1273 and had an affair with Valdemar.[93] This was a particularly bad scandal: not only was this a public humiliation for the queen, but this was also a case of incest, as per the Church's definition. A sixteenth-century Danish historian, Arild Huitfeldt, claims that the illicit couple had a child together, for which Valdemar had to go on pilgrimage to Jerusalem in 1274.[94] The veracity of this tale cannot be confirmed, however. In any case, after he was deposed as king in 1275, and Sofia lost her queenship, Valdemar is said to have neglected her and instead began to live openly with his mistresses, whom "Erikskrönikan" claims he later married following the queen's death.[95] Sofia remained engaged in her husband's political affairs, however, and as the conflict with his brothers kept raging, she co-issued with him a letter pawning Gotland to their allies in Brandenburg dated to 1277.[96] As mentioned previously, the marriages of her daughter Ingeborg to Gerhard of Holstein and Marina to Rudolf of Diepholz were also strategic alliances aiming at shoring up support for her husband.

These efforts were ultimately vain and by 1280, Valdemar's abdication became official and Sofia lost her queenship. The royal couple separated around this time or shortly after. They never co-issued documents again after this date. Several charters survive in which Sofia is directly mentioned. While Valdemar was king, she was always mentioned alongside him as "the queen," or as "his wife." Following his fall from grace, however, she remained socially active, and a couple of charters issued by her survive to this day. One of them, dated to 1283, contains the very first mention of Norrköping.[97] Both charters involve the giving of land and in them, she styles herself "formerly queen" and "senior queen" (*Regina quondam Sweorum, Sophia senior regina*). These were not formal titles, and she chose them herself. The idea of "senior queen" is particularly interesting because it does not mean anything concrete. Instead, it reflects Sofia's bid to remain relevant.

This might have worked, as in 1284 she was finally granted her share of her father's inheritance in Denmark, which had been the object of a long-standing dispute.[98] She appears in correspondence as late as 1285 but died in 1286 according to later medieval sources, including *Vetus Chronica Sialandie*.[99] Her place of burial is not known.

4.8   Helvig of Holstein

Helvig of Holstein was the daughter of Count Gerhard I of Holstein and Elisabeth of Mecklenburg, which made her a woman of very high status.[100] Her date of birth is unclear, but considering that she married Magnus Ladulås in 1276, she may have been born sometime in the second half of the 1250s, or in the early 1260s. She was the sister of Gerhard II of Holstein, mentioned above, who also married into Swedish royalty. Helvig of Holstein is one of Sweden's most important queens, being the earliest royal wife for which there is clear evidence that she was crowned during a ceremony. The complete lack of sources mentioning similar ceremonies for previous queens seems to suggest that this was a new practice. Indeed, a charter sealed by the king himself states that Helvig's crowning took place in Södertälje on 29 July 1281.[101] Annals also confirm the event, and show that she was crowned by the archbishop of Uppsala.[102]

Interestingly, however, she had married Magnus Ladulås a few years prior in Kalmar.[103] "Erikskrönikan" states that he was then only still a duke, and shortly after the marriage was elected king. Other sources claim instead that when Magnus was crowned in May 1276 at the old cathedral of Uppsala, he was not married yet to Helvig, whom he married in November of the same year.[104] On her marriage, she received the estate of Dåvö in Västmanland as well as three nearby hundreds as a morning gift.[105] This is confirmed by surviving charters which she wrote from there. Regardless of the marriage's chronology, it is not clear why it took several more years for the queen to be crowned. Later examples (as well as similar instances elsewhere in Europe) suggest that it was not unusual to have a delay between the royal wedding and the coronation. The case of Märta and Birger, studied next, shows that there could be political reasons for this. Sometimes, despite one's election as king, it was preferable to secure the support of the realm's other grandees before organising a coronation ceremony, which served as a public confirmation of the king's power. However, Helvig's case was different in that her husband had already been crowned on his own. As we have seen with previous women, in those cases, the queen was normally not crowned.

The fact that Helvig was given her own ceremony several years after her wedding suggests that there was a shift in tradition precisely during her reign. In other words, she was probably not initially meant to be crowned, which is why there was such a lengthy delay. Why and how it was decided to organise a coronation specifically for the queen remains unclear. There might be a link between Helvig and her stepmother-in-law, Mechtild, who had been crowned as Queen of Denmark in 1250. Indeed, elsewhere in Scandinavia and Europe, female coronations had become commonplace.[106] The Swedish court was perhaps inspired by such close examples to take up the practice, which arguably served to strengthen the standing of the monarchy. Helvig herself, or her family, might have insisted on it. Regardless of the reasons for it, this ceremony was an important turning point in queenly customs, and all most other medieval queens of Sweden were also formally crowned.

Coronations were important events, as they formally inaugurated a monarch, or their spouse, into their new public role. In medieval Europe, they also had a strong religious element, and emphasised the God-given (and therefore indubitable) nature of the monarch's power.[107] In the context of medieval Sweden, where pre-Christian marital customs (including having concubines and legitimising their children) endured long, having a coronation had an additional layer of symbolism attached to it. It showed that *this* queen was the true queen, the most important queen, in a royal family where one might have become accustomed to having multiple cohabiting royal partners. The circumstances of the union itself are worth commenting on as well. Magnus required a dispensation from the Pope to legitimise his marriage. This was eventually granted in 1288, no less than 12 years after the union was contracted. The dispensation was required because Helvig was related in the fourth degree to Magnus' former betrothed, a noblewoman named Sofia who is known only from this charter. This was within the seven degrees forbidden by the Church's laws against incest but the marriage was confirmed by the Pope on the basis that the spouses had been unaware of the women's link, and that an annulment might have had serious diplomatic consequences.[108] This is an interesting detail, which underlines the political importance of this union, and by extension the importance of forging strong alliances with the German elite.

With Magnus, Helvig had several children, all of whom are well documented and later became powerful actors in European politics. In chronological order, their sons were Erik, who died as an infant; Birger, who became king; another Erik, Duke of Södermanland (for whom "Erikskrönikan" was written), and his brother Valdemar, Duke of Finland. The royal couple also had two daughters. Ingeborg was born around 1277 and became Queen of Denmark in 1296. She will be mentioned again in relation to her brothers and their relationship with the Danish Crown, but she is best studied in a Danish context. Another daughter, Rikissa, was entrusted to Clara Priory in Stockholm as a child. The house had been founded by Magnus himself. She later became its abbess and died there in 1348.[109]

There are few mentions of Helvig in surviving contemporary charters dating from the reign of Magnus who, like his father Birger Jarl, was a powerful and dominant character in Swedish politics. Nevertheless, despite the relative stability of her husband's authority, Helvig's reign also saw some turbulent periods. According to "Erikskrönikan," in the late 1270s, she escaped an attempted kidnapping by seeking refuge in a convent near Skara.[110] However, it is after Magnus' death in 1290 that Helvig appears more regularly in the sources. In 1291, for instance, she was appointed to arrange the funeral procession of a canon of Linköping Cathedral named Stenar.[111] It is possible that she played similar roles behind-the-scenes and organised other events which we do not have surviving evidence for.

In terms of public image, Helvig's seal depicts her kneeling next to the Virgin Mary. Both women wear similar attire, and both are shown wearing a crown in what is a clear comparison being drawn between the two.[112] Her hands are joined in prayer – which is also a symbol of intercession.[113] This type of representation is far from an isolated example in Europe, and the identification of medieval queens with the Virgin Mary both in theory and in material culture has been extensively discussed elsewhere. It is widely acknowledged that because the Virgin Mary was considered the Queen of Heaven (an idea which became particularly popular from the twelfth century onwards), secular queens across Europe were expected to follow her example.[114] Marian traits (humility, gentleness, compassion) were considered highly desirable in women in general. In the case of queens, there was also a clear parallel between Mary's intercessory role between God and people, and a queen's mediation between king and subjects.[115] Naturally, secular queens also relied on this holy association to enhance their public image. Helvig's seal therefore fits in with wider queenly practices, which may also reflect her continental background.

This religious association fits particularly well with Helvig's quiet persona. While not as flamboyant as other women of her time such as the two Duchesses Ingeborg (studied below), Helvig had a steady influence on the political landscape of the realm. She was a foster-mother to her future daughter-in-law Märta who, according to "Erikskrönikan," had arrived at the court of Sweden as a child in anticipation of her marriage to Helvig's son, Birger.[116] The details of this arrangement are not known, but it is difficult not to see it as an experienced queen training a future queen. It was the first time in Sweden that a future bride was brought up in the court that she was due to join to learn its language and customs. Yet, elsewhere in Europe, this was common.[117] Aristocratic girls on the continent were sometimes taken into the care of another high-status family to receive their education.[118] It is unclear whether similar practices were common in Sweden, although the queens studied in this monograph, most of whom came from outside Sweden, were certainly familiar with the concept. In any case, this arrangement in a Swedish context was extraordinary enough to be noted by the writer. Education was still very much the remit of mothers and other maternal figures.

Even in royal circles, where girls often spent time in convents to be educated, the household's mistress was still responsible for the overall trajectory of a girl's education, sometimes through the employment of private tutors. This education included learning domestic skills such as sewing and cooking, reading, writing, and basic maths; but could also include finance and household management.[119]

Helvig may also have been involved in the care of her grandson, Magnus Eriksson, following the death of his father Duke Erik in 1318. The circumstances of Magnus' accession to the throne will be discussed in connection with his mother, Ingeborg Håkonsdatter, who is studied later in this chapter. Helvig's exact position in the regency is unclear, but she appears in documents from that period. This means that Helvig is the first woman in Swedish history to reign as consort and to remain politically active during a relative's reign. It is also worth noting that she lived a very long life, and thus was part of Swedish politics for over more than 50 years – which itself might explain her continued involvement in royal affairs. She never took centre stage as other women of the same era, but remained a constant presence, advising several generations of royal figures. She may have finished her life on her estate in Västmanland, from where her last known charters were issued, and died in 1324.[120] She is now buried in Riddarholm Church in Stockholm.

4.9   Märta Eriksdatter

Märta (known in Danish as Margrete, and in other sources as Margareta and Marita) was the daughter of King Erik V of Denmark and his wife Agnes of Brandenburg. Several basic details about her life are given in late medieval annals including the fourteenth-century "Incerti Scriptoris Sveci Chronicon Rerum Sveo-Gothicarum." Firstly, we know that she was born sometime between 1277 and 1280 as her older brother Christopher's date of birth is firmly given as 1277, while Petrus Olai's chronicle tells us that the union with Birger was already arranged in 1280.[121] The fourteenth-century "Erikskrönikan" claims that upon her engagement, she immediately left Denmark and was raised alongside her future husband at the court of Sweden. In any case, they definitely married in Stockholm in 1298.[122] The festivities which accompanied the event are described in "Erikskrönikan." They involved artists such as jugglers, musicians, jesters, and others commonly associated with medieval fests. An interesting detail is that the king is said to have given his bride's clothes to the jesters who performed at the wedding: an unusual step which perhaps aimed at showcasing the royal couple's generosity. This description provides further evidence that courtly culture was well established by the end of the thirteenth century and early fourteenth century in Sweden.

Furthermore, the chronicle tells us that Märta initially refused to receive a morning gift. This presented her as a humble woman who did not seek to enrich herself. This was a common motif found in many other medieval Christian societies, whereby medieval queens were expected to content themselves with little, to emulate Christian ideals. Queens served as role models for the women of the realm, and humility was one of women's most desirable attributes. This was, however, purely performative, and Märta received a significant morning gift consisting of Fjädrundaland in Uppland, as well as the city of Enköping as her personal property.[123] She was presumably always going to receive those lands, which was not only a custom but also an important geo-political asset for the bride's family who, without a good dower, would probably not agree to the union. Thus, the queen's pretence that she did not require a dower highlights the conflicting relationship between Christian ethos and political reality, and a queen's role in mediating between the two.

Instead of a morning gift, Märta is said to have pleaded for the release of a certain Magnus Algotsson, who had been imprisoned for reasons which remain unclear, but might concern his possible involvement in the abduction of Ingrid Svantepolkesdotter, mentioned previously.[124] From the thirteenth century onwards, it became common across Europe for a queen to start her new office by asking for the release of prisoners. Many contemporary examples are known from Britain and modern-day France in particular. Both male and female prisoners could be released, and the seriousness of their crime varied greatly.[125] Rooted in biblical ideals of female gentleness and mercifulness, this is a prime example of a queen's role as intercessor and peacemaker. It gave her an avenue for decision-making – or at least for influencing it – and could serve an important diplomatic function, effectively reconciling parties and improving the people's relations with the Crown.

As her mother-in-law Helvig before her, Märta was also crowned upon becoming queen. Her coronation took place alongside that of her husband in Söderköping in 1302.[126] This second public coronation certainly cemented the new custom and like that of Helvig, there was a significant delay between Märta's marriage and her coronation. In this case, it has been suggested that this was for political reasons. Indeed, the unstable political circumstances in which Birger was elected king (detailed below) mean that he may not have had the support necessary to officially take up the throne until 1302.[127] Yet, Birger had used his royal titles in charters issued long before the coronation, as he had effectively been lawfully chosen as king independently of the coronation ceremony. Yet, the coronation itself was an important event which performed a function: here, that of *confirming* a king's authority. The coronation was deemed a sufficiently crucial element of his kingship for Birger to delay it by several years. It is less clear from the surviving material whether Märta was known as "queen" for administrative purposes before 1302, but she frequently appears in surviving charters following her coronation.

Märta was known for being politically active, a common trait among royal women of the second half of the thirteenth century. We know for instance that she attended an important meeting between her husband King Birger and her brother King Erik VI of Denmark in 1304, which is evidence that she played a role in politics.[128] It is also likely that her close ties to both men were seen as a good diplomatic tool. Much of what we know of her time as queen comes from "Erikskrönikan," a chronicle written in the fourteenth century by allies of her brother-in-law Duke Erik as a work of propaganda which aimed to tell (and certainly embellish) his story. It shows that she was notably deeply involved in the disputes between her husband Birger and his two younger brothers, the dukes Erik of Södermanland and Valdemar of Finland. Birger worried that they may try to overthrow him. In 1304, he had them relinquish their possessions, after which they fled to Norway. Shortly after, they reconciled and the dukes returned to Sweden, where they agreed to a set of rules aiming at curbing their own power.[129] In the meantime, Erik had also been gifted extensive lands in Halland and Bohuslän, which both belonged to Norway.[130] In 1306, the dukes toppled King Birger. This event, which is known as the Håtuna Games, is related in several sources including "Erikskrönikan" and contemporary charters and chronicles.[131] Birger and Märta organised a party at their estate in Håtuna to which they invited the dukes. The dukes took the opportunity to capture the royal couple and hold them hostage in nearby Nyköping Castle. Their son, Magnus Birgersson, was reportedly saved by a courtier and taken to safety in Denmark.[132]

A full-blown international conflict ensued. The king of Denmark, Erik VI, supported Birger. The king of Norway, Håkon V, supported the dukes. However, following their sealing of a peace treaty with Denmark behind Håkon's back, both kings turned against the dukes, and peace negotiations led to the release of Birger and Märta after two years of captivity.[133] According to "Erikskrönikan," King Håkon of Norway tried to claim some of his gifts back, but Erik of Södermanland refused to return the land, which led to war between the two factions.[134] In 1310, following a short but intense war, peace was agreed upon which Sweden was divided among the three brothers, with Birger and Märta retaining their royal titles.[135] In December 1317, King Birger organised a Christmas feast, known as the Nyköping Banquet after its location, where he invited his two younger brothers. Taking them by surprise, he arrested them, imprisoned them, and allegedly starved them to death. They were certainly both dead within a few months.[136]

"Erikskrönikan" mentions Märta several times in connection with these events. Of course, she was on the wrong side of the story from the author's point of view, and what the chronicle says about her should be considered accordingly, but the text implies that she was one of the masterminds behind this event. It says that she was cheerful during the banquet, knowing the upcoming fate of her guests. The chronicle implicitly depicts her as cruel and calculating, and is a damning depiction of the royal couple.[137] As mentioned previously, the author is clearly biased. It is quite ironic that he fails to offer similar criticism of the dukes, despite them doing much the same against Birger and Märta at the Håtuna Games ten years prior. The *Annales Lubicenses*, compiled c. 1330, are less partial but nevertheless confirm that Märta was actively involved in the event.[138] It is not surprising that the queen should have been aware of what was about to happen. Whether she directly helped plan the scheme is unknown, but it is completely plausible that she should have discussed the plot with her husband. This was, after all, a question of life and death. The violence of the conflict in the preceding years, which had already led to much blood being shed on both sides, made it clear that either the dukes, or the king, could survive. Märta was always going to support her husband, it would have been extremely strange not to. Her own status was at stake as well: if her husband lost his crown, she lost hers.

She eventually did. Despite the dukes' questionable deeds, this double murder provoked outrage, and Märta and her husband were forced to flee first to Gotland, and then to Denmark with their children.[139] Back in Sweden, Duke Erik's son was elected heir with his mother Ingeborg – discussed below – and his grandmother Helvig of Holstein as regents. This means that Märta and Birger effectively ceased to be queen and king in 1318. The same year, in Denmark, Märta's brother King Erik VI granted her a manor in Hjarup on Jylland, which was to provide financially for her. She had staff at her disposal and clearly lived comfortably.[140] Märta evidently never returned to Sweden, and neither did her husband. He died in 1321.[141] Both their sons died around the same time as well. Erik, who had been a deacon at the cathedral in Uppsala, died while in exile in Denmark in 1319.[142] Magnus, who had fled to Denmark already in 1306 following the Håtuna Games, returned to Sweden after the Nyköping Banquet, presumably with the hope of regaining his royal status. However, he was captured as his parents and the rest of his siblings fled to Denmark, and was eventually executed in Stockholm in 1320.[143]

The 1320s were difficult years for Märta. In addition to the loss of her children and husband, she was forced to leave Denmark in 1326 when her brother Christopher II, who had so far guaranteed her protection, was himself forced into exile in Germany.[144] While it is unclear, she might have followed him to Germany and stayed there for a few years. In 1329, she was guaranteed the return of her properties in Denmark, which is probably about when she moved back.[145] Very little is known about her after this. There is evidence that she spent some time towards the end of her life in Denmark at Skovkloster Abbey in Næstved, but the details of her activities there are not known. She died in 1341 and was buried in St. Bendt's Church in Ringsted.[146] Both her daughters survived her, although little is known about them. Agnes was the eldest, and Catherine the youngest. About Catherine, virtually nothing can be said. Lastly, all we know of Agnes is that King Valdemar IV granted lands to Slangerup Abbey to secure her upkeep.[147] It is possible that she spent her whole life as a nun.

4.10   Ingeborg Håkonsdatter (and Ingeborg Eriksdatter)

Ingeborg Håkonsdatter and to a lesser extent her cousin Ingeborg Eriksdatter are the last royal women to be discussed in this book. Both held powerful leadership positions through their respective marriages to two of Sweden's most influential dukes (Erik and Valdemar Magnusson, sons of Magnus Ladulås), but especially so following their deaths. As will be shown shortly, it is in fact Ingeborg Håkonsdatter who held power in Sweden between 1318 and 1322. She was the only known legitimate child of King Håkon V of Norway and Eufemia of Rügen. As such, her family background is well documented, and we know from several medieval Icelandic annals that she was born in 1301, which fits neatly with what "Erikskrönikan" tells us about her age.[148] The question of her betrothal, however, is more complicated due to the turbulent relationship between Duke Erik and King Håkon, notably captured in "Erikskrönikan." Multiple Icelandic annals say that she was betrothed to Erik as soon as September 1302. This is confirmed by a letter from Erik to Håkon from 1306 in which he refers to him as his "father-in-law" (*pater noster*).[149] However, a charter from 1309, which lays out various conditions for peace between Norway, Denmark, and Sweden, states instead that she was then betrothed to Magnus Birgersson, the son and heir of King Birger

Magnusson and Märta. It was subsequently confirmed multiple times as late as July 1310.[150] Eventually, instead of the heir, she married Erik. The wedding took place sometime between 1311 and 1313 in Oslo, when Ingeborg was only about eleven and Erik was in his thirties.[151] During the same occasion, her cousin Ingeborg Eriksdatter married Valdemar (more on this below).

We previously mentioned that Ingeborg was betrothed to Erik just a year after her birth, although over the course of ten years, the engagement was broken off, and reinstated. Considering this troubled context, Erik and Ingeborg's marriage may well have been the most politically sensitive event studied in this book so far. It has recently been suggested that it is in preparation for her daughter's marriage to a Swedish grandee that Queen Eufemia commissioned her famous romances, which notably would explain why they were translated into Old Swedish rather than Old Norwegian. These three texts may have served as tools through which to teach the young Ingeborg the values and principles of courtly life.[152] This corpus of texts may have deeply influenced the young Ingeborg, especially as her mother died already in 1312, just about when her daughter was married away. Upon becoming the wife of Erik, aged only eleven, Ingeborg gained considerable power and influence over vast estates. It also made Erik a possible pretender to the Norwegian throne, in addition to being very close himself to the Swedish Crown. They became a veritable power couple of the Middle Ages. As mentioned previously, this was in fact a double wedding, during which Ingeborg's cousin, Ingeborg Eriksdatter, got married to Erik's brother, Valdemar.[153] Ingeborg Eriksdatter was the daughter of King Erik II of Norway and the Scottish princess Isabel Bruce. Her father and Ingeborg Håkonsdatter's father were brothers. She was born between 1297, the year of her parents' wedding, and 1300, when she was initially betrothed to the earl of Orkney Jan Magnusson in 1300.[154] It is her eventual marriage to Duke Valdemar that launched Ingeborg Eriksdatter in the public eye.

With Erik, Ingeborg Håkonsdatter had two children. The first was Magnus, born in 1316 and named after his Swedish grandfather, who later became King Magnus Eriksson (known notably for establishing the first national law code of Sweden). The second was Eufemia, born in 1317 and named after her Norwegian grandmother, who became Duchess of Mecklenburg and whose son Albert became king in 1364.[155] With Valdemar, Ingeborg Eriksdatter had at least one son, born in 1316, but about whom nothing is known. She may have had more children, as charters from 1344 and 1345 mention inheritance that she received from her children, who therefore must have died before her.[156]

It is the capture of their husbands that sparked the true beginning of the duchesses' political lives. Indeed, as news spread of the Nyköping Banquet (discussed previously in Märta's biography), their supporters rallied behind their wives. The two widows took over the management of their late husbands' assets, which automatically granted them a significant level of authority and agency. Duke Erik, in particular, had been at the head of a considerable fortune and was the second most powerful landowner in Sweden after the king. Both women confirmed arrangements which had been made by their husbands prior to their deaths, which mostly included donations of land to various parties such as the cathedral of Linköping, which was a recurrent beneficiary, as well as to political allies of the late dukes. The women's campaign to free their husbands is evidenced by a letter from 16 April 1318 in which Duke Kristoffer of Halland, the archbishop of Lund, and their allies, promised to help the duchesses. In exchange, a few days later, the duchesses pledged support for the archbishop in anticipation of the release of their husbands.[157] It is worth remembering that by this point, Ingeborg Håkonsdatter was still only about 17. Ingeborg Eriksdatter was barely older. Following the confirmation that their husbands had died, both duchesses then embarked on a prolific partnership as they worked towards a common goal: deposing King Birger.

It did not take long for the king to be ousted by his brothers' supporters. Erik's son, Magnus, was then chosen as heir in the summer 1319.[158] The same year, he had also been elected king of Norway following the death of his grandfather, King Håkon V. This made Ingeborg Håkonsdatter's regent in both kingdoms. This biography focuses on her life in Sweden but it must be understood in the context of her being active over both sides of the border. Many of the problems associated with her regency, detailed shortly, were exacerbated by the relationships that she maintained with Norwegian courtiers, which sometimes led to conflicts of interests. Ingeborg Håkonsdatter did not solely manage her husband's fortunes, but directly acted as the leader of the Swedish realm, and formulated her documents as such. She also personally managed her son's estates, giving and exchanging properties in his name; and supervised monetary affairs. She had full authority over local leaders such as bailiffs, and maintained far-reaching diplomatic relationships with magnates both within and outside Sweden. Some of her decisions were quite radical, such as clearing the citizens of Riga of their debt to her late husband in exchange for annulling Sweden's debt to them.[159] As was common across Europe in cases of royal minorities, many charters were written to read as if the king himself had personally made decisions or approved of them. However, he was then a toddler and there is no doubt that his name and seal were used by his mother and her followers to justify their actions (Figure 4.3).

Without context, Ingeborg's behaviour can seem erratic, but it was the result of external factors. Indeed, all of Ingeborg's decisions and granting of lands benefitted powerful noblemen who had supported Duke Erik during his conflict with his brother King Birger. The names cited alongside hers in surviving charters give us an idea of the type of people with whom she surrounded herself. Knud Porse, whom she eventually married in 1327, was a Danish nobleman whose father had been involved in the murder of King Erik V of Denmark in 1286.[160] He had notably led the troops which had removed Birger from power in 1318, which led him to fleeing to Denmark. He is a recurring signatory of Ingeborg's charters, and clearly influenced her deeply. She is known to have distributed estates to her followers as rewards, as well as exempted some from taxes, which may provide a motive as to their support of the duchess. Ingeborg Eriksdatter engaged in the same practice, although to a lesser extent.[161]

Not all of Ingeborg Håkonsdatter's dealings were benign. In April 1321, the Norwegian regency council complained about the imprisonment of a fellow Norwegian man by foreign youths in Ingeborg's Varberg fief, where she had established her private

FIGURE 4.3   Seal of Ingeborg Håkonsdatter. Original in Hesburgh Library.

court. It is unclear what the incident truly was about, but the letter urges her to listen to experienced advisers rather than foreigners. This suggests that members of Ingeborg's entourage, who may not have been Swedish or Norwegian, acted against the interests of both kingdoms.[162] It is probably not the presence of outsiders which was a problem in itself but rather the influence that they had on Sweden. A similar problem had emerged during the reign of Magnus Ladulås who himself had been known to have foreign favourites.[163] A few months after the Varberg incident, when Ingeborg directly arranged her daughter's wedding to Albert of Mecklenburg in 1321, the marriage came with significant conditions: that his father as well as his allies support her conquest of Skåne. In exchange, she promised assistance against the King of Denmark in hers, her son's, and Norway's name.[164] In 1322, with the support of Knud Porse (but not that of the foreign parties mentioned above, who betrayed her), she launched a military operation in Skåne with the aim of claiming the region for herself. This did not work and caused serious and long-lasting diplomatic problems with Denmark. In retaliation, her fief in Axvalla (Västergötland) was seized in 1323 by members of her own political entourage – more on this below. As part of peace negotiations conducted in 1326, she received the Dåvö estate in modern-day Munktorp, in the same region.[165] This sort of eccentric and rash decision-making, in addition to the reported disturbances in her fiefs, is what led experienced and long-tenured political councillors to start worrying about the duchess's power and manoeuvring to diminish her authority.

Indeed, despite her apparent autonomy, Ingeborg did not operate in a vacuum but was part of two regency councils: one in Sweden, and one in Norway. The lack of sources makes it difficult to ascertain how the Swedish council worked but several of her charters mention the fact that the council had approved the content of the document. The surviving sources give us an idea of what kind of person sat on the council. Mats (or Matthias) Kettilmundsson, a Swedish nobleman, is introduced in one charter from 1319 as *dapifer* and *capitanus*, two titles with no modern equivalent which roughly correspond to a steward and seneschal, respectively. Another charter, from 28 July 1319, which confirms the Church's privileges, names him *hoffmestere* which suggests that he may have been the highest-ranked member of the council.[166] Indeed, Kettilmundsson appears in many charters from the period, dating back long before Duke Erik's death, and was deeply involved in the regency of King Magnus. In the same charter, another councillor, Birger Persson, is introduced as *lagman i Upland*, making him one of the realm's most powerful judges. A series of other names is also listed showing that other councillors were lawmen, such as Knut Jonsson, ecclesiastics, such as the bishop of Linköping, and powerful landowners, although not all these men have left as rich a paper trail as Kettilmundsson.[167] The charter also makes clear the existence of other councillors who are not named at all. These nameless figures may well include some of the problematic foreign men who exerted influence over Ingeborg while operating in the shadows. The Danish knight (*miles*) Knud Porse was certainly associated with the most important men of the realm without being formally part of the council. We know from other charters that the other Duchess Ingeborg was part of the council too, or at least closely associated with it. Queen Helvig also makes some appearances in charters which show that she was associated with her son Duke Erik's business dealings, and that some of her estates (including Dåvö) were passed to Ingeborg Håkonsdatter upon her death. Her exact role within the regency, however, is difficult to describe.[168]

This means that there were certainly checks and locks on Ingeborg Håkonsdatter's power. Following her attack on Skåne, processes were put in place to stop her from repeating such an act. From 1322 onwards, Ingeborg seems to have needed to ask the council to approve her legal acts. When she decided to give land, which had belonged to her husband, to a nun in Gudhem Abbey, she specifically asked the Council to approve the gift and confirm it with the king's seal.[169] A few years prior, she probably would have done so without anyone's approval. As mentioned previously, her castle in Axvalla was attacked, possibly by members of the regency council themselves, in 1323. This is related in several annals, and probably contributed to Ingeborg's decision to relinquish the property, which had high strategic value, in 1326.[170] The document formally enunciating the need to counteract Ingeborg's influence reveals that many of the councillors which had previously served her eventually turned against her. In the charter from 1326, in which the regency council discussed protective measures and reparations against Ingeborg, Knud was formally banned from Sweden, except for his estates which he was free to use.[171] This was a brutal fall from grace for a man who had flirted so closely with power. Yet, he married Ingeborg shortly after, in 1326 or 1327, and thereafter Knud went by the title of Duke of Halland and Samsö.[172] Porse later found favour with the new king of Denmark, while Ingeborg remained involved in Swedish politics. With Porse, she had two more sons: Håkan and Knut, who were both born between 1327 and 1330. In 1330, Porse was murdered, leading to a repeat of Ingeborg's younger years, whereby she again inherited large amounts of land, including properties in Denmark which had belonged to Porse, and which she administered on behalf of her infant sons.[173] She notably kept using the title of Duchess of Halland and Samsö.[174]

Her royal powers were all but curtailed upon the majority of her eldest son Magnus, around 1331, but as a duchess owning vast tracts of land in both Sweden and Denmark, she remained an important political player until her death. The rest of her life is outside the scope of this monograph, but it is worth summarising because of the extraordinary nature of her possessions and influence. In 1332, Skåne was finally secured in the name of King Magnus.[175] We also know, thanks to the late fourteenth-century chronicler Detmar, that she had her own fleet, which she flaunted upon meeting her daughter Eufemia and her husband Albert of Mecklenburg on the occasion of Magnus' coronation in 1336.[176] This was not just a ceremonial fleet either, as she actively took part in a war against the Hanseatic League and some of its allies just a few years later in 1341.[177] In 1350, following the deaths of both sons that she had had with Knud, she permanently received their estates as her personal property. Surviving documents show that she remained economically active, proactively dealing with her estates, and maintaining relationships with ecclesiastical institutions and other political actors of the time until her death in 1361.

Ingeborg had a long-reaching political legacy – albeit a mostly negative one. Her son Magnus Eriksson is most famous for the national law that he implemented around 1350. The law contains a clause which explicitly stipulates that the realm should be steered by Swedes and not foreigners.[178] It is difficult not to see there a reference to his mother's court (and to other known precedents such as Magnus Ladulås' affinity for Germans). Women are also oddly absent from his royal provisions. When they are mentioned, it is only as wives and daughters, never as potential political actors, and an ominous clause also firmly stipulates that the queen must never act against the interests of the kingdom.[179] Again, his mother's shadow lurks behind the wording of the law. Ingeborg's way of conducting business, and her friendships, were thus considered damaging enough for national sovereignty that it had to be officially banned for future generations.

Yet, not everything was negative about her, and Ingeborg's contribution to Swedish history goes beyond her political dealings.

Ingeborg was a leader both in public, and in private. She headed her own personal court in Varberg, no doubt modelled on that of Norway to which her own mother, Eufemia, had herself hugely contributed through the introduction of courtly literature.[180] She was not just an impetuous and rash leader, but a figure well integrated within European courtly culture. Above all, Duchess Ingeborg was the first female leader of Sweden. She never received the title of Queen (although the Pope once mistakenly called her that),[181] but performed the function of a male monarch while transcending her gender's expectations. Her decisions were certainly not always popular, she may have been naïve in some respects, but she was also a young woman entrusted with immense powers at an extremely young age, in a very turbulent political landscape. It is not certain that a more experienced leader would have fared much better. Yet, in light of the long series of powerful women that had preceded her, a woman such as Ingeborg's ascent to power is not very surprising. Indeed, we must note that there is no contemporary evidence that she was belittled for being a woman. There is no trace of her contemporaries complaining about her gender. She was judged solely on the soundness of her decisions. She is an iconic female figure not only of the Middle Ages, but of European history as a whole. Never before had a woman had so much power in Scandinavia.

4.11   Concluding Remarks

This last chapter presented the most prominent royal women of thirteenth and fourteenth-century Sweden. This period witnessed the consolidation of royal power with a new administrative apparatus at its core. It is during this period that some of the most characteristic attributes of queenship were introduced: courtly culture and coronation ceremonies. These two elements cemented the queen's status as a public figure and queenship as a public office of its own. It is likely that these were based on continental models. On one hand, coronation ceremonies – which appeared in Sweden in 1281 – were widespread in continental Europe and had first been held for Danish queens earlier in the thirteenth century. On the other hand, the holding of a court, best exemplified by Ingeborg Håkonsdatter, was clearly based on foreign examples – Ingeborg herself was raised in Norway in what was then a very sophisticated court setting. It is thus important to underline the significant contribution of foreign customs and ideas of queenship in defining the role in a Swedish context.

This study also leads us to the surprising observation that these women's gender was less limiting than what modern scholars might expect. The royal women of this period exerted a significant degree of autonomy both in the political and economic spheres, as witnessed by the charters issued on their behalf. While it is likely that earlier women had also managed their own affairs to an extent, it became common from the thirteenth century onwards for female figures of authority to overtly manage their money, lead their households, and conduct business in a personal capacity. Some queens and regents of this period are also credited with exerting considerable political influence. This is especially true of Queen Märta and Duchess Ingeborg Håkonsdatter, who are both shown in contemporary and later sources to have made political decisions with tangible (and sometimes deadly) consequences. Ingeborg, in particular, effectively reigned independently. Her tenure is thus a fitting end to this catalogue of Swedish royal women, who emerged from relative obscurity to reach remarkable positions of power.

Notes

1 For a thorough literature review and overview of the state of research in this area, see Attila Barany, "Medieval Queens and Queenship: The Present Status of Research in Income and Power," *Annual of Medieval Studies at the CEU* 19 (2013), 149–199.
2 SDHK nr 510; 519.
3 Axel Ahlström, "Klosterrovisorna," *Samlaren* 14 (1933), 26.
4 Johannes Messenius, "Chronologiæ Scondiæ," in *Johannes Messenius. Scondia Illustrata, vol. I–X*, ed. Johan Peringskiöld (Stockholm: Olavi Enaei, 1700–1703), 26.
5 Bror Emil Hildebrand, *Svenska sigiller från medeltiden, vol. 1* (Stockholm: Vitterhetsakademien, 1862), PL. 1, seal 10.
6 Ahlström, "Klosterrovisorna," 26.
7 SDHK nr 653.
8 SDHK nr 680.
9 SDHK nr 798.

10 Karsten Friis-Jensen, ed. and Peter Fisher, trans., Saxo Grammaticus. *Gesta Danorum: The History of the Danes, Volume II* (Oxford: Clarendon Press, 2015), 1041, 1045.
11 Messenius, "Chronologiæ Scondiæ," 26.
12 Messenius, "Chronologiæ Scondiæ," 41. They were married by 1253, as attested by their seals on a charter from that year: SDHK nr 680.
13 Göta Paulsson, ed., "Annales 916–1430," in *Annales Suecici Medi Ævii*, ed. Göta Paulsson (Lund: Gleerup, 1974), 297; "Ex Chronica regni Gothorum," 365.
14 SDHK nr 2515.
15 Agneta Conradi Mattson, *Riseberga Kloster. Birger Brosa och Filipssönerna* (Örebro: Örebro Läns Museum, 1998), 410–413.
16 Caroline Dunn, *Stolen Women in Medieval England: Rape, Abduction, and Adultery, 1100–1500* (Cambridge: Cambridge University Press, 2013), 82–97.
17 Tryggve Lundén, ed., *Sankt Nikolaus av Linköping kanonisationsprocess* (Stockholm: Bonnier, 1963), 153.
18 Dunn, *Stolen Women*, 82–97.
19 This law is called "kvinnofrid." Its dating is unclear, but it is recorded in a statue issues by Birger Jarl's son King Magnus Ladulås from 1279 (SDHK nr 1122).
20 Line, *Kingship and State Formation*.
21 Sten Engström, "Birger Magnusson," in *Svenskt biografiskt lexikon bd. 4*, ed. Bertil Boëthius (Stockholm: Bonnier, 1924), 418.
22 G. E. Klemming, ed., *Olai Petri Svenska Krönika* (Stockholm: H. Klemming, 1860), 59.
23 SDHK nr 1735.
24 Klemming, *Svenska Krönika*, 71.
25 SDHK nr 216 and 268.
26 Ingrid Gustin, *Tornet till Bjälbo Kyrka* (Linköping: Östergötland Länsmuseum, 2006), 5.
27 Gustin, *Tornet till Bjälbo Kyrka*, 8.
28 This is known thanks to a psalter kept at the British Museum. See Gottfrid Carlsson, "En svensk drottnings andaktsbok? Några anteckningar om en medeltidshandskrift i British Museum," *Nordisk tidskrift för bok- och bibliotekshistoria* 41 (1954).
29 Hans Gillingstam, "Folkungaätten," in *Svenskt biografiskt lexicon band 16*, ed. Erik Grill (Stockholm: Kulturdepartementet, 1964–1966), 260.
30 Jakob Langebek, ed., "Chronicon Erici Regis," in *Scriptores rerum danicarum medii ævi tomus I*, ed. Jakob Langebek (Copenhagen: Godiche, 1772), 169.
31 Gustin, *Tornet till Bjälbo Kyrka*, 8.
32 Stephen Mitchell, *Witchcraft and Magic in the Nordic Middle Ages* (Philadelphia: University of Pennsylvania Press, 2011), x.
33 Elizabeth Tucker, "Antecedents of Contemporary Witchcraft in the Middle Ages," in *Popular Culture in the Middle Ages*, ed. Josie P.

Campbell (Bowling Green: Bowling Green State University Press, 1986), 40–45.

34 Messenius, "Chronologiæ Scondiæ," 39.

35 Gustin, *Tornet till Bjälbo Kyrka*, 5.

36 Grant Loomis, *White Magic: An Introduction to the Folklore of Christian Legend* (Cambridge, MA: Mediaeval Academy of America, 1948).

37 Mitchell, *Witchcraft and Magic*, 217.

38 Elin Andersson, ed., *Gråbrödernas diarium: Ett vittnesbörd från senmedeltidens Stockholm* (Stockholm: Kungliga Bibliotek, 2017), 35. Messenius, "Chronologiæ Scondiæ," 39.

39 Ellen Jørgensen, ed., "Annales 67–1287," in *Annales Danici Medii Ævi: Editionem Nouam Curauit*, ed. Ellen Jørgensen (Copenhagen: I Kommission Hos G. E. C. Gad, 1920), 136. Martin Clarentius Gertz, ed., "Tabula Ringstadiensis," in *Scriptores minores historiæ Danicæ medii ævi ex codicibus denuo, vol. II*, ed. Martin Clarentius Gertz (Copenhaghen: I. Kommission hos G. E. C. Gad, 1917), 83.

40 Paulsson, "Annales 1208–1288," 258; "Chronica Visbycensis 815–1444," 315–316; "Annales 826–1415," 381.

41 Anders Magnus Strinnholm, *Svenska folkets historia från äldsta till närwarande tider del 4* (Stockholm: Hörsberg, 1854), 241–242.

42 Jakob Langebek, ed., "Petri Olai Excerpta ex Historicis Danorum a Svenone Tiugskaeg ad Ericum Menved," in *Scriptores rerum Danicarum medii aevi tomus II*, ed. Jakob Langebek (Copenhagen: Godiche, 1773), 256.

43 SDHK nr 1182.

44 Friedrich Wigger, "Stammtafeln des Großherzoglichen Hauses von Meklenburg," *Jahrbücher des Vereins für Mecklenburgische Geschichte und Altertumskunde* 50 (1885), 262–263.

45 Genealogists such as Wilhelm Karl von Isenburg maintained that she was a Swedish princess, but she could be several different women. See Martin Wehrmann, *Genealogie des pommerschen Herzogshauses* (Stettin: Leon Sauniers, 1937), 48–49.

46 SDHK nr 4843 and 4844.

47 This is related in multiple sources. See for instance Jørgensen, "Annales Sorani 1202–1347," in *Annales Danici*, 142. Also, "Annales Nestvedienses 821–1300," 104, and "Annales Ludenses," 105. Also Paulsson, "Ex Chronica regni Gothorum," 359.

48 This can be guessed from various charters including SDHK nr 510; 519; 642; 653.

49 Paulsson, "Annales 1160–1336," in *Annales Suecici Medi Ævii*, 269 and "Annales 1208–1288," 260. Jørgensen, "Ex Annalibus Dano-Suecanis 826–1415," in *Annales Danici Medii Ævii*, 140.

50 SDHK nr 642.

51 Erik Carlquist and Peter Hogg, trans., *The Chronicle of Duke Eric: A Verse Epic from Medieval Sweden* (Lund: Nordic Academic Press, 2011), 34.

52 Carlquist and Hogg, *Chronicle of Duke Eric*, 32–33.

53 This is related in a great many different documents which can all be found in Jørgensen, *Annales Danici* and Paulsson, *Annales Suecici Medi Ævii*.

54 See, for instance, the contributions to Cathleen Sarti, ed., *Women and Economic Power in Premodern Royal Courts* (2020) and Theresa Earenfight, *Women and Wealth in Late Medieval Europe* (2010) which provide many examples across Europe.

55 SDHK nr 642.

56 Andersson, *Gråbrödernas diarium*, 35. Karl Fredrik Wasén, trans., "1252," in *Skänningeannalerna*, http://wadbring.com/historia/sidor/skanninge2.htm.

57 Joakim Carlson, "Sunesdotter – en drottning i det fördolda," *Historiska Museet*, https://rattvishistoria.historiska.se/2017/03/06/katarina-sunesdotter/, accessed 23 April 2024.

58 Carlquist and Hogg, *Chronicle of Duke Eric*, 34.

59 Sharon Farmer, "Persuasive Voices: Clerical Images of Medieval Wives," *Speculum* 61, no. 3 (1986), 534–543.

60 Farmer, "Persuasive Voices," 517–521. For examples of contemporary queenly intercession in the early fourteenth century in England, see Lisa Benz St John, *Three Medieval Queens: Queenship and the Crown in Fourteenth-Century England* (New York: Palgrave Macmillan, 2012).

61 Carlquist and Hogg, *Chronicle of Duke Eric*, 41; 46.

62 Hildebrand, *Medeltida sigiller*, PL. 3, seal 12.

63 Wasén, "1254," in *Skänningeannalerna*.

64 Sofia Gustafsson, "Svenska städer i medeltidens Europa: En komparativ studie av stadsorganisation och politisk kultur" (PhD Diss., Stockholm University, 2009), 21–27.

65 Gustafsson, "Svenska städer," 21–27.

66 SDHK nr 199 and 44456.

67 Gustafsson, "Svenska städer," 24–25; 31–32.

68 Mia Korpiola, "High and Late Medieval Scandinavia: Codified Vernacular Law and Learned Legal Influence," in *Oxford Handbook of European Legal History*, ed. Heikki Pihlajamäki (Oxford: Oxford University Press 2018), 389–390.

69 Elias Wessén, *Om det tyska inflytandet på svenskt språk under medeltiden* (Stockholm: Kungl. Boktryckeriet, 1970).

70 J. M. Lappenberg, ed., "Annales Stadenses," in *Monumenta Germaniae Historica Scriptores vol. XVI*, ed. Georg Heinrich Pertz (Hannover: Impensis Bibliopolii Avlici Hahniani, 1859), 363–373. For a slightly earlier dating, see Jørgensen, "Annales Ripenses," 152.

71 Jakob Langebek, ed., "Processus litis inter Christophorum I et Jacobum Erlandi," in *Scriptores rerum danicarum medii ævi tomus V*, ed. Jakob Langebek (Copenhagen: Godiche, 1783), 610.

72 Jørgensen, "Annales Ryenses," 113.

73 Kai Hørby, *Status Regni Dacie: Studier i Christofferlinjens ægteskabs- og alliancepolitik 1252–1319* (Copenhagen: Den danske historike forening, 1977), 27–28.

74 Jørgensen, "Annales Ripenses," 150; "Annales Ryenses," 89.

75 Hørby, *Status Regni Dacie*, 27–28.

76 Jørgensen, "Annales Ryenses," 89.

77 Jørgensen, "Annales Ripenses," 150; "Annales Ryenses," 89.

78 Lappenberg, "Annales Stadenses," 363–373.

79 Sven Axelson, *Sverige i Utländsk Annalistisk 900–1400* (Stockholm: Appelbergs, 1955), 80.

80 Torbjörn Ahlström, *Skeletten från jarlen Birger Magnussons grav i Varnhems klosterkyrka. Osteologiska resultat och historiska konsekvenser baserade på undersökningen i maj 2002* (Skara: Västergötlands museum, 2002).

81 Jan Svanberg, "Folkungatumban i Varnhems klosterkyrka," *Konsthistorisk tidskrift* 37, no 2 (1968).

82 Jørgensen, "Annales Ryenses," 111.

83 Carlquist and Hogg, *Chronicle of Duke Eric*, 50.

84 Hildebrand, *Medeltida sigiller*, PL. 4, seal 20.

85 Hildebrand, *Medeltida sigiller*, 57. It is not clear whether Abel truly did it or if the rumour was politically motivated. See, Kerstin Hundahl, "Placing Blame and Creating Legitimacy: The Implications of Rügish Involvement in the Struggle over the Succession amidst the Danish Church Strife c.1258–1260," in *Denmark and Europe in the Middle Ages, c.1000–1525. Essays in Honour of Professor Michael H. Gelting*, ed. Kerstin Hundahl, Lars Kjær, Niels Lund (London: Routledge, 2014), 284–285.

86 Hildebrand, *Svenska sigiller*, PL. 4, seal 20.

87 Carlquist and Hogg, *Chronicle of Duke Eric*, 56.

88 Alexander Bugge, ed., "Magnus Haakonssøns saga," in *Norges kongesagaer*, ed. Alexander Bugge (Copenaghen: I. M. Stenersen, 1914), 299.

89 Carlquist and Hogg, *Chronicle of Duke Eric*, 14–15.

90 Carlquist and Hogg, *Chronicle of Duke Eric*, 60; 258.

91 Paulsson, "Annales 916–1430," 297; "Ex Chronica regni Gothorum," 365. Wilhelmina Stålberg and P. G. Berg, *Anteckningar om svenska qvinnor* (Stockholm: P. G. Berg, 1864), 255.

92 Paulsson, "Annales 1208–1288," 261; "Annales 266–1430," 279; "Ex Chronica regni Gothorum," 361.

93 Carlquist and Hogg, *Chronicle of Duke Eric*, 58–60. *Rimkrönikan* gives similar information. See also Langebek, "Chronicon Skibyense Restitut," in *Scriptores II*, 556–557.

94 Arild Huitfeldt, *Danmarckis Rigis Krønicke* (Copenhaghen: Joachim Moltken, 1652), 275.

95 Carlquist and Hogg, *Chronicle of Duke Eric*, 82–83.

96 SDHK nr 1022.

97 SDHK nr 1236.

98 SDHK nr 1274.

99 Martin Clarentius Gertz, ed., "Vetus Chronica Sialandie," in *Scriptores minores historiæ Danicæ medii ævi ex codicibus denuo*, ed.

Martin Clarentius Gertz (Copenhagen: I Kommission hos G. E. C. Gad, 1917), 70.

100 Carlquist and Hogg, *Chronicle of Duke Eric*, 67.

101 SDHK nr 1181.

102 Paulsson, "Annales 31–1463," in *Annales Suecici Medii Aevii*, 336.

103 Paulsson, "Chronica Visbycensis 815–1444," in *Annales Suecici Medii Aevii*, 316.

104 Jørgensen, "Ex Annalibus Dano-Suecanis 826–1415," in *Annales Danici*, 140.

105 Carlquist and Hogg, *Chronicle of Duke Eric*, 67–68.

106 Multiple examples and case studies are given in *Queens and Queenship in Medieval Europe: Proceedings of a Conference Held at King's College London, April 1995*, ed. Anne Duggan (Woodbridge: Boydell Press, 1997).

107 See the contributions to *Coronations Medieval and Early Modern Monarchic Ritual*, ed. János M. Bak (Berkeley: California University Press, 1990) and *Royal Divine Coronation Iconography in the Medieval Euro-Mediterranean Area*, ed. Mirko Vagnoni (MDPI, 2020).

108 SDHK nr 1404.

109 Stålberg and Berg, *Anteckningar*, 316.

110 Carlquist and Hogg, *Chronicle of Duke Eric*, 79.

111 SDHK nr 1512.

112 Hildebrand, *Medeltida sigiller*, PL. 6, seal 36.

113 Parsons, "The Queen's Intercession," 156.

114 Janet L. Nelson, "Medieval Queenship," in *Women in Medieval Western European Culture* (reprint), ed. Linda E. Mitchell (Abingdon: Routledge, 2011), 186.

115 Parsons, "The Queen's Intercession," 159–162. Also Anne Duggan, "Introduction," in *Queens and Queenship in Medieval Europe: Proceedings of a Conference Held at King's College London April 1995*, ed. Anne Duggan (Woodbridge: The Boydell Press, 1997), xvii. Many scholars have also written about representations of queens and Mary in art and iconography. For a material perspective, see Grzegorz Pac, "The Attire of the Virgin Mary and Female Rulers in Iconographical Sources of the Ninth to Eleventh Centuries: Analogues, Interpretations, Misinterpretations," in *Medieval Clothing and Textiles 12*, ed. Robin Netherton and Gale R. Owen-Crocker (Martelsham: Boydell and Brewer, 2016).

116 Carlquist and Hogg, *Chronicle of Duke Eric*, 87.

117 Duggan, "Introduction," xviii.

118 Mary Martin McLaughlin, "Survivors and Surrogates: Children and Parents from the Ninth to Thirteenth Centuries," in *Medieval Families: Perspectives on Marriage, Household, and Children*, ed. Carol Neel (Toronto: University of Toronto Press, 2004), 107.

119 Sandy Bardsley, "Education and Work, Multiple Tasks and Lowly Status," in *A Cultural History of Women in the Middle Ages*, ed. Kim M. Phillips (London: Bloomsbury, 2013), 134–135.

120 Paulsson, "Annales 266–1430," in *Annales Suecici Medii Aevii*, 285.
121 Jakob Langebek, ed., "Petri Olai Minoritae Roskildensis Annales Rerum Danicarum," in *Scriptores rerum danicarum medii ævi vol. 1*, ed. Jakob Langebek (Copenhagen: Godiche, 1772), 188.
122 Among others in Paulsson, *Annales Suecici Medii Aevi*, "Chronica Visbycensis 815–1444," 318; "Annales 266–1430," 282; "Annales 916–1430," 297; "Annales 1298–1473," 302.
123 Klemming, *Olai Petri Svenska Krönikan*, 100.
124 Sven-Bertil Jansson, trans., *Erikskrönikan* (Stockholm: Tiden, 1987), 74–75; 211. Carlquist and Hogg, *Chronicle of Duke Eric*, 98.
125 Gwen Seabourne, *Imprisoning Medieval Women: The Non-Judicial Confinement and Abduction of Women in England, C. 1170–1509* (Abingdon: Routledge, 2016), 184–186.
126 Jakob Langebek, ed., "Incerti Scriptoris Sveci Chronicon Rerum Sveo-Gothicarum," in *Scriptores rerum danicarum medii ævi tomus IV*, ed. Jacob Langebek (Copenhagen: Godiche, 1776), 595.
127 Jansson, *Erikskrönikan*, 213–214.
128 Jørgensen, "Annales Ripenses," 154.
129 SDHK nr 2059.
130 Carlquist and Hogg, *Chronicle of Duke Eric*, 132; 138. *Diplomatarium Norvegicum*, nr 60, https://www.dokpro.uio.no/dipl_norv/diplom_felt.html, accessed 23 April 2024.
131 SDHK nr 41011, 2181, among others. Jørgensen, "Annales Ripenses," 154.
132 Carlquist and Hogg, *Chronicle of Duke Eric*, 145–146. "Annales 1298–1473," 303, and "Annales 916–1430," 298, among others in Paulsson, *Annales Suecici Medii Aevi*.
133 SDHK nr 40726; 2238. Axelson, *Sverige i Utländsk Annalistik*, 126–129.
134 Carlquist and Hogg, *Chronicle of Duke Eric*, 151–180.
135 SDHK nr 2372; 2373; 2375; 2376; 41027; 41032 and others.
136 Jakob Langebek, ed., "Incerti Auctoris Chronicon Danorum ab An. 936 ad An. 1317," in Scriptores *II*, 176.
137 Carlquist and Hogg, *Chronicle of Duke Eric*, 198–199.
138 J. M. Lappenberg, ed., "Annales Lubicenses," in *Monumenta Germaniae Historica Scriptores vol. XVI*, 427.
139 Jørgensen, "Annales Ripenses," 155.
140 Franz Blatt, ed., *Danmarks Riges Breve 1318–1322* (Copenhagen: Det Danske Sprog- og Litteraturselskab, 1953), 38; 315–316.
141 Jørgensen, "Annales Ripenses," 155.
142 Jerker Rosén, "Erik Birgersson d. y.," in *Svenskt Biografiskt Lexicon band 13*, ed. Bengt Hildebrand (Stockkholm: Bonnier, 1953), 313.
143 Among others in *Annales Suecici Medii Aevi* edited by Paulsson, "Annales 1208–1434," 349; "Chronica Visbycensis 815–1444," 319; "Annales 31–1463," 336.
144 Jørgensen, "Chronica Sialandie," 170–171.

145 Franz Blatt, ed., *Danmarks Riges Breve 1328–1332* (Copenhagen: Det Danske Sprog- og Litteratureselskab, 1948), 155.
146 Jakob Langebek, ed., "Calendarium Nestvediense," in *Scriptores IV*, 297; 312.
147 Franz Blatt, ed., *Danmarks Riges Breve, 1344–1347* (Copenhagen: Det Danske Sprog- og Litteraturselskab, 1959), 9–10.
148 Erich Christian Werlauff, ed., *Íslenzkir Annálar sive Annales Islandici ab anno Christi 803 ad annum 1430 (Annales Islandici)* (Copenhagen: Sumptibus Legati Arnæ-Magnæni, 1847), 181. Gustav Storm, ed., "Flatøannalerna," in *Islandske Annaler indtil 1578*, ed. Gustav Storm (Copenhagen: Grøndal, 1888), 388. In the same edition, "Annales Vetustissimi," 52; "Annales Regi," 146, and several others.
149 See the references above. Axelson, *Sverige i Utländsk Annalistik*, 124–125. Diplomatarium Norvegicum nr 37.
150 SDHK nr 2293; 2351 and 2373. Werlauff, *Annales Islandici*, 181.
151 Werlauff, *Annales Islandici*, 201. Axelson, *Sverige i Utländsk Annalistik*, 136–137.
152 William Layher, *Queenship and Voice in Medieval Northern Europe* (New York: Palgrave-Macmillan, 2010), 91–115.
153 Werlauff, *Annales Islandici*, 201.
154 Storm, "Annales Vestutissimi," 52; "Flatøannalerna," 387, and others.
155 Sven Tunberg, "Albrekt," in *Svenskt Biografiskt Lexicon, bd 1*, ed. Bertil Boëthius (Stockholm: Bonnier, 1918), 368.
156 Storm, "Flatøannalerna," 393. SDHK nr 4966; 5202.
157 SDHK nr 2868 and 2867.
158 SDHK nr 2931.
159 See for instance SDHK nr 3074, 3028, and many others.
160 Jørgensen, "Ex Annalibus Dano-Suecanis 826–1415," 141.
161 There are many surviving charters concerning property dealings. For examples of the duchesses' gifts to political allies, see SDHK nr 3078, 3057, and 2892. For a case of tax exemption, see SDHK nr 2901.
162 SDHK nr 3085.
163 Carlquist and Hogg, *Chronicle of Duke Eric*, 74–78.
164 SDHK nr 40687 and 40688.
165 SDHK nr 3389.
166 SDHK nr 2928 and 2937.
167 SDHK nr 2937.
168 SDHK nr 3389.
169 SDHK nr 3156.
170 Paulsson, "Annales 266–1430," 284. SDHK nr 3390.
171 SDHK 3389.
172 Jørgensen, "Chronica Sialandie," 171–172. Axelson, *Sverige i Utlandsk Annalistisk*, 180.
173 Axelson, *Sverige i Utlandsk Annalistisk*, 180.
174 SDHK nr 3834.

175 SDHK nr 3893.
176 Ferdinand Heinrich Grautoff, ed., *Detmar von Lübeck: Chronik des Franciscaner Lesemeisters Detmar vol. 1* (Hamburg: Perthes, 1829), 239–240.
177 SDHK nr 4725.
178 Åke Holmbäck and Elias Wessén, trans, *Magnus Erikssons Landslag i Nusvensk Tolkning* (Lund: Institutet för Rättshistorisk Forskning, 1962), 5.
179 Holmbäck and Wessén, *Magnus Erikssons Landslag*, 9.
180 David Brégaint, *Vox Regis: Royal Communication in High Medieval Norway* (Leiden: Brill, 2015), 225–226.
181 SDHK nr 7254.

5

CONCLUSION

In conclusion, queenship, both in its definition and its performance, changed dramatically between the late Viking Age and the fourteenth century in Sweden. As time progressed, and important changes such as Christianisation took place, the position became better defined and increasingly documented. We have seen that little is known about the earliest recorded queens, which has sometimes led to their lives being rewritten and reinterpreted by later historians for various purposes. One can nevertheless discern some basic characteristics of queenship during this time. While there does not seem to have been as rigid a set of expectations surrounding Viking Age royal women as there would be for their successors, their role as political and cultural intercessors can be seen in the diplomatic functions that they had: as peacemakers and hostesses. This is illustrated by the importance that women held in the custom of feasting, and the relative power they could exert over the household. However, concubinage remained the norm well into the eleventh century, leading to a somewhat blurred distinction between formal and informal royal partners. "Queens" of that period often were in fact the victims of kidnappings who had been brought over to Scandinavia after a successful raid, usually in the eastern Baltic region. There may have been almost no difference in the treatment of an official wife, who had been lawfully wed, and a concubine. The royal women of tenth- and eleventh-century Sweden were therefore far remote from later queens whose coming to power, role, and legacy were more strictly defined and channelled. Nevertheless, these early

DOI: 10.4324/9781003392200-5

examples are no less interesting. They illustrate the geo-political dynamics of the time. Indeed, most royal wives of that period came from Slavic lands, with which Scandinavian rulers had long had exchanges, and sought to form alliances. Their foreignness was an asset, not only politically but possibly religiously too, as sacral kingship sought to distance itself from the people it governed, notably by forging ties with far-away dynasties. These early queens also highlight vastly different cultural norms and attitudes towards inheritance and succession, and how pre-Christian ideas impacted women's lives. This is best illustrated by Sigrid Storråda who has become an iconic literary character known for her fierceness and free-spirited behaviour, which is completely at odds with later Christian ideals. While her biography is contested, she may be representative of the more liberal attitudes towards women which were prevalent during the Viking Age.

The spread of Christianity undoubtedly played an important role in redefining women's social roles, and it is during the long twelfth century that the office of "queen" as it is most often understood today began to flourish in Sweden, as it did elsewhere in Latin Christendom. This period represents the peak of monasticism in Europe, and much of a queen's working life revolved around maintaining good relations with monastic institutions. It is during this century that many of Sweden's great monastic houses were founded, often with the help of a queen and sometimes explicitly at her request, such as in the case of Queen Ulvhild and Alvastra. This represents an important shift from Viking Age queens whose main political role was still fully dependent on that of their husband, even after his death. With the spread of ecclesiastical institutions, women now had external actors with which to engage independently of their domestic status.

The twelfth century is the most difficult period of Sweden's medieval history, not least because so many kings replaced each other in quick succession. It is nearly impossible to keep track of who was king, where, and when, and who they married. The lack of contemporary sources and the relative unreliability of later documents do not help either. However, it seems that royal women were considerably quieter during this period than during the late Viking Age. While present in the sources, they often serve as exemplars of Christian ideals – which emphasised the inferiority of woman to man – and are shown as benefactors of the Church. Few are credited with having any political influence, and there is little evidence that this was expected of them. Indeed, it is also during the twelfth century that the Church refined its position on gender roles, not only in Sweden but elsewhere in Europe too. Women were now expected to be chaste, humble, obedient, and pious, much like the Virgin Mary. Physical beauty was thought to represent these qualities. Kings were expected to be generous, merciful, and monogamous. Clerical celibacy was introduced, while the definition of incest was extended up to seven degrees. These changes all had profound effects on the institution of marriage which became strictly regulated and led to a streamlining of succession, with fewer pretenders to the throne and fewer potential partners for them. It is during this period that the nuclear family took on its sacred character as a social, economic, and symbolic unit, with women's role within that unit firmly defined.

There was a clear shift sometime around the beginning of the thirteenth century, when royal women suddenly (or seemingly) became a lot more public. They appear more regularly in charters. They witnessed the writing of them and affixed their own seal. Some, like Ingrid Ylva, amassed considerable personal prestige and economic power, to the point of eclipsing their husbands. From the middle of the century onwards, queens had actual political power as well, and not only mere "influence." There is evidence that they stood behind some decisions, or at the very least that they worked together with their husbands. This all culminated with the advent, in the early fourteenth century, of women whose powers approximated those of a king. The main question to derive from these observations is simply, why? What happened to explain this extraordinary, and very quick change in the condition of Swedish royal women? No single answer can be given with certainty at this stage, and further research into the background of thirteenth-century politics may help elucidate the matter. Nevertheless, some possibilities can be put forward.

We have seen throughout this monograph that Swedish noble-men relied on foreign women of royal pedigree to legitimise their power. Up until 1280, when Magnus Ladulås created an armed aristocracy, Sweden's elites derived their status mainly from landownership and from immemorial prestige rooted in the kingdom's past as a warrior society. The local chiefs dwelling in modern-day Svealand (and mainly Uppland) derived their power from their belonging to the warrior class, a pre-Christian system which emphasised one's ability to fight as the basis of one's social standing. We know that the people of Uppland struggled with the shift from a pagan, warrior society to that of a Christian, bureau-cratic kingdom with new social classes, new mentalities, and a new administrative elite with the power to overrule traditional prerogatives. In Götaland, which was closer to the continent and an early adopter of Christianity, elites mostly based their power on their economic status, normally achieved through landown-ership. Many of the kingdom's earliest recorded kings were not warriors as found in France or England, but land administrators who ruled over vast family estates in southern Sweden. That is to say that these men, although wealthy and influential at local level, had little credibility in the eyes of the military aristocracies of their better-connected neighbouring countries. Marrying women of royal or noble descent from foreign kingdoms, where the mon-archy and aristocracy were better established and recognised, was thus an easy way to legitimise one's line.

As a result, most of the queens discussed in this book came from countries with much more developed royal families, and more intricate aristocratic networks. Nevertheless, Swedish king-ship remained fragile throughout the entire period studied. It was not as elusive a concept in the thirteenth and fourteenth centuries as it had been in previous times, but Valdemar's fall from grace, and Birger's delayed coronation are nevertheless evidence that a king's authority still relied enormously on several other factors, such as the approval of his brothers. In this context, could it be that their queens were in fact more powerful precisely because of their family heritage, and because their husbands were weak? Sofia was the daughter of a Danish king and his politically active Saxon wife, Jutta. Helvig of Holstein was the daughter of the count of Holstein, who was one of the most powerful men in Europe. Märta was the daughter of the king of Denmark, and the granddaughter of his regent, Margaret Sambiria, herself from Pomerania, and a competent female ruler. Ingeborg was the daughter of the illustrious Håkon V of Norway, who strengthened kingship in Norway, and the German-born Queen Eufemia, a famous patron of courtly literature. The Swedish kings' pedigrees paled in contrast. None had received as good a political education as the women they married. They also could not take the risk of angering their in-laws, whose political support they needed. This suggests that the royal women of this period may have had a lot more freedom to play politics alongside their husbands because they had experience of doing so from their upbringing in prestigious environments, and because they personally had the authority to impose themselves as political actors.

From the second half of the twelfth century onwards, noble Swedish girls were often sent to monastic houses to receive an education. Vreta was a common choice for royal girls. What exactly they were taught is less clear, although female education in general typically included domestic skills such as sewing and cooking, and religious and moral education. They sometimes also learn to read and write, as well as the basics of household management, especially when homeschooled. This education usually ended when they reached teenagehood, around which time they normally got married. Thirteenth-century women were in fact the first generation of women to have received an education on par with that traditionally afforded to the boys. Their education did not stop at the monastery, however, and they kept receiving support from their birth families. Ingeborg Håkonsdatter, for example, still benefitted from the schooling of her late mother Queen Eufemia through her publications of courtly literature. In this context, the women of the late thirteenth and fourteenth centuries were given all the tools to compete on the same stage as the men, which they decidedly did.

In conclusion, is it possible to define queenship during the period studied? This depends on how strict a definition is required, but some characteristics of queenship can be found as much in the Viking Age as in the fourteenth century. Firstly, legitimacy was always of the utmost importance, starting with the king's perceived authority when claiming power. It remains unclear what made a union "lawful" in the tenth and early eleventh centuries, but it seems to have been a major criterion for a woman to be recognised as an official royal partner, and for her children to be considered more attractive matches than those of concubines. From the turn of the twelfth century onwards, a canonically valid marriage was required. Furthermore, while not strictly needed to become queen, coronations became the norm from the late thirteenth century onwards. There is thus clear continuity in the requirement for a queen to be a lawful partner of the king, and to be perceived as such by the people who were subjected to her. Royal widows from all periods also seem to have retained their prestige after the death of their husbands. While some retreated from political life, others remained economically and politically active, and sometimes remarried as well. This is best evidenced by Mechtild of Holstein's effigy which represents her crowned despite dying as a noblewoman, rather than as a queen.

While not a strict requirement for queenship, Sweden's political circumstances during the period studied meant that having a foreign queen was a particularly welcome development. Unlike in some other areas of Europe where foreign women were treated with suspicion or even rejected for not belonging to their new environment, the foreign origins of Sweden's queens do not seem to have ever been problematic. It is what these queens did with their foreign links which mattered. A consequence of this constant influx of foreign women into the highest levels of Swedish society may have been a greater openness to continental ideas, and their adoption. There is no doubt that the introduction of coronations for queens, for instance, was inspired by European examples. This opens up new research questions, which cannot be answered here, about the extent to which the Swedish monarchy was influenced and shaped by foreign customs.

Despite the popular view, before the wide adoption of the Church's views on marriage and family, producing an heir was not always important for a queen to be legitimate. Viking Age customs allowed for children born of concubines to inherit – even if they were not necessarily the preferred candidates to do so – and the option to form new political alliances through multiple late-in-life marriages led some queens into childless unions without it diminishing their legitimacy. Nonetheless, if giving birth was not always required, legal submission to male power was another constant feature of medieval queenship. Despite often being the origin of a family's prestige through their systematic royal heritage, none of the queens covered in this collection directly inherited the throne in her own name, and none was able to make executive decisions concerning foreign affairs without the approval of a male council or male advisors. In spite of the popularity of the concept of "female king," it does not apply in a Swedish context, as none of the women studied, including the very powerful Ingeborg Håkonsdatter, truly ever exerted the sort of unbridled power associated with kings.

In sum, I propose the following definition for a queen in Sweden between the late Viking Age and the early fourteenth century: a woman lawfully married or otherwise joined in a formal union to a king himself recognised by at least part of the population. She may or may not use titles normally associated with royalty, although she may be referred to in literature with such titles. She may or may not actively impact on politics (both foreign and domestic) and may or may not own land either in her name or in her capacity as royal partner. However, she consistently performs functions commensurate with the expectations of her time, which can include religious duties, diplomatic intercession, and procreation. Crucially, she is the maternal head of the royal household and is recognised by outsiders and later generations as part of a royal line of succession.

Even though this study only superficially presented Sweden's medieval queens, some patterns and motifs already emerged. It is notably clear that queenship developed in Sweden along much the same lines as elsewhere in Europe. In many cases, this development was slower – not least because Sweden was Christianised significantly later than most of Europe – which means that Swedish queens reached the peak of their power precisely as their European counterparts' influence was starting to wane. Notwithstanding the shift in chronology, nothing about the women introduced in this book will have shocked scholars of medieval

European queenship. Royal women were important communicators and intercessors, serving as link between the king, the Church, and people. During all periods studied, they were closely associated with religious activities, especially in the twelfth century, which was a time of rapid ecclesiastical growth everywhere in Europe. Royal women also had personal economic agency and could be influential business leaders. It is therefore unwise not to give as much weight to the study of queens as to that of kings in medieval Sweden, because many of these women were evidently important political actors. The last few women studied in this monograph clearly carried the kingdom on their shoulders, sometimes for years in the absence of a male king.

We must nonetheless also acknowledge the difficulties encountered throughout this study. It has been exceedingly hard to find precise information about queens, who are often not named in the charters. When documents do exist, they often are filed under other categories but the woman's identity, as queens have normally been seen, both by medieval writers and modern historians, as extensions of their husbands, and indeed as accessories to their reign. In some cases, this was true, and it was not the goal of the present monograph to exaggerate the historical importance of some women who may not have had much influence in their own time. Nevertheless, some kings also had very little influence and yet we know about them. There is therefore a need for the whole field to reevaluate our approach to studying women in Sweden and to find ways of concretely facilitating research into them by reorganising our collections and understanding of archival practices.

Much remains to be studied which was only superficially covered – if at all – in this book. While it has focused on the biographical background of these medieval queens and has mostly presented the salient aspects of their lives, it is possible to study them at a much deeper level, even considering the scarcity of sources. Two subjects deserve urgent attention. A few surviving seals have been mentioned. These are hugely interesting. Different seals could be used for different occasions and allow us to get an understanding of how queens wanted to present themselves in various circumstances. Elsewhere in Europe, women's seals, which are naturally quite rare compared to men's seals, have been studied by scholars such as Brigitte Bedos-Rezak.[1] The British Library has also recently digitised over a hundred women's seals from its collections. Nearly nothing has been done in a Swedish context, however, which leaves room for further research. Much more can also be said about the political and economic significance of the morning gifts which deserve a separate study. These were not just symbolic gestures but important land transactions which could have long-term consequences for the political and economic power, not just of the recipient, but of her entire lineage for generations to come. The limited scope of this book has made it impossible to map these morning gifts in Sweden, but they do need to be investigated, as they have been elsewhere notably by the "Examining the Resources and Revenues of Royal Women in Premodern Europe" project.[2] It is hoped that this brief overview of Sweden's medieval queens will inspire other researchers to dig deeper into what is a fascinating, rich, and enlightening subject, which will no doubt improve our understanding of society and politics in northern Europe during the Middle Ages.

Notes

1 Among Brigitte Bedos-Rezak's many publications on seals, see "Women, Seals and Power in Medieval France, 1150–1350," in *Women and Power in the Middle Ages*, ed. Mary Carpenter Erler and Maryanne Kowaleski (Athens: University of Georgia Press, 1988), 61–82; and "Medieval Women in French Sigillographic Sources," *Medieval Women and the Sources of Medieval History*, ed. Joel T. Rosenthal (Athens: University of Georgia Press, 1990), 1–36.
2 Resources and Revenues of Royal Women project, "Examining the Resources & Revenues of Royal Women in Premodern Europe: An International Research Project Investigating the Economic Agency and Activities of Royal Women in Premodern Europe," https://www. queensresources.org/, accessed 23 April 2024.

BIBLIOGRAPHY

Primary Sources

Adam of Bremen. *The History of the Archbishops of Hamburg-Bremen.* Translated by Francis Tschan. New York: Columbia University, 1959.

Adam of Bremen. *Adami Gesta Hammaburgensis ecclesiae pontificum ex recensione Lappenbergii.* Edited by Georg Waitz. Hannover: Impensis Bibliopolii Hahniani, 1876.

Aili, Hans, Olle Ferm, and Helmer Gustavson, eds., *Röster från svensk medeltid: Latinska Texter i Original och Översättning.* Stockholm: Natur och Kultur, 1990.

Andersson, Elin, ed., *Gråbrödernas diarium: Ett vittnesbörd från senmedeltidens Stockholm.* Stockholm: Kungliga Bibliotek, 2017.

Axelson, Sven, ed., *Sverige i Utländsk Annalistik 900–1400.* Stockholm: Appelbergs, 1955.

Bjarni Aðalbjarnarson, ed., *Snorri Sturluson. Heimskringla vol. 2.* Reykjavik: Hið Íslenzk Fornritafélag, 1945.

Brask, Hans. *Biskop Hans Brasks registratur.* Edited by Hedda Gunneng. Uppsala: Svenska fornskriftsällsk, 2003.

Brate, Erik, ed., *Sveriges Runinskrifter III. Runinskrifter från 1000-talet.* Stockholm: Natur och Kultur, 1922.

Bugge, Alexander, ed., "Magnus Haakonssøns saga." In *Norges kongesagaer,* edited by Alexander Bugge, 296–305. Copenhagen: I. M. Stenersen, 1914.

Campbell, Alistair, ed. and trans., *Encomium Emmae Reginae.* London: Royal Historical Society, 1949.

Carlquist, Erik, and Peter Hogg, trans., *The Chronicle of Duke Eric: A Verse Epic from Medieval Sweden.* Lund: Nordic Academic Press, 2011.

Dahlberg, Erik. *Suecia Antiqua et Hodierna vol. III.* Stockholm: 1726.

de Gray Birch, Walter, ed., *Liber Vitae: Register and Martyrology of New Minster and Hyde Abbey, Winchester.* London: Simkin & Co. 1892.

Detmar of Lübeck. *Chronik des Franciscaner Lesemeisters Detmar vol. 1*. Edited by Ferdinand Heinrich Grautoff. Hamburg: Perthes, 1829.

Finlay, Alison, trans., *Fagrskinna: A Catalogue of the Kings of Norway: A Translation with Introduction and Notes*. Leiden: Brill, 2003.

Gertz, Martin Clarentius, ed., *Scriptores minores historiæ Danicæ medii ævi ex codicibus denuo*. Copenhagen: I Kommission hos G. E. C. Gad, 1917.

Griesser, Bruno, ed., *Exordium Magnum Cisterciense, sive, Narratio de Initio Cisterciensis Ordinis*. Rome: Editiones Cistercienses, 1961.

Grønlie, Siân, ed., *The Book of the Icelanders — The Story of the Conversion*. London: Viking Society for Northern Research, 2006.

Hazzard Cross, Samuel, and Olgerg Sherbowitz-Wetzor, eds. and trans., *The Russian Primary Chronicle: Laurentian Text*. Cambridge, MA: The Medieval Academy of America, 1953.

Hermann Pálsson and Paul Edwards, trans., *Knýtlinga saga: The History of the Kings of Denmark*. Odense: Odense University Press, 1986.

Hermann Pálsson and Paul Edwards, trans., *Orkneyinga saga: The History of the Earls of Orkney*. London: Penguin Books, 1978.

Hildebrand, Bror Emil. *Svenska sigiller från medeltiden, vol. 1*. Stockholm: Vitterhetsakademien, 1862.

Hollis, Stephanie, ed., *Writing the Wilton Women: Goscelin's Legend of Edith and Liber Confortatorius*. Turnhout: Brepols, 2004.

Holmbäck, Åke and Elias Wessén, trans, *Magnus Erikssons Landslag I Nusvensk Tolkning*. Lund: Institutet för Rättshistorisk Forskning, 1962.

Huitfeldt, Arild. *Danmarckis Rigis Krønicke*. Copenhagen: Joachim Moltken, 1652.

Ibn Fadlan. *Ibn Fadlan's Journey to Russia: A Tenth-Century Traveler from Baghdad to the Volga River*. Translated by Richard Frye. Princeton: Marjus Wiener Publishers, 2005.

Jansson, Sven-Bertil, trans., *Erikskrönikan*. Stockholm: Tiden, 1987.

Jordanes. *Romana and Getica*. Translated by Peter Van Nuffelen and Lieve Van Hoof. Liverpool: Liverpool University Press, 2020.

Jordanes. *Romana et Getica*. Edited by Theodor Mommsen. Berlin: Weidmann, 1882.

Jørgensen, Ellen, ed., *Annales Danici Medii Ævi: Editionem Nouam Curauit*. Copenhagen: I Kommission Hos G. E. C. Gad, 1920.

Karl Jónsson. *Konung Sverre Sigurðssons saga efter Flatöboken* ("Sverris saga"). Translated by Hermann Vendell. Helsinki: Xylografiska atelierns tryckpräss, 1885.

Klemming, Gustaf Edvard, ed., *Småstycken på Forn Svenska*. Stockholm: Kungl. Boktryckeriet, 1881.

Klemming, Gustaf Edvard, ed., *Svenska Medeltidens Rimkrönikor*. Stockholm: Norstedt & Söner, 1865.

Kroman, Erik, ed., *Corpus codicum Danicorum medii aevi vol. I: Necrologium Lundense*. Copenhagen: Ejnar Munksgaard, 1960.

Kunin, Devra, trans., and Carl Phelpstead, ed., *A History of Norway and the Passion and Miracles of the Blessed Óláfr.* London: Viking Society for Northern Research, 2001.

Langebek, Jakob, ed., *Scriptores rerum danicarum medii ævi tomus V.* Copenhagen: Godiche, 1783.

Langebek, Jakob, ed., *Scriptores rerum danicarum medii ævi tomus IV.* Copenhagen: Godiche, 1776.

Langebek, Jakob, ed., *Scriptores rerum Danicarum medii aevi tomus II.* Copenhagen: Godiche, 1773.

Langebek, Jakob, ed., *Scriptores rerum danicarum medii ævi tomus I.* Copenhagen: Godiche, 1772.

Lindkvist, Thomas, ed. and trans., *The Västgöta Laws.* Abingdon: Routledge, 2021.

Lundén, Tryggve, ed., *Sankt Nikolaus av Linköping kanonisationsprocess.* Stockholm: Bonnier, 1963.

Magnus, Johannes. *Göternas och svearnas historia.* Translated by Kurt Johannesson and edited by Hans Helander. Stockholm: Michaelisgillet and Kungl. Vitterhets Historie och Antikvitets Akademien, 2018.

Messenius, Johannes. *Scondia Illustrata, vol. I–X.* Edited by Johan Peringskiöld. Stockholm: Olavi Enæi, 1700–1703.

Nilsson Nylander, Eva, ed., *Mellan Evighet och Vardag. Lunds domkyrkas martyrologium Liber daticus vestustior: Studier och faksimilutgava.* Lund: Universitetsbiblioteket, 2015.

Oddr Snorasson, "Yngvar's saga." In *Vikings in Russia: Yngvar's Saga and Eymund's Saga.* Edited and translated by Hermann Pálsson and Paul Edwards, 44–69. Edinburgh: Edinburgh University Press, 1989.

Paulsson, Göta, ed., *Annales Suecici Medi Ævii.* Lund: Gleerup, 1974.

Peel, Christine, ed. and trans. *Guta Lag and Guta Saga: The Law and History of the Gotlanders.* Abingdon: Routledge, 2015.

Pertz, Georg Heinrich, ed., *Monumenta Germaniae Historica Scriptores vol. XVI.* Hannover: Impensis Bibliopolii Avlici Hahniani, 1859.

Peringskiöld, Johan. *Monumenta Sveo-Gothicum.* Stockholm: Olavi Enæi, 1710.

Petri, Olaus. *Svenska Krönika.* Edited by G. E. Klemming. Stockholm: H. Klemming, 1860.

Ptolemy. *Geography.* Edited by Bill Thayer. https://penelope.uchicago.edu/Thayer/E/Gazetteer/Periods/Roman/_Texts/Ptolemy/home.html#Text. Accessed 14 January 2024.

Rasmus Ludvigsson. "Brevis historica narration." Edited by Nils Ahlund in "Vreta Klosters Äldsta Donatorer." *Historisk Tidskrift* 65 (1945), 301–351.

Rimbert. *Anskar, the Apostle of the North, 801–865.* Translated by Charles H. Robinson. Toronto: Toronto University Press, 1921.

Snorri Sturluson. *Heimskringla Volume III. Magnús Óláfsson to Magnús Erlingsson.* Translated by Alison Finlay and Anthony Faulkes. London: Viking Society for Northern Research, 2015.

Snorri Sturluson. *Heimskringla Volume II. Óláfr Haraldsson (The Saint).* Translated by Alison Finlay and Anthony Faulkes. London: Viking Society for Northern Research, 2014.

Snorri Sturluson. *Heimskringla Volume I. The Beginnings to Óláfr Tryggvason.* Translated by Alison Finlay and Anthony Faulkes. London: Viking Society for Northern Research, 2011.

Storm, Gustav, ed., *Islandske Annaler indtil 1578.* Copenhagen: Grøndal, 1888.

Tacitus. *The Agricola and the Germania.* Edited by James Rives and translated by Harold Mattingly. London: Penguin Classics, 2010.

Tacitus. *Germania.* Edited by J. G. C. Anderson. Bristol: Bristol Classical Press, 1998.

Thietmar of Merseburg. *Ottonian Germany. The Chronicon of Thietmar of Merseburg.* Translated by David Warner. Manchester: Manchester University Press, 2001.

Thietmar of Merseburg. *Die Chronik des Bischofs Thietmar von Merseburg und ihre Korveier Überarbeitung.* Edited by Robert Holtzmann. Berlin: Weidmann, 1935.

Tolkien, Christopher, ed. and trans., *Saga of King Heidrik.* London: Thomas Nelson & Sons, 1960.

Wasén, Karl Fredrik, trans., *Skänningeannalerna.* http://wadbring.com/historia/sidor/skanninge2.htm. Accessed 13 January 2024.

Webbe Dasent, George, trans., "The Saga of Hacon, Hacon's Son." In: *Icelandic Sagas and Other Historical Documents Relating to the Settlements and Descents of the Northmen of the British Isles, vol. 4,* edited by George Webbe Dasent, 1–373. Cambridge: Cambridge University Press, 2012.

Werlauff, Erich Christian, ed., *Íslenzkir Annálar sive Annales Islandici ab anno Christi 803 ad annum 1430 (Annales Islandici).* Copenhagen: Sumptibus Legati Arnæ-Magnæni, 1847.

Wolter, Heinrich. "Chronica Bremensis." In: *Rerum Germanicarum tomi II. Scriptores Germanicos,* edited by Heinrich Meibom, 19–82. Rome: Collegio Romano, 1688.

Secondary Sources

Ahlström, Axel. "Klosterrovisorna." *Samlaren* 14 (1933), 25–54.

Ahlström, Torbjörn. *Skeletten från jarlen Birger Magnussons grav i Varnhems klosterkyrka. Osteologiska resultat och historiska konsekvenser baserade på undersökningen i maj 2002.* Skara: Västergötlands museum, 2002.

Ahnlund, Nils. "Vreta Klosters Äldsta Donatorer." *Historisk Tidskrift* 65 (1945), 301–351.

Alm, Henrik. *Drottning Ragnhild och hennes gravskrift i Tälje.* Sträng-näs: Tidnings Tryckeri, 1931.

Andersson, Catharina. "Cistercian Monasteries in Medieval Sweden. Foundations and Recruitments, 1143–1420." *Religions* 12, no. 8: 582 (2021), 1–18.

Arnold, John. *What Is Medieval History?* Hoboken: Wiley, 2008.

Auður Magnúsdóttir. "Friends, Foes, and Followers. Power, Networks, and Intimacy in Medieval Iceland." In: *Nordic Elites in Transformation, c. 1050–1250, Volume II. Social Networks*, edited by Kim Esmark, Lars Hermanson, and Hans-Jacob Orning, 1–22. Abingdon: Routledge, 2020.

Auður Magnúsdóttir. "Frillor och fruar: politik och samlevnad på Island 1120–1400." PhD Diss., Gothenburg University, 2001.

Axel Kristinsson. *Expansions: Competition and Conquest in Europe since the Bronze Age.* Reykjavik: Reykjavíkur Akademían, 2010.

Bagge, Sverre. *From Gang Leader to the Lord's Anointed: Kingship in "Sverris saga" and "Hákonar saga Hákonarsonar."* Odense: Odense University Press, 1996.

Bailey, Mark. *The English Manor C.1200–c.1500.* Manchester: Manchester University Press, 2002.

Bak, János M., ed., *Coronations Medieval and Early Modern Monarchic Ritual.* Berkeley: California University Press, 1990.

Barany, Attila. "Medieval Queens and Queenship: The Present Status of Research in Income and Power." *Annual of Medieval Studies at the CEU* 19 (2013), 149–159.

Bardsley, Sandy. "Education and Work, Multiple Tasks and Lowly Status." In: *A Cultural History of Women in the Middle Ages*, edited by Kim M. Phillips, 125–152. London: Bloomsbury, 2013.

Barnish, S. J. B. "The Genesis and Completion of Cassiodorus' 'Gothic History'." *Latomus* 43 (1984), 336–361.

Bedos-Rezak, Brigitte. "Medieval Women in French Sigillographic Sources." In: *Medieval Women and the Sources of Medieval History*, edited by Joel T. Rosenthal, 1–36. Athens: University of Georgia Press, 1990.

Bedos-Rezak, Brigitte. "Women, Seals and Power in Medieval France, 1150–1350." In: *Women and Power in the Middle Ages*, edited by Mary Carpenter Erler and Maryanne Kowaleski, 61–82. Athens: University of Georgia Press 1988.

Beem, Charles. *The Lioness Roared: The Problems of Female Rule in English History.* New York: Palgrave Macmillan, 2006.

Benz St John, Lisa. *Three Medieval Queens: Queenship and the Crown in Fourteenth-Century England.* New York: Palgrave Macmillan, 2012.

Berend, Nora, Przemysław Urbańczyk, and Przemysław Wiszewski. *Central Europe in the High Middle Ages: Bohemia, Hungary and Poland, c. 900-c.1300*. Cambridge: Cambridge University Press, 2013.

Berend, Nora, ed., *Christianization and the Rise of Christian Monarchy: Scandinavia, Central Europe and Rus' c. 900–1200*. Cambridge: Cambridge University Press, 2007.

Berglund, Louise. "Queen Philippa and Vadstena Abbey: Royal Communication on a Medieval Media Platform." In: *Media and Monarchy in Sweden*, edited by Mats Jönsson and Patrik Lundell, 21–32. Göteborg: Nordicom, 2009.

Berglund, Louise. "Medeltidens diskreta makthavare: om abbedissan Ragnhild och andra kvinnor i Riseberga kloster." In: *Patroner, gästgivare och andra kvinnor*, edited by Gunnela Björk, Håkan Henriksson, and Sture Isaksson, 7–20. Örebro: Lokalhistoriska sällskapet i Örebro län, 2008.

Bisson, Thomas. "Medieval Lordship." *Speculum* 70, no. 4 (1995), 743–759.

Bjørgo, Narve. "Margrete Eriksdotter." *Store Norske Leksikon*. https://snl.no/Margrete_Eriksdotter. Accessed 13 January 2024.

Blomkvist, Nils, Stefan Brink, and Thomas Lindkvist. "The Kingdom of Sweden." In: *Christianization and the Rise of Christian Monarchy Scandinavia, Central Europe and Rus' C.900–1200*, edited by Nora Berend, 167–213. Cambridge: Cambridge University Press, 2007.

Bordawé, Katrinette. "Abbesses." In: *Women and Gender in Medieval Europe: An Encyclopedia*, edited by Margaret Schaus, 1–4. London: Taylor & Francis, 2006.

Boureau, Alain. "How Christian was the Sacralization of Monarchy in Western Europe (Twelfth-Fifteenth Centuries)?" In: *Mystifying the Monarch: Studies on Discourse, Power, and History*, edited by Jeroen Deploige and Gita Deneckere, 25–34. Amsterdam: Amsterdam University Press, 2006.

Brégaint, David. *Vox Regis: Royal Communication in High Medieval Norway*. Leiden: Brill, 2015.

Bricka, Carl Frederik. *Dansk Biografisk Lexikon, vol. XVII*. Copenhagen: Gyldendalske Boghandels Forlag, 1905.

Brink, Stefan. *Thraldom: A History of Slavery in the Viking Age*. Oxford: Oxford University Press, 2021.

Brink, Stefan. "The Creation of a Scandinavian Provincial Law: How Was It Done?." *Historical Research* 86 (2013), 432–444.

Buckley, Veronica. *Christina, Queen of Sweden: The Restless Life of a European Eccentric*. New York: HarperCollins, 2004.

Burton, Janet and Julie Kerr. *The Cistercians in the Middle Ages*. Woodbridge: The Boydell Press, 2011.

Carlson, Joakim. "Sunesdotter – en drottning i det fördolda." *Historiska Museet.* https://rattvishistoria.historiska.se/2017/03/06/katarina-sunesdotter/. Accessed 14 January 2024.

Carlsson, Gottfrid. "En svensk drottnings andaktsbok? Nagra anteckningar om en medeltidshandskrift i British Museum," *Nordisk tidskrift för bok- och bibliotekshistoria* 41 (1954), 101–110.

Castor, Helen. *She-Wolves: The women who Ruled England before Elizabeth.* London: Faber & Faber, 2010.

Charpentier Ljungqvist, Fredrik. *Quantitative Approaches to Medieval Swedish Law.* Newcastle: Cambridge Scholars Publishing, 2022.

Charpentier Ljungvist, Fredrik. *Lagfäst kungamakt under högmedeltiden: en komparativ internordisk studie.* Stockholm: Institutet för Rättshistorisk Forskning, 2016.

Cherezińska, Elżbieta. *Harda.* Poznan: Zysk i S-ka, 2016.

Chibnall, Marjorie. *The Empress Matilda: Queen Consort, Queen Mother and Lady of the English.* Oxford: Blackwell, 1991.

Christiansen, Eric. *The Northern Crusades,* 2nd edn. London: Penguin, 1997.

Clunies Ross, Margaret. "Realism and the Fantastic in the Old Icelandic Sagas." *Scandinavian Studies* 74, no. 4 (2002), 443–454.

Clunies Ross, Margaret. "Concubinage in Anglo-Saxon England." *Past and Present* 108 (1985), 3–34.

Conradi Mattson, Agneta. *Riseberga Kloster. Birger Brosa och Filipssönerna.* Örebro: Örebro Läns Museum, 1998.

Curman, Sigurd, and Erik Lundberg. *Sveriges Kyrkor. Östergötland, vol. II.* Stockholm: Esselte AB, 1935.

Curta, Florin, ed., *Eastern Europe in the Middle Ages (500–1300).* Leiden: Brill, 2019.

Dabrowski, Patrice M. *Poland: The First Thousand Years.* Ithaca: Cornell University Press, 2014.

Davies, Rees. "The Medieval State: The Tyranny of a Concept?" *Journal of Historical Sociology* 16, no. 4 (2003), 280–300.

Deploige, Jeroen, and Gita Deneckere, eds, *Mystifying the Monarch: Studies on Discourse, Power, and History.* Amsterdam: Amsterdam University Press, 2006.

Dimnik, Martin. *The Dynasty of Chernigov, 1146–1246.* Cambridge: Cambridge University Press, 2003.

Dobat, Andres Siegfried. "Viking Stranger-kings: The Foreign as a Source of Power in Viking Age Scandinavia, or, Why There Was a Peacock in the Gokstad Ship Burial?" *Early Medieval Europe* 23, no. 2 (2015), 161–201.

Duby, Georges. *Love and Marriage in the Middle Ages.* Translated by Jane Dunnett. Chicago: University of Chicago Press, 1994.

Duggan, Anne, ed., *Queenship in Medieval Europe: Proceedings of a Conference Held at King's College London April 1995*. Woodbridge: The Boydell Press, 1997.

Duggan, Anne. "Introduction." In: *Queens and Queenship in Medieval Europe: Proceedings of a Conference Held at King's College London April 1995*, edited by Anne Duggan, xv–2. Woodbridge: The Boydell Press, 1997.

Dunn, Caroline. "Serving Isabella of France: From Queen Consort to Dowager Queen." In: *Royal and Elite Households in Medieval and Early Modern Europe: More Than Just a Castle*, edited by Theresa Earenfight, 169–201. Leiden: Brill, 2018.

Dunn, Caroline. *Stolen Women in Medieval England: Rape, Abduction, and Adultery, 1100–1500*. Cambridge: Cambridge University Press, 2013.

Dzhakson, T. N. "Elizaveta Iaroslavna, koroleva norvezhskaia." In: *Vostochnaia Evropa v istoricheskoi retrospektive: K 80-letiiu V.T. Pashuto*, 63–71. Moscow: Iazyki russkoi kul'tury, 1999.

Earenfight, Theresa. *Medieval Queenship: Queenship and Power*. New York: Palgrave Macmillan, 2017.

Earenfight, Therea, ed., *Women and Wealth in Late Medieval Europe*. New York: Palgrave Macmillan, 2010.

Earenfight, Theresa, ed., *Queenship and Political Power in Medieval and Early Modern Spain*. Abingdon: Routledge, 2005.

Edberg, Rune. *Viking Princess, Christian Saint: Ingegerd, a woman in the 11ᵗʰ century*, 2nd edn. Translated by Theodosia Tomkinson. Sigtuna: Sigtuna Museum, 2005.

Ellis Nilsson, Sara. *Creating Holy People and Places on the Periphery: A Study of the Emergence of Cults of Native Saints in the Ecclesiastical Provinces of Lund and Uppsala from the Eleventh to the Thirteenth Centuries*. Gothenburg: University of Gothenburg, 2015.

Engström, Sten. "Birger Magnusson." In: *Svenskt biografiskt lexikon bd. 4*, edited by Bertil Boëthius, 418–424. Stockholm: Bonnier, 1924.

Esmark, Kim, Lars Hermanson, and Hans Jacob Orning, eds., *Nordic Elites in Transformation, c. 1050–1250, Volume II: Social Networks*. Abingdon: Routledge, 2020.

Facinger, Marion. "A Study of Medieval Queenship: Capetian France, 987–1237." *Studies in Medieval and Renaissance History* 5 (1968), 1–48.

Farmer, Sharon. "Persuasive Voices: Clerical Images of Medieval Wives." *Speculum* 61, no. 3 (1986), 521–543.

Ferrer, Marlen. "State Formation and Courtly Culture in the Scandinavian Kingdoms in the High Middle Ages." *Scandinavian Journal of History* 37, no. 1 (2012), 1–22.

Fischer Drew, Katherine. *The Law of the Franks*. Philadelphia: University of Pennsylvania Press, 1991.

Forde, Simon, Lesley Johnson, and Alan Murray, eds., *Concepts of National Identity in the Middle Ages*. Leeds: Leeds University, 1995.

Fordyce, William. *The History and Antiquities of the County Palatine of Durham*. Newcastle: A. Fullerton & co, 1857.

France, James. *The Cistercians in Scandinavia*. Kalamazoo: Cistercian Publications, 1992.

Fröjmark, Anders. "Ragnhild." In: *Svenskt biografiskt lexicon band 29*, edited by Göran Nilzén, 613–615. Stockholm: Norstedt Tryckeri, 1995–1997.

Gaethke, Hans-Otto. *Die Eheschließung Herzog Bolesław III. von Polen mit der Grafentochter Salome von Berg in Schwaben*. Hamburg: Verlag Dr. Kovač, 2022.

Gahrn, Lars. "Sparrsätra och Gata skog: Två fältslag som har utkämpats i Uppland." In: *Kärnhuset i riksäpplet*, edited by Karin Blent, Elisabeth Svalin, and Iréne Andersson Flygare, 75–104. Uppsala: Upplands fornminnesförening och hembygdsförbund, 199).

Garver, Valerie L., Penelope Nash, Elena Woodacre, Janet L. Nelson; Charlotte Cartwright, Theresa Earenfight, Phyllis Jestice, Simon MacLean, Lucy K. Pick, Dana Polanichka, Katherine Weikert, and Megan Welton. "Forum: Pauline Stafford's Queens, Concubines, and Dowagers Thirty-Five Years On." *Medieval People*, 35, no. 1 (2020), article 3. https://scholarworks.wmich.edu/medpros/vol35/iss1/3. Accessed 23 April 2024.

Gelting, Michael H. "Scandinavian and the North Sea World." In: *The Cambridge Companion to the Age of William the Conqueror*, edited by Benjamin Pohl, 52–72. Cambridge: Cambridge University Press, 2022.

Gillingstam, Hans. "Magnus Henriksson." In: *Svenskt Biografiskt Lexicon bd 24*, edited by Birgitta Lager-Kromnow, 646. Stockholm: Bonnier, 1986.

Gillingstam, Hans. "Utomnordiskt och nordiskt i de äldsta svenska dynastiska förbindelserna." *Personhistorisk tidskrift* 77 (1981), 17–28.

Gillingstam, Hans. "Folkungaätten." In: *Svenskt biografiskt lexikon band 16*, edited by Bertil Boëthius, 260–265. Stockholm: Bonnier, 1964–1966.

Gineste, Bernard. "Thibaud d'Étampes." *Les Cahiers d'Étampes-Histoire* 10 (2009), 43–58.

Griffiths, Fiona. "The Mass in Monastic Practice: Nuns and Ordained Monks, c. 400–1200." In: *The Cambridge History of Medieval Monasticism in the Latin West, vol. 1 and 2*, edited by Alison I. Beach and Isabelle Cochelin, 729–746. Cambridge: Cambridge University Press, 2020.

Gustafsson, Sofia. "Svenska städer i medeltidens Europa: En komparativ studie av stadsorganisation och politisk kultur." PhD Diss., Stockholm University, 2009.

Gustin, Ingrid. *Tornet till Bjälbo Kyrka*. Linköping: Östergötland Museum, 2006.

Hauberg, Peter Christian. *Myntforhold og udmyntninger i Danmark indtil 1146*. Copenhagen: B. Lunos, 1900.

Haverkamp, Alfred. *Medieval Germany 1056–1273*, 2nd edn. Oxford: Oxford University Press, 1992.

Hedenstierna-Jonson, Charlotte. "Spaces and Places of the Urban Settlement of Birka." In: *New Aspects on Viking Age Urbanism c. AD 750–1100: Proceedings of the International Symposium at the Swedish History Museum, April 17th–20th 2013*, edited by Lena Holmquist, Sven Kalmring, and Charlotte Hedenstierna-Jonson, 23–34. Stockholm: Archaeological Research Laboratory, 2016.

Herlihy, David. *Medieval Households*. Cambridge, MA: Harvard University Press, 1985.

Hermanson, Lars, and Auður Magnúsdóttir, eds., *Medeltidens genus: Kvinnors och mäns roller inom kultur, rätt och samhälle. Norden och Europa ca 300–1500*. Gothenburg: Acta Universitatis Gothoburgensis, 2016.

Hermanson, Lars. "Släkt, vänner och makt: en studie av elitens politiska kultur i 1100-talets Danmark." PhD Diss., University of Gothenburg, 2000.

Hildebrand, Hans. *Sveriges medeltid: kulturihistorisk skildring* (in 2 vols). Stockholm: P. A. Norstedt & Söner, 1879.

Hildebrandt, Johanne. *Estrid*. Stockholm: Forum, 2016.

Hildebrandt, Johanne. *Sigrid*. Stockholm: Forum, 2014.

Hill, Joyce. "Pilgrimage and Prestige in the Icelandic Sagas." *Saga-Book* 23 (1990–1993), 433–453.

Hørby, Kai. *Status Regni Dacie: Studier i Christofferlinjens ægteskabs- og alliancepolitik 1252–1319*. Copenhagen: Den danske historike forening, 1977.

Hornaday, Aline G. "Early Medieval Kinship Structures as Social and Political Controls." In *Medieval Family Roles: A Book of Essays*, edited by Cathy Jorgensen Itnyre, 21–37. Abingdon: Routledge, 1996.

Hundahl, Kerstin. "Placing Blame and Creating Legitimacy: The Implications of Rügish Involvement in the Struggle over the Succession amidst the Danish Church Strife c.1258–1260." In: *Denmark and Europe in the Middle Ages, c.1000–1525. Essays in Honour of Professor Michael H. Gelting*, edited by Kerstin Hundahl, Lars Kjær, and Niels Lund, 269–286. London: Routledge, 2014.

Huneycutt, Lois. "Intercession and the High-Medieval Queen: The Esther Topos." In: *Power of the Weak: Studies on Medieval Women*, edited by Jennifer Carpenter and Sally-Beth MacLean, 126–146. Chicago: University of Illinois Press, 1995.

Imsen, Steinar. "Late Medieval Scandinavian Queenship." In: *Queens and Queenship in Medieval Europe. Proceedings of a Conference Held at King's College London, April 1995*, edited by Anne Duggan, 53–74. Woodbridge: Boydell Press, 1997.

"Inge." In: *Nordisk Familjebok, bd. 12*, edited by Theodor Westrin, 620–622. Stockholm: Nordisk Familjeboks förlags aktiebolag, 1910.

Ingvorsen, Leif. *Mythen om Dronning Thyra*. Copenhagen: Wormanium, 1988.

Janse, Otto. "Erik den helige såsom historisk person: några synpunkter." *Fornvännen* 49 (1954), 91–115.

Jasiński, Kazimierz. *Rodowód pierwszych Piastów*. Krakow: Avalon, 2007.

Jesch, Judith. *Women in the Viking Age*. Woodbridge: The Boydell Press, 1991.

Jezierski, Wojtek, Kim Esmark, Hans Jacob Orning, and Jón Viðar Sigurðsson, eds., *Nordic Elites in Transformation, c. 1050–1250, Volume III: Legitimacy and Glory*. Abingdon: Routledge, 2022.

Johansen, Birgitta, and Ing-Marie Pettersson. *Från borg till bunker: Befästa anläggningar från förhistorisk och historisk tid*. Stockholm: Riksantikvarieämbetet, 1993.

Jón Viðar Sigurðsson. "The Viking Age and the Scandinavian Peace." In: *Viking Encounters: Proceedings of the Eighteenth Viking Congress*, edited by Anne Pedersen and Søren Sindbæk, 23–33. Aarhus: Aarhus University Press, 2020.

Jones, Gwyn. *A History of the Vikings*, 2nd edn. Oxford: Oxford University Press, 2001.

Kerr, Berenice M. *Religious Life for Women c.1100–c.1350: Fontevraud in England*. Oxford: Oxford University Press, 1999.

Kjellström, Anna. "From Saint to Anthropological Specimen: The Transformation of the Alleged Skeletal Remains of Saint Erik." In: *Interdisciplinary Explorations of Postmortem Interaction. Dead Bodies, Funerary Objects, and Burial Spaces Through Texts and Time*, edited by Estella Weiss-Krejci, Sebastian Becker and Philip Schwyzer, 166–188. Cham: Springer, 2022.

Kloczowski, Jerzy. *A History of Polish Christianity*. Cambridge: Cambridge University Press, 2000.

Korpiola, Mia. "High and Late Medieval Scandinavia: Codified Vernacular Law and Learned Legal Influence." In: *Oxford Handbook of European Legal History*, edited by Heikki Pihlajamäki, 378–403. Oxford: Oxford University Press, 2018.

Korpiola, Mia. *Between Betrothal and Bedding Marriage: Formation in Sweden 1200–1600*. Leiden: Brill, 2009.

Kraft, Salomon. "Vreta klosters äldre historia." *Kyrkohistorisk årsskrift* 45 (1945), 230–249.

Krakow, Annett. "On the Influence of Adam's *Gesta* on Yngvars saga víðförla." In: *Adam of Bremen's* Gesta Hammaburgensis Ecclesiae Pontificum: *Origins, Reception and Significance*, edited by Grzegorz Bartusik, Radosław Biskup and Jakub Morawiec, 146–157. Abingdon: Routledge, 2022.

Laidoner, Triin. *Ancestor Worship and the Elite in Late Iron Age Scandinavia: A Grave Matter*. Abingdon: Routledge, 2020.

Lawson, Michael Kenneth. *Cnut: England's Viking King*. Cheltenham: Tempus, 2004.

Layher, William, *Queenship and Voice in Medieval Northern Europe*. New York: Palgrave-Macmillan, 2010.

Lind, John H. "Consequences of the Crusades in Target Areas: The Case of Karelia." In: *Crusade and Conversion on the Baltic Frontier, 1150–1500*, edited by Alan Murray, 133–150. Aldershot: Ashgate, 2001.

Lindkvist, Thomas. "Crusades and Crusading Ideology in the Political History of Sweden, 1140–1500." In: *Crusade and Conversion on the Baltic Frontier, 1150–1500*, edited by Alan Murray, 119–130. Aldershot: Ashgate, 2001.

Lindkvist, Thomas. "Kungamakt, kristnande, statsbildning." In: *Kristnandet i Sverige. Gamla källor och nya perspektiv*, edited by Bertil Nilsson, 217–241. Uppsala: Lunne Böcker, 1996.

Line, Philip. *Kingship and State Formation in Sweden: c.1130–1290*. Leiden: Brill, 2007.

Ljungkvist, John and Per Frölund. "Gamla Uppsala – The Emergence of a Centre and a Magnate Complex." *Journal of Archaeology and Ancient History* 16 (2015), 1–29.

Longfellow, Henry Wadsworth. *Tales of a Wayside Inn*. Boston: Ticknor and Fields, 1864.

Lönnroth, Lars. *Isländska mytsagor*. Stockholm: Atlantis, 1995.

Loomis, Grant. *White Magic: An Introduction to the Folklore of Christian Legend*. Cambridge, MA: Mediaeval Academy of America, 1948.

Lovén, Christian. "Sigridlev och godsrikedomen i Stenkilsätten." In: *Medeltida storgårdar. 15 uppsatser om ett tvärvetenskapligt forskningsproblem*, edited by Olof Karsvall and Kristofer Jupiter, 145–164. Uppsala: Kungl. Gustav Adolfs Akademien, 2014.

Lundén, Tryggve. *Sveriges missionärer, helgon och kyrkogrundare. En bok om Sveriges kristnande*. Helsingborg: Artos, 1983.

Lundh-Eriksson, Nanna. *Den glömda drottningen: Karl XII:s syster Ulrika Eleonora d. y. och hennes tid*. Norrtälje: Nanna Lundh-Eriksson, 1976.

Lundh-Eriksson, Nanna. *Sveriges drottningar, 1531–1860*. Stockholm: Magn. Bergvalls förlag, 1916.

Lyle, Emily. "The Scylding Dynasty in Saxo and Beowulf as Disguised Theogony." In: *Myth and History in Celtic and Scandinavian Traditions*, edited by Emily Lyle, 235–250. Amsterdam: Amsterdam University Press, 2021.

Mägi, Marika. *In Austrvegr: The Role of the Eastern Baltic in Viking Age Communication across the Baltic Sea*. Leiden: Brill, 2018.

Malm, Wilhelm. *Svenska drottningar: porträtter och biografier*. Stockholm: Hörbergska boktryckeriet, 1844.

Malone, Kemp. "The Suiones of Tacitus." *The American Journal of Philology* 46, no. 2 (1925), 170–176.

Martin, Therese. *Queen as King: Politics and Architectural Propaganda in Twelfth-Century Spain*. Leiden: Brill, 2006.

Martling, Carl Henrik. *En svensk helgonkrönika*. Skellefteå: Artos, 2001.

Mazo Karras, Ruth. "Concubinage and Slavery in the Viking Age." *Scandinavian Studies* 62, no. 2 (1990), 141–162.

McGuire, Brian Patrick. "Vretas nonner i europæisk perspektiv." In: *Fokus Vreta kloster. 17 nya rön om Sveriges äldsta kloster*, edited by Göran Tagesson, 243–255. Stockholm: Historiska Museet, 2010.

McGuire, Brian Patrick. "Cistercian Origins in Denmark and Sweden: The Twelfth Century Founders." In: *Itinéraires du savoir de l'Italie à la Scandinavie (Xe-XVIe Siècle)*, edited by Corinne Péneau, 85–97. Paris: Editions Sorbonne, 2009.

McLaughlin, Mary Martin. "Survivors and Surrogates: Children and Parents from the Ninth to Thirteenth Centuries." In: *Medieval Families: Perspectives on Marriage, Household, and Children*, edited by Carol Neel, 20–124. Toronto: University of Toronto Press, 2004.

McMahon, Keith. *Celestial Women: Imperial Wives and Concubines in China from Song to Qing*. Lanham: Rowman and Littlefield, 2016.

Metzler, Irina. "Sex, Religion, and the Law." In: *A Cultural History of Sexuality in the Middle Ages*, edited by Ruth Evans, 101–119. London: Bloomsbury, 2012.

Mitchell, Stephen. *Witchcraft and Magic in the Nordic Middle Ages*. Philadelphia: University of Pennsylvania Press, 2011.

Mortensen, Lars Boje, ed., *The Making of Christian Myths in the Periphery of Latin Christendom*. Copenhagen: Museum Tusculanum Press, 2006.

Mundal, Else. "The Double Impact of Christianization for Women in Old Norse Culture." In: *Gender and Religion*, edited by Kari E. Børresen, 238–253. Rome: Carocci, 2001.

Nelson, Janet L. "Medieval Queenship." In: *Women in Medieval Western European Culture* (reprint), edited by Linda E. Mitchell, 179–208. Abingdon: Routledge, 2011.

Neville, Kristoffer, and Lisa Skogh, eds., *Queen Hedwig Eleonora and the Arts Court Culture in Seventeenth-Century Northern Europe*. Abingdon: Routledge, 2017.

Nilsson, Bertil. *Sveriges Kyrkohistoria. Missionstid och Tidig Medeltid.* Stockholm: Verbum, 1998.

Nilsson, Bertil, ed., *Kristnandet i Sverige: gamla källor och nya perspektiv.* Lund: Lunne, 1996.

Nisbeth, Åke. *Enångers Kyrkor.* Stockholm: Riksantikvarieämbetet, 1994.

Nolan, Kathleen. *Capetian Women.* New York: Palgrave Macmillan, 2003.

North, Michael. *The Baltic: A History.* Cambridge, MA: Harvard University Press, 2015.

Nyberg, Tore. *Monasticism in North-Western Europe, 800–1200.* Aldershot: Ashgate, 2000.

Ohlmarks, Åke. *Våra Kungar från äldsta till våra dagar.* Stockholm: Sureförlaget, 1972.

Olfsson, Stefan. *The Hostages of the Northmen: From the Viking Age to the Middle Ages.* Stockholm: Stockholm University Press, 2019.

Olofsson, Sven Ingemar. "Sankt Olofs stad." In: *Södertälje stads historia del. 1,* edited by Alf Nordström, 127–144. Stockholm: Södertälje stads drätselkammare, 1968.

Olrik, Hans. "Knud Magnussen." In: *Dansk Biografisk Lexicon, vol. IX,* edited by Carl Frederick Bricka, 263–264. Copenhagen: Gyldendalske Boghandels Forlag, 1895.

Pac, Grzegorz. *Women in the Piast Dynasty: A Comparative Study of Piast Wives and Daughters (c. 965–c. 1144).* Translated by Anna Kijak. Leiden: Brill, 2022.

Pac, Grzegorz. "The Attire of the Virgin Mary and Female Rulers in Iconographical Sources of the Ninth to Eleventh Centuries: Analogues, Interpretations, Misinterpretations." In: *Medieval Clothing and Textiles 12,* edited by Robin Netherton and Gale R. Owen-Crocker, 1–26. Martlesham: Boydell and Brewer, 2016.

Paciocco, Roberto. "The Canonization of Saints in the Middle Ages: Procedure, Documentation, Meanings." In: *A Companion to Medieval Miracle Collections,* edited by Sari Katajala-Peltomaa, Jenni Kuuliala and Iona McCleery, 54–77. Leiden: Brill, 2021.

Parsons, John Carmi. "The Queen's Intercession." In: *Power of the Weak: Studies on Medieval Women,* edited by Jennifer Carpenter and Selly-Beth MacLean, 147–177. Chicago: University of Illinois Press, 1995.

Parsons, John Carmi, ed., *Medieval Queenship.* New York: Palgrave-Macmillan, 1990.

Poulsen, Bjørn, Helle Vogt, and Jón Viðar Sigurðsson, eds., *Nordic Elites in Transformation, c. 1050–1250, Volume I: Material Resources.* Abingdon: Routledge, 2019.

Prestwich, Michael. *Edward I.* New Haven: Yale University Press, 2008.

Pringle, Denys. "Scandinavian Pilgrims and the Churches of the Holy Land in the Twelfth and Thirteenth Centuries." In: *Tracing the Jerusalem Code Volume 1: The Holy City Christian Cultures in*

Medieval Scandinavia (ca. 1100–1536), edited by Kristin B. Aavitsland and M. Bonde, 199–217. Berlin: De Gruyter, 2021.

Prinke, Rafał. "Świętosława, Sygryda, Gunhilda. Tożsamość córki Mieszka I i jej skandynawskie związki." *Roczniki Historyczne* 70 (2004), 81–110.

Pryce, Huw. *Native Law and the Church in Medieval Wales*. Oxford: Oxford University Press, 1993.

Räf, Erika. *Alvastra Kloster*. Stockholm: Riksantikvarieämbetet, 2000.

Raffield, Ben, Neil Price, and Mark Collard. "Polygyny, Concubinage, and the Social Lives of Women in the Viking Age." *Viking and Medieval Scandinavia* 13 (2017), 165–209.

Rawska-Mrożkiewicz, Maria. *Świętosława: Córka Mieszka I, żona, matka skandynawskich Konungów*. London: Oficyna Poetów i Malarzy, 1987.

Resources and Revenues of Royal Women Project, "Examining the Resources & Revenues of Royal Women in Premodern Europe: An International Research Project Investigating the Economic Agency and Activities of Royal Women in Premodern Europe." https://www.queensresources.org/. Accessed 23 April 2024.

Reynolds, Philip. *How Marriage Became One of the Sacraments: The Sacramental Theology of Marriage from Its Medieval Origins to the Council of Trent*. Cambridge: Cambridge University Press, 2016.

Reynolds, Susan. "The Historiography of the Medieval State." In: *Companion to Historiography*, edited by Michael Bentley, 117–138. London: Routledge, 1997.

Riis, Thomas. "The Significance of 25 June, 1170." In: *Of Chronicles and Kings: National Saints and the Emergence of Nation States in the High Middle Ages*, edited by John Bergsagel, David Hiley and Thomas Riis, 91–102. Copenhagen: Museum Tusculanum Press, 2015.

Rodrigues, Ana Maria S. A. "Gender and Feminine Identity in the Middle Ages." In: *Identity in the Middle Ages: Approaches from Southwestern Europe*, edited by Flocel Sabaté, 123–136. Leeds: Arc Humanities Press, 2021.

Rosén, Jerker. "Erik Birgersson d. y." In: *Svenskt Biografiskt Lexicon band 13*, edited by Bengt Hildebrand, 313. Stockholm: Bonnier, 1953.

Rübekeil, Ludwig. "Scandinavia in the Light of Ancient Tradition." In: *The Nordic Languages: An International Handbook of the History of the North Germanic Languages vol. I*, edited by Oskar Bandle, 594–605. Berlin: De Gruyter, 2002.

Rüdiger, Jan. *All the King's Women: Polygyny and Politics in Europe, 900–1250*. Leiden: Brill, 2020.

Sahlin, Claire. "Holy Women of Scandinavia." In: *Medieval Holy Women in the Christian Tradition, c. 1100–1500*, edited by Alastair Minnis and Rosalynn Voaden, 689–724. Turnhout: Brepols, 2010.

Saint Petersburg State University. "Rikissa/Ryksa of Poland." https://medieval-princesses.spbu.ru/en/articles/richezaryksa-of-poland. Accessed 13 January 2024.

Salmesvuori, Päivi. *Power and Sainthood: The Case of Birgitta of Sweden.* New York: Palgrave Macmillan, 2014.

Sarti, Cathleen, ed., *Women and Economic Power in Premodern Royal Courts.* Leeds: Arc Humanities Press, 2020.

Sawyer, Birgit. *Kvinnor och familj i det forn- och medeltida Skandinavien,* 2nd edn. Ebook, 2015. https://www.academia.edu/15124871/Kvinnor_och_familj_i_det_forn-_och_medeltida_Skandinavien. Accessed 14 January 2024.

Sawyer, Birgit. "Late Viking-Age Rune-Stones in Scandinavia." Unpublished paper, 2001.

Sawyer, Birgit. "Marriage, Inheritance, and Property in Early Medieval Scandinavia." Unpublished paper, 2001.

Sawyer, Birgit and Peter Sawyer. *Medieval Scandinavia: From Conversion to Reformation circa 800-1500.* Minneapolis: University of Minnesota Press, 1993.

Sawyer, Birgit. "Valdemar, Absalon and Saxo: Historiography and Politics in Medieval Denmark." *Revue belge de Philologie et d'Histoire* 63, no. 4 (1985), 685–705.

Sawyer, Peter. *När Sverige blev Sverige.* Alingsås: Viktoria Bokförlag, 1991.

Seabourne, Gwen. *Imprisoning Medieval Women: The Non-Judicial Confinement and Abduction of Women in England, C. 1170–1509.* Abingdon: Routledge, 2016.

Sedlar, Jean W. *East Central Europe in the Middle Ages, 1000–1500.* Seattle: University of Washington Press, 2013.

Selart, Anti. *Livonia, Rus' and the Baltic Crusades in the Thirteenth Century.* Leiden: Brill, 2015.

Semple, Sarah, Alex Sanmark, Frode Iversen, and Natascha Mehler. *Negotiating the North: Meeting-Places in the Middle Ages in the North Sea Zone.* Abingdon: Routledge, 2021.

Silber, Ilana F. "Gift-Giving in the Great Traditions: The Case of Donations to Monasteries in the Medieval West." *European Journal of Sociology* 36, no. 2 (1995), 209–243.

"Sitones." In: *Real-Encyclopädie der classischen Altertumswissenschaft in alphabetischer Ordnung, vol. 6. Pra-Stoai,* edited by August Pauly, Christian Walz and W.S. Teuffel, 1226. Stuttgart: Metzler, 1852.

Skovgaard-Petersen, Inge. "Queenship in Medieval Denmark." In: *Medieval Queenship,* 2nd edn, edited by John Carmi Parsons, 25–42. New York: St Martin's Press, 1998.

Stålberg, Wilhelmina, and Per Gustaf Berg. *Anteckningar om svenska qvinnor.* Stockholm: P. G. Berg, 1864.

Stafford, Pauline. *Queens, Concubines and Dowagers: The King's Wife in the Early Middle Ages*. Athens: University of Georgia Press. 1983.

Stone, Gerald. *Slav Outposts in Central European History*. London: Bloomsbury Academic, 2016.

Storm, Gustav. "Den 'buxelöse Jarl' i Sverige." *Historisk tidskrift* 23 (1903), 89–90.

Strickland, Agnes. *Lives of the Queens of England vol. 1*. London: H. Colburn, 1841.

Strinnholm, Anders Magnus, *Svenska folkets historia från äldsta till närwarande tider del 4*. Stockholm: Hörsberg, 1854.

Svanberg, Jan. "Folkungatumban i Varnhems klosterkyrka." *Konsthistorisk tidskrift* 37, no. 2 (1968), 131–145.

Sverrir Jakobsson, *The Varangians: In God's Holy Fire*. New York: Springer International, 2020.

Tagesson, Göran. *Vreta Klosters Kyrka*. Linköping: Svenska Kyrkan, 2007.

Tanner, Heather J., Laura L. Gathagan and Lois Huynecutt. "Introduction." In: *Medieval Elite Women and the Exercise of Power, 1100–1400: Moving beyond the Exceptionalist Debate*, edited by Heather J. Tanner, 1–18. Cham: Springer, 2019.

Tegenborg Falkdalen, Karin. *Svenska Drottningar*. Lund: Historiska Media, 2020.

Tegenborg Falkdalen, Karin. *Vasadrottningen: En biografi över Katarina Stenbock 1535–1621*. Lund: Historiska Media, 2015.

Tegenborg Falkdalen, Karin. *Vasadöttrarna*. Lund: Historiska Media, 2010.

Tesch, Sten. "Sigtuna: Royal Site and Christian Town and the Regional Perspective, c. 980–1100." In: *New Aspects on Viking Age Urbanism c. AD 750–1100: Proceedings of the International Symposium at the Swedish History Museum, April 17th–20th 2013*, edited by Lena Holmquist, Sven Kalmring, and Charlotte Hedenstierna-Jonson, 115–150. Stockholm: Archaeological Research Laboratory, 2016.

Tucker, Elizabeth. "Antecedents of Contemporary Witchcraft in the Middle Ages." In: *Popular Culture in the Middle Ages*, edited by Josie P. Campbell, 39–47. Bowling Green: Bowling Green State University Press, 1986.

Tunberg, Sven. "Ragnvald Knapphövde: Ett bidrag till diskussionen om Sveriges medeltida konungalängd." *Svensk Tidskrift* 41 (1954), 35–40.

Tunberg, Sven. "Albrekt." In: *Svenskt Biografiskt Lexicon, bd 1*, edited by Bertil Boëthius, 368. Stockholm: Bonnier, 1918.

Turner Camp, Cynthia. *Anglo-Saxon Saints Lives as History Writing in Late Medieval England*. Cambridge: D.S. Brewer, 2015.

Turvey, Roger. *The Welsh Princes: The Native Rulers of Wales 1063–1283* (reprint). Abingdon: Routledge, 2013.

University of Copenhagen. "Dictionary of Old Norse Prose." https://onp. ku.dk/onp/onp.php?q. Accessed 12 January 2024.

Vagnoni, Mirko, ed., *Royal Divine Coronation Iconography in the Medieval Euro-Mediterranean Area*. MDPI, 2020.

Viennot, Éliane. *La France, les femmes et le pouvoir: l'invention de la loi salique (V-XVI siècle)*. Paris: Perrin, 2006.

Vogt, Helle. *The Function of Kinship in Medieval Nordic Legislation*. Leiden: Brill, 2010.

Wågman, Frans Oscar. *Vreta kloster. Historik jämte vägledning vid besök i Vreta klosters kyrka och dess omgifningar*. Stockholm: Norstedt, 1904.

Wehrmann, Martin. *Genealogie des pommerschen Herzogshauses*. Stettin: Leon Sauniers, 1937.

Weibull, Lauritz. *Kritiska undersökningar i Nordens historia omkring år 1000*. Lund: Lybecker, 1911.

Wessén, Elias. *Om det tyska inflytandet på svenskt språk under medeltiden*. Stockholm: Kungl. Boktryckeriet, 1970.

Wigger, Friedrich. "Stammtafeln des Großherzoglichen Hauses von Meklenburg." *Jahrbücher des Vereins für Mecklenburgische Geschichte und Altertumskunde* 50 (1885), 111–326.

Wilhelmsson, Caroline. "The Concept of Swedish Identity, c. 800–1288." PhD Diss., University of Aberdeen, 2022.

Wilkinson, Louise. "Royal Daughters and Diplomacy at the Court of Edward I." In: *Edward I. New Interpretations*, edited by Andy King and Andrew Spencer, 84–104. York: York Medieval Press, 2020.

Wiszewski, Przemyslaw. *Domus Bolezlai: Values and Social Identity in Dynastic Traditions of Medieval Poland (c.966–1138)*. Leiden: Brill, 2010.

Witte, John. *From Sacrament to Contract: Marriage, Religion, and Law in the Western Tradition*, 2nd edn. Louisville: Westminster John Knox Press, 2012.

Woodacre, Elena. *Queens and Queenship*. Leeds: ARC Humanities Press, 2021.

Zachrisson, Terese. "The Saint in the Woods: Semi-Domestic Shrines in Rural Sweden, c. 1500–1800." *Religions* 10, no. 6: 386 (2019), 1–15.

Zajac, Talia. "The Social-Political Roles of the Princess in Kyivan Rus." In: *A Companion to Global Queenship*, edited by Elena Woodacre, 125–146. Amsterdam: Amsterdam University Press, 2018.

Zajac, Talia. "Gloriosa Regina or 'Alien Queen'? Some Reconsiderations on Anna Yaroslavna's Queenship (r. 1050-1075)." *Royal Studies Journal* 3, no. 1 (2016), 28–70.

Zori, Davide. *Age of Wolf and Wind: Voyages Through the Viking World*. Oxford: Oxford University Press, 2024.

APPENDIX

Maps

MAP 1   Sweden's traditional provinces and their districts c. 1300 with main monasteries, castles, and manors © National Archives, Stockholm

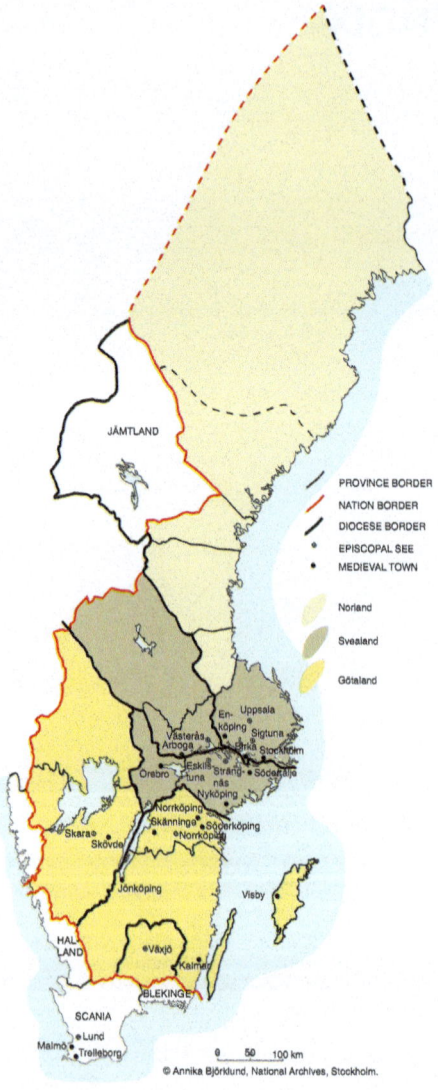

MAP 2   Towns and dioceses in Sweden c. 1300 © National Archives,
Stockholm

List of Kings

"King" (and approximate dating)	Associated royal woman
Erik Segersäll (d. 995)	Sigrid Storråda
Olof Skötkonung (r. 995–1022)	Estrid, Edla
Anund Jacob (r. 1022–1050)	Gunnhild
Emund the Old (r. 1050–1060)	Estrid Njalsdatter
Stenkil (r. 1060–1066)	Ingamoder
Erik and Erik (disputed) (c. 1066–1067)	n.a.
Halsten (disputed) (c. late 1060s)	n.a.
Anund Gårdske (disputed) (c. late 1060s, early 1070s)	n.a.
Håkan the Red (disputed) (r. 1070s)	n.a.
Inge the Elder (r. late 1070s–1080s)	Helena (Maer)
Blót-Sven (r. 1080s)	n.a.
Inge the Elder (1080s–c. 1110)	Helena (Maer), Margareta Fredkulla
Filip (r. c.1110–1118)	Ingegerd Haraldsdatter
Inge the Younger (r. 1110–1120s)	Ragnhild of Tälje, Ulvhild Håkonsdatter
Magnus Nielsen (r. c. 1130–1132)	Rikissa of Poland
Sverker the Elder (r. c.1132–1156)	Ulvhild Håkonsdatter, Rikissa of Poland, Ingegerd Sverkersdotter, Helena Sverkersdotter of Denmark
Erik Jedvardsson (r. c. 1156–1160)	Kristina Bjørnsdatter
Magnus Henriksson (disputed, r. 1160)	Brigida Haraldsdatter
Karl Sverkersson (r. 1161–1167)	Kristina Stigsdatter Hvide
Knut Eriksson (1167–1195)	Cecilia
Sverker the Younger (1196–1208)	Ingegerd Birgersdotter, Benedicta Ebbesdatter Hvide, Helena Sverkersdotter of Sweden
Erik Knutsson (1208–1216)	Rikissa Valdemarsdatter
Johan Sverkersson (1216–1222)	n.a.
Erik Eriksson (c. 1222–1224; 1229–1250)	Katarina Sunesdotter
Valdemar Birgersson (1250–1275)	Sofia Eriksdatter, Ingrid Ylva
Magnus Ladulås (1276–1290)	Helvig of Holstein, Ingrid Ylva
Birger Magnusson (1290–1318)	Märta Eriksdatter
Magnus Eriksson (1319–1364)	Ingeborg Håkonsdatter

Family Trees

Family trees of Swedish queens and female regents (the consorts of Olof Skötkonung, Stenkil, and Knut I are omitted due to the complete lack of information about their background. Sigrid Storråda's genealogy is tentative).

Sigrid Storråda

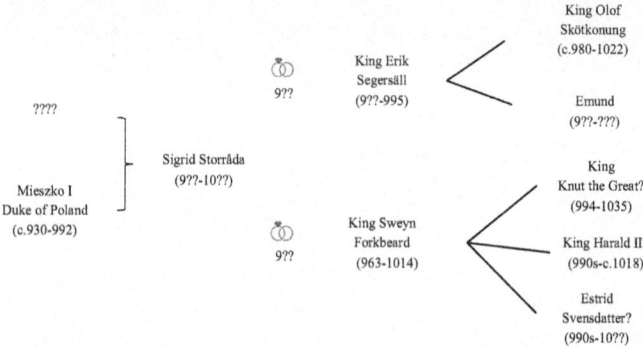

Helena

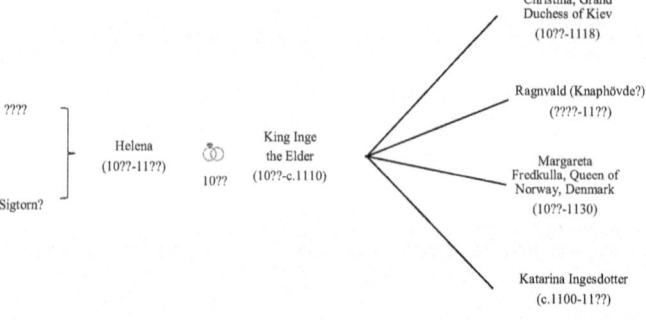

Ingegerd Haraldsdatter

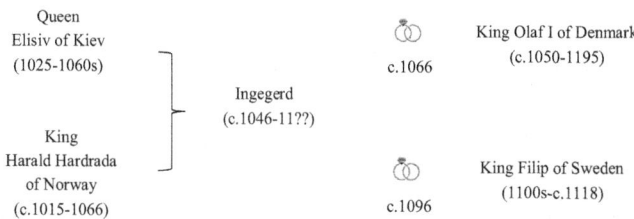

Ulvhild Håkonsdatter

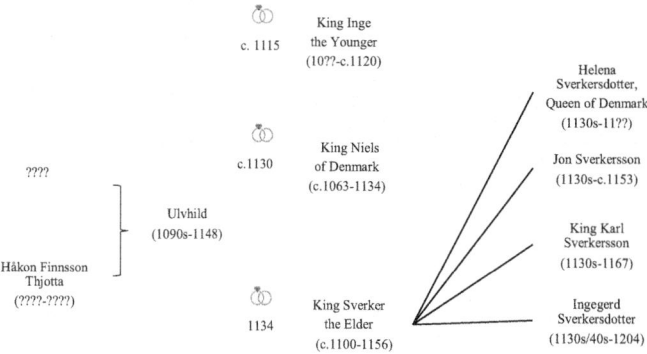

Rikissa of Poland

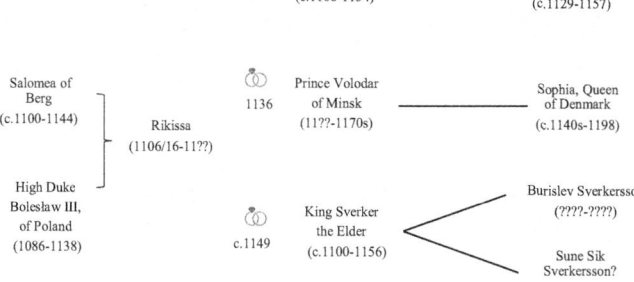

Kristina Bjørnsdatter

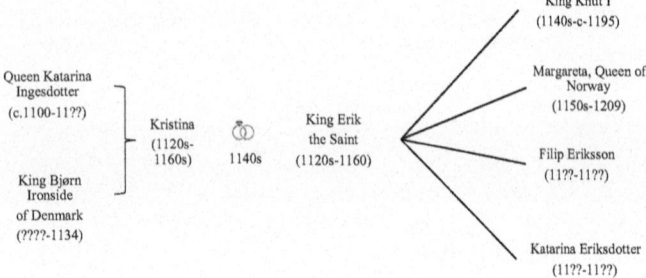

Brigida Haraldsdatter

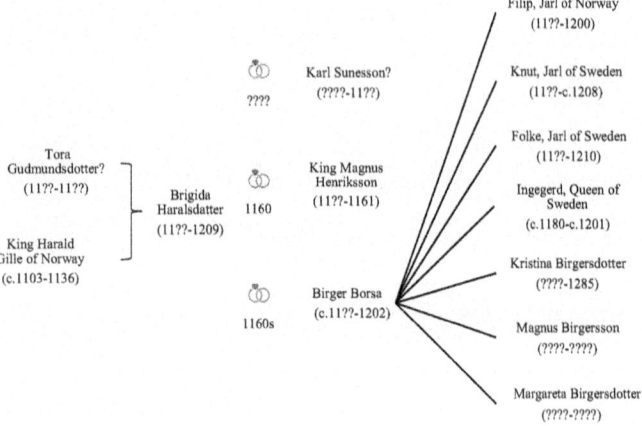

Kristina Stigsdatter Hvide

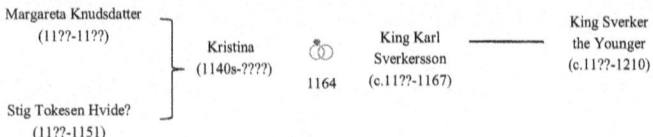

Ingegerd Birgersdotter

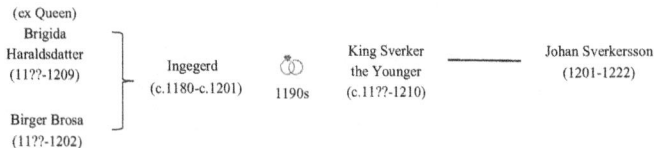

Benedicta Ebbesdatter Hvide

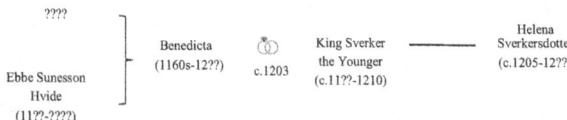

Rikissa Valdemarsdotter

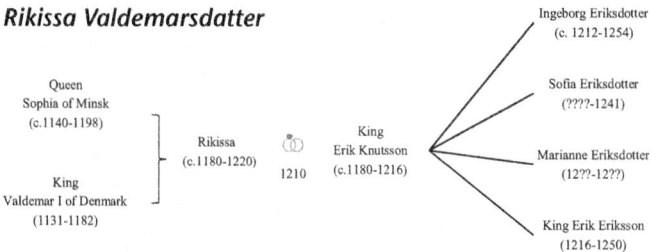

Katarina Sunesdotter

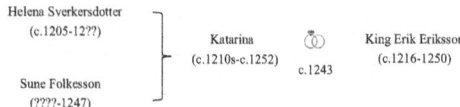

Sofia Eriksdatter

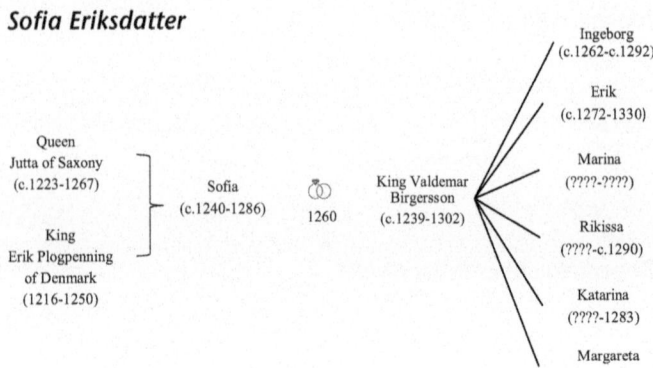

Queen
Jutta of Saxony
(c.1223-1267)

King
Erik Plogpenning
of Denmark
(1216-1250)

Sofia
(c.1240-1286)

1260

King Valdemar
Birgersson
(c.1239-1302)

Ingeborg
(c.1262-c.1292)

Erik
(c.1272-1330)

Marina
(????-????)

Rikissa
(????-c.1290)

Katarina
(????-1283)

Margareta
(????-????)

Helvig of Holstein

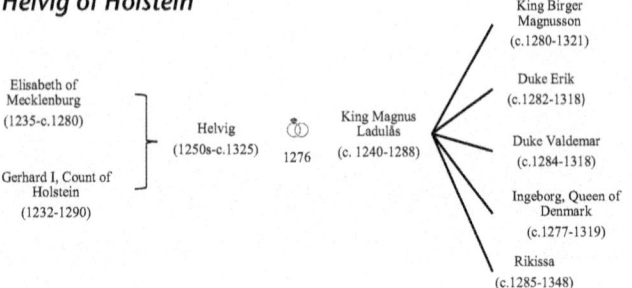

Elisabeth of
Mecklenburg
(1235-c.1280)

Gerhard I, Count of
Holstein
(1232-1290)

Helvig
(1250s-c.1325)

1276

King Magnus
Ladulås
(c. 1240-1288)

King Birger
Magnusson
(c.1280-1321)

Duke Erik
(c.1282-1318)

Duke Valdemar
(c.1284-1318)

Ingeborg, Queen of
Denmark
(c.1277-1319)

Rikissa
(c.1285-1348)

Märta Eriksdatter

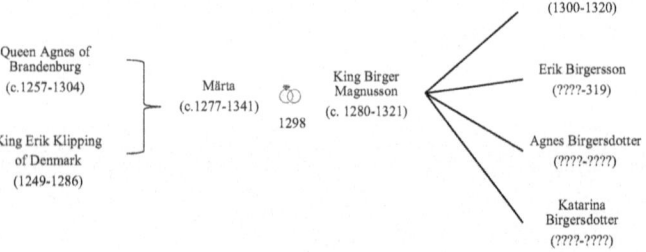

Queen Agnes of
Brandenburg
(c.1257-1304)

King Erik Klipping
of Denmark
(1249-1286)

Märta
(c.1277-1341)

1298

King Birger
Magnusson
(c. 1280-1321)

Magnus Birgersson
(1300-1320)

Erik Birgersson
(????-319)

Agnes Birgersdotter
(????-????)

Katarina
Birgersdotter
(????-????)

Ingeborg Håkonsdatter

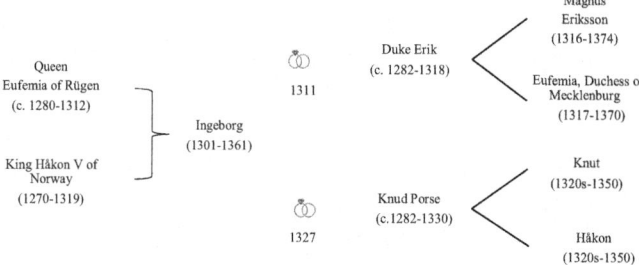

Queen
Eufemia of Rügen
(c. 1280-1312)

King Håkon V of
Norway
(1270-1319)

Ingeborg
(1301-1361)

1311

Duke Erik
(c. 1282-1318)

Magnus
Eriksson
(1316-1374)

Eufemia, Duchess of
Mecklenburg
(1317-1370)

1327

Knud Porse
(c.1282-1330)

Knut
(1320s-1350)

Håkon
(1320s-1350)

Index

For Product Safety Concerns and Information please contact our EU
representative GPSR@taylorandfrancis.com Taylor & Francis Verlag GmbH,
Kaufingerstraße 24, 80331 München, Germany

Printed and bound by CPI Group (UK) Ltd, Croydon, CR0 4YY
26/02/2026
02061077-0001